Healing the Racial Divide

Healing the Racial Divide
A Catholic Racial Justice Framework
Inspired by Dr. Arthur Falls

LINCOLN RICE

PICKWICK *Publications* · Eugene, Oregon

HEALING THE RACIAL DIVIDE
A Catholic Racial Justice Framework Inspired by Dr. Arthur Falls

Copyright © 2014 Lincoln Rice. All rights reserved. Except for brief quotations in critical publications or reviews, no part of this book may be reproduced in any manner without prior written permission from the publisher. Write: Permissions. Wipf and Stock Publishers, 199 W. 8th Ave., Suite 3, Eugene, OR 97401.

Pickwick Publications
An Imprint of Wipf and Stock Publishers
199 W. 8th Ave., Suite 3
Eugene, OR 97401

www.wipfandstock.com

ISBN 13: 978-1-62564-474-9

Cataloguing-in-Publication Data

Rice, Lincoln

> Healing the racial divide : a Catholic racial justice framework inspired by Dr. Arthur Falls / Lincoln Rice.
>
> p. ; cm. —Includes bibliographical references and index.
>
> ISBN 13: 978-1-62564-474-9
>
> 1. African American Catholics—History—20th century. 2. Civil rights workers—United States—Biography. 3. Church and social problems—Catholic Church. I. Title.

BX4705.F3 R49 2014

Manufactured in the U.S.A.   10/13/2014

Scripture texts in this work are taken from the New American Bible, revised edition © 2010, 1991, 1986, 1970 Confraternity of Christian Doctrine, Washington, D.C. and are used by permission of the copyright owner. All Rights Reserved. No part of the New American Bible may be reproduced in any form without permission in writing from the copyright owner.

Contents

Acknowledgments | vii
List of Abbreviations | ix
Introduction | xi

1 Black Experience and Empowerment in Catholic Thought | 1
2 The Life of Dr. Arthur G. Falls | 32
3 The Thought and Writings of Dr. Arthur G. Falls | 92
4 A New Understanding of Catholic Racial Justice—Inspired by Falls | 122
5 Virtues for the Oppressed | 150

Afterword | 165
Bibliography | 167
General Index | 193

Acknowledgments

FIRST, I WOULD LIKE to thank Arthur Grand Pré Falls. The passion and vigor behind his life and writings has been an inspiration for me. The decades of his life that he dedicated to racial justice were a constant source of reinvigoration in getting back to work on this project. Furthermore, Arthur's own unique vision of the Catholic Worker movement continues to challenge my own appropriation of this movement.

Professionally, I owe my eternal gratitude to Bryan Massingale—my dissertation director. My initial interest at St. Francis Seminary had been in spirituality and scripture. His obvious enthusiasm for moral theology and its importance for twenty-first century Catholicism are in no small way responsible for my further studies in the subject. I also owe my gratitude to the rest of my dissertation board. Patrick Carey was supportive of a PhD student who came into his office wanting to write a paper on Arthur Falls, without any real sources at that moment. Daniel Maguire is a testament to the importance of conscience and the need to intelligently—and at times humorously—interact with our great Catholic tradition. Jon Nilson's own willingness to become an apprentice to James Cone and black Catholic thought serves as an example par excellence for how white Catholic theologians should address racism. I would also like to thank Karen A. Johnson, a fellow researcher at Wheaton College, who was willing to share with me her own discoveries related to Falls.

I am also thankful to the Marquette Theology Department for its commitment to high academic quality and its generous funding of my classes. I am thankful to the family of Cyril E. Smith (1900–1969) for funding my first year of dissertating in the form of the Smith Family Fellowship, which allowed me to perform research in Chicago.

I am thankful to the many faith communities that have supported me over the years: the Casa Maria Catholic Worker, St. Michael Catholic

Acknowledgments

Church, and Blessed Trinity Parish in Milwaukee; St. John the Evangelist Catholic Church and Catholic Central Grade School in Green Bay; and, of course, my parents, Curt and Cele Rice—and their parents, who passed on to them a faith that they in turned passed on to me.

Lastly, I would like to thank my wife, Laura Pope. She has always supported me on this project. No words can express my sincere gratitude for her.

Abbreviations

AAC: Archdiocese of Chicago's Joseph Cardinal Bernardin Archives and Records Center

AGF: Arthur G. Falls, Reminiscence. Raynor Memorial Libraries, Special Collections and University Archives, Marquette University

CUL: Chicago Urban League Records, Richard J. Daley Library, University of Illinois at Chicago

DDCW: Dorothy Day-Catholic Worker Collection, Raynor Memorial Library, Marquette University

WSHS: Western Springs Historical Society, Western Springs, Illinois

Introduction

THE REASON FOR THIS BOOK

THE BROAD CONTEXT FOR the writing of this book is a desire to share the story of Arthur Grand Pré Falls (1901–2000) with as many people as possible. Falls, a black Catholic medical doctor, devoted his days to bettering the lives of African Americans and poor people of all races. In addition to admiring his keen mind and witty personality, I was moved by his activities and his writings to consider the plight of African Americans on a much deeper level. Falls's dedication to living out his Catholic faith despite onerous challenges has all the indications of sainthood. It is my belief and hope that every reader of this book will come to the same conclusion.

The immediate context for the writing of this book was the discovery of a manuscript that Falls composed in 1962—a draft of his unpublished memoir. This manuscript is a *new* source of information about a man who has been largely absent in writings on black and Catholic American history. While doing research during spring 2009 for a doctoral seminar in American Catholic Theology with Dr. Patrick W. Carey, I learned about the edited draft (about 620 pages, typed) when I made an unsolicited phone call to Falls's favorite niece, Vilma Childs, an octogenarian living in Kalamazoo, Michigan. I then aided the head of the Raynor Library Archives at Marquette University in obtaining this draft for Raynor's Social Action Collection. Certain pieces are missing from this source, so I also consulted a very incomplete first draft of Falls's memoir (about 180 pages) that is part of the August Meier Papers at the New York Public Library.[1] Falls's extensive

---

1. Falls, Reminiscence, 1962; Unpublished Autobiography, 1962. These two sources are two parts of a memoir that is not available in one complete copy. I will only use the second source to fill in missing parts of the first source. Falls made notes and corrections to the first source. The second source of the memoir has no corrections.

Introduction

writings include articles in publications such as the *New York Catholic Worker*, the *Chicago Catholic Worker*, the *St. Elizabeth Chronicle*, the *Interracial Review*, the *Chicago Defender*, the *Sign*, and *America*. Moreover, numerous archives in the Chicago area aided me in confirming many of the episodes relayed by Falls in his memoir and in piecing together those parts of his life not covered in the memoir. My use of all these sources—especially the newly discovered manuscript—make this book unique as a contribution to the field of racial justice.

**Dr. Falls at his office desk. Chicago Illinois: 1941.
Courtesy of the Library of Congress, LC-USF34-038696-D.**

Falls is best known for founding the first Catholic Worker in Chicago in 1936 and working tirelessly on racial justice issues within the Catholic Church and the Chicago area from the late 1920s through the 1960s.

Introduction

Historical references to Falls are often limited to a few sentences; even Cyprian Davis's *The History of Black Catholics in the United States*, which is the first and only work dealing with the entire history of black Catholics in America, does not mention Falls.

The newly discovered manuscript documents Falls's family background and his life until the mid-1940s. It chronicles the activities of a man who dedicated almost every spare minute of his adult life to improving the situation of African Americans in the Chicago area. To list some (but not all) of the organizations and groups that Falls was involved with: the Catholic Worker movement, the Chicago Urban League, the Federated Colored Catholics (later the National Catholic Federation for the Promotion of Better Race Relations), the American League Against War and Fascism, the Chicago Catholic Worker Credit Union, the Cooperative Wholesale and Consumer Cooperative Services, the People's Consumer Cooperative, the Chicago Catholic Interracial Council, the Citizens Committee for Adequate Medical Care, the Ogden Park Citizens Committee, the Cook County Physicians Association, the National Medical Association, the Illinois State Commission on the Urban Colored Population, the Fellowship of Reconciliation, the Congress of Racial Equality, the Chicago chapter of the Post War World Council, and St. John of the Cross Catholic Church in Western Springs, Illinois.

The doctrine of the mystical body of Christ permeates Falls's life and writings, both implicitly and explicitly. Falls viewed racism as rooted in a heretical understanding of Christianity that was foreign to Christianity's true nature. Falls dedicated his life to fighting this evil with the same tenacity that early Christian saints dedicated themselves to fighting their contemporary heresies. His vision for Catholic racial justice brought together both theory and active struggle, and it is this vision that is needed as a corrective and inspiration for contemporary Catholic thought on racial justice. His emphasis on struggle could help bridge the divide that often exists in theology between esoteric thought and action. This combination of thought and action echoes liberation theology's notion of "practical mediation" or theological praxis.[2]

Despite the work of Falls and countless others like him, racial injustice continues to pervade American society: being black means that one will

---

2. For more information on the notions of theological praxis and practical mediation, see McAuliffe, *Fundamental Ethics*, 130–43; Boff and Boff, *Introducing Liberation Theology*, 1–42.

experience "racial prejudice, discrimination, rejection, and hostility" and being white means that one will experience "*the presumption of dominance and entitlement . . . [and being] the measure of normativity*."[3] For those who think that racism ceased to be a problem when Barack Obama was elected president of the United States, Bryan N. Massingale gives countless examples of racist acts that occurred within the first two hundred days of Obama taking office, including the "resurgence of race-based hate groups and militia movements." Obama also received more death threats than any previous presidential candidate, president-elect, or president.[4] Bishop Dale Melczek of Gary, Indiana, points out that the "very existence of segregated communities is a sad testimony to the fact that people of faith have not translated religious values into action."[5] More recently, there was national outrage and tension over the murder of Trayvon Martin, an unarmed seventeen-year-old African American. He was shot by a neighborhood watch volunteer who stated that he killed Trayvon in self-defense. The twenty-eight-year-old volunteer had followed Trayvon because he believed the teenager looked suspicious and a number of break-ins had recently occurred in the community. The volunteer was later found innocent of any wrongdoing.[6] These examples point not only to blatant explosions of racial tension in the United States, but also to a more subtle racism below the surface that can be more difficult to discern since it is not as blatant as the Jim Crow system that preceded it.

For over the last hundred years, Catholic ethical thought in the area of racism—when it has been addressed—has consisted almost exclusively of white clergy writing and speaking about how whites should be more civil in their personal interactions with blacks. In other words, the remedies put forth can be distilled almost solely to moral suasion, or trying to convince whites to behave better toward other races. No one saw a need to make use of African American sources or to advocate for any active agency, or role, on the part of blacks. Over the past twenty years, a shift has begun among Catholic ethicists who engage with the topic of racism, toward employing African American sources and promoting black agency (i.e., a role for African Americans to play in furthering their liberation), but there is essentially a great inadequacy in Catholic ethical reflection regarding racism.

3. Massingale, *Racial Justice*, 19, 24. Italics in the original.
4. Ibid., 6-8.
5. Melczek, "Created in God's Image," 17.
6. Preston and Moynihan, "Death of Florida Teen."

Introduction

This inadequacy also extends to official Catholic reflection as found in documents from the Vatican and from U.S. bishops. As with most Catholic scholarly reflection over the past one hundred years, none of the statements make any serious use of black or black Catholic sources. This omission of African American resources is a damning indictment of Catholic leaders: it betrays a worldview in which white European reflection is sufficient for all times and places.

A rethinking of racial justice requires more attentive engagement with black Catholic thought. Falls represents a shift from Catholic ethical thought on racial justice by seamlessly connecting traditional dogmas and doctrines with the everyday experiences of African Americans. Although his writings did not always indicate the role of black agency, his very active pursuit of racial justice speaks volumes. This book's ethical framework, which is grounded in the life and thought of Falls, is part of the necessary retrieval of black voices—particularly black Catholic voices. Scholarship in the area of black Catholic history is only beginning to realize the richness of the all but forgotten history of black Catholics in the United States. In studying the newly discovered manuscript and Falls's other forgotten writings, there is an opportunity to retrieve an important voice that was almost lost.

HISTORICAL RETRIEVAL AND LIBERATION THEOLOGY[7]

The central thesis guiding this work is that the retrieval of Dr. Arthur G. Falls as a new source of information will bring a fuller and deeper understanding to current notions of Catholic racial justice. This renewed understanding will view racism not only as sinful, but rooted in a heretical understanding of Christianity—specifically a denial of the mystical body of Christ. Such a view will provide new types of practices for combating racism.

First and foremost, this central thesis will be fulfilled vis-à-vis the newly discovered manuscript of Falls's memoir, in tandem with the draft archived

---

7. This book will stay within the confines of the United States and focus almost exclusively on racism against African Americans. Although current immigration controversies and a growing Latino population add a new and important dimension to the discussion, it would make this work too large and unmanageable. Also, as Bryan Massingale has pointed out, "the estrangement between black and white Americans has shaped American life in decisive ways not matched by either the estrangement between whites and other racial/ethnic groups, or the tensions among the 'groups of color.'" Massingale, *Racial Justice*, xi.

Introduction

at the New York Public Library. Together, these eight-hundred-plus pages are a rich and abundant resource on Falls's activities and his inner motivations. Since Falls has been largely forgotten, this project is the first to use his life and writings to inform a theological racial justice framework.

Two theoretical methodologies inform my approach and perspective: (1) critical historical retrieval and (2) liberation theology's "practical mediation" or theological praxis. Historical retrieval allows for the recovery of important sources and figures that have been omitted, ignored, or silenced. Theologian Stacey Floyd-Thomas employs a similar method with her womanist ethical methodology. Floyd-Thomas believes that it is essential in ethics to examine the lives of oppressed black women so that one can understand how they "survived and subverted" the advances of racism and sexism. She points to the stories of Harriet Jacobs and Sojourner Truth as examples of black women with the "ability to maintain—or even attain—a sense of dignity and self-worth that is in contradistinction to her social station."[8] In surveying the slave narratives of black women, Floyd-Thomas posits that "the moral system(s) of these enslaved black women formed, informed, and transformed not only their moral systems and those of others around them, but often altered their social circumstances as well." Within the context of her retrieval of female African American voices, she asks, "*How do you resurrect the ethical realities and concerns of black women from the 'underside of history'?*"[9] This question is just as relevant for this study if it is slightly rephrased: how do you resurrect the ethical realities and concerns of African American Catholics from the "underside of history"? The assumption here is that the ignoring of African American figures by white Catholic ethicists has led to an inadequate and often harmful vision of racial justice, when the topic is addressed at all. Therefore, a retrieval of the life and writings of Falls will be an important step in rectifying this situation. Through critical historical retrieval, I hope to contribute to an American Catholic historical, ethical, and theological field that has often ignored black sources.

Liberation theology's theological praxis allows a new experience to inform a new understanding and practice, which leads to an improved theological framework. In addition, a liberationist ethic believes that an ethic that

---

8. Floyd-Thomas, *Mining the Motherlode*, 105, 120. Harriet Jacobs (1813–1897) was born as a slave in North Carolina and was most famous for her book, *Incidents in the Life of a Slave Girl*. Sojourner Truth (1797–1883) was a famous abolitionist and speaker who had escaped slavery in 1826.

9. Ibid., 105. Italics in the original.

Introduction

does not address suffering "cannot be taken seriously."[10] This understanding of ethics privileges the poor as an essential source of knowledge regarding injustice, since it is the poor who experience suffering firsthand. With this in mind, genuine responses to suffering must be willing to go beyond standard academic responses and be willing to integrate new data.[11] Within the context of this book, the life and writings of Falls will act as a new experience. As a new source of information, the life narrative and ethical thought presented by Falls introduce new types of thought and practices for understanding and combating racism. These practices and writings can then be integrated into an improved theological framework for addressing racial justice in Catholic ethical thought. A *more* relevant approach to dealing with the evil of racism is the most that this work can hope to accomplish. And, of course, as more retrieval and listening to African American figures occur, even more relevant and adequate frameworks can be proposed.

This book has been divided into five chapters. The first chapter assesses the main movements of Catholic racial justice over the past one hundred years, especially concerning the notions of black agency and the retrieval of African American sources. The second chapter retrieves the life of Dr. Arthur G. Falls by covering his upbringing, discussing the movements with which he was involved, and highlighting the segments of his life that exhibit his work for racial justice. The third chapter investigates the major themes in his writings. Particular attention is given to religious themes and the implications his writings have for Catholic racial justice. The fourth chapter proposes a new definition of Catholic racial justice based on the analysis in the first three chapters. Falls is used as the primary inspiration for this definition, and his life and writings are given the opportunity to provide insights on the challenges of the twenty-first century. The final chapter, which proposes virtues for the oppressed, is an attempt to provide a concrete example of how a vision of Catholic racial justice inspired by Falls may be meaningful today.

By using the resources and methods listed above, it is my hope that this book can make the following three contributions: (1) draw attention to the necessity of African American sources and black agency in Catholic racial justice, (2) reveal the life of Arthur Grand Pré Falls to a new generation of Catholics, and (3) deepen our current understanding of Catholic racial justice.

---

10. McAuliffe, *Fundamental Ethics*, x, 134. For liberationists, suffering is foundational for ethics.

11. Ibid., 34 n10, 127–28.

1 Black Experience and Empowerment in Catholic Thought

THIS CHAPTER WILL EXAMINE more deeply the current state of Catholic racial justice—particularly as it pertains to the role of black agency and the use of black sources in Catholic racial justice. "Black agency" refers to the role that African Americans are deemed to possess in working toward racial justice in society, and "the use of black sources" refers to the extent that the intellectual, cultural, and ecclesial experiences of African Americans are incorporated into a theological framework of racial justice. The first section of this chapter will survey authors who offer a more limited view of African American sources and black agency. The latter section will consider authors who make greater use of and give greater legitimacy to black agency and experience. The first section will begin with an examination of the life and writings of John LaFarge, who, in addition to being a contemporary of Falls, was the most prominent American exponent of Catholic racial justice during the first half of the twentieth century, and whose impact is still discernible in the documents of American bishops. This section will then appraise documents from the United States Conference of Catholic Bishops, the Vatican's Pontifical Council for Justice and Peace, and the statements of individual American bishops. The second section will examine James Cone, Shawn Copeland, Bryan Massingale, and Jon Nilson.

LIMITED USE OF BLACK AGENCY AND EXPERIENCE

John LaFarge

John LaFarge, S.J. (1880–1963), a contemporary of Falls, was the most famous Catholic champion of racial justice during the first half of the twentieth century. He rose to prominence in the interracial relations movement when he became involved with the Federated Colored Catholics (FCC). The FCC was founded in 1924 by Dr. Thomas Wyatt Turner (1877–1978), a biologist, to further the cause of African American Catholics in the Catholic Church, as well as to promote self-worth and to provide leadership opportunities.[1] The independence of this group from clerical leadership and its methods of self-determination to solve the oppression of blacks made LaFarge uncomfortable. As historian David Southern observes, "LaFarge simply disliked protest with an African American accent."[2] He believed that the FCC should have clerical leadership and focus primarily on employing moral suasion and appealing to white sympathy to bring about racial justice.[3] In 1932, after garnering enough support from black Catholics within the FCC, LaFarge and fellow Jesuit William Markoe orchestrated a constitutional revision of the FCC, which resulted in a change of aims and leadership for the organization.[4] As Southern notes, after LaFarge took over the movement, "instead of raising a cadre of black leaders, the Catholic interracial movement actually helped create a vacuum of black leadership in the church."[5]

In his 1937 book, *Interracial Justice*, LaFarge advocated for the integration of public and Catholic schooling in the United States, well before the 1954 *Brown v. Board of Education of Topeka* court case, which ruled that separate but equal was unconstitutional. *Interracial Justice* pointed to a twofold approach for Catholic action in the attainment of interracial justice: (1) "the *combating of race prejudice*," and (2) "the *establishment of social justice*."[6] LaFarge defined racial justice as an "equality of opportunity" for all groups or individuals, regardless of race.[7] LaFarge's understanding of racism did not address how to create an equality of opportunity when great

---

1. Nilson, *Hearing past the Pain*, 31. The FCC will be mentioned only briefly here; the focus in this section will be the theology and praxis of LaFarge. The FCC will be addressed more concretely in the next two chapters through Arthur's involvement with the organization.

2. Southern, *John LaFarge*, 362.

3. Massingale, *Racial Justice*, 47–50.

4. Nilson, *Hearing past the Pain*, 32. The organization eventually became known as the Catholic Interracial Council. Markoe would leave the organization in the fall of 1935. Nickels, *Black Catholic Protest*, 206.

5. Southern, *John LaFarge*, 361.

6. John LaFarge, *Interracial Justice*, 152–61, 172. Emphasis in the original.

7. LaFarge, *The Race Question and the Negro*, 84.

economic disparity already exists between blacks and whites.[8] Southern notes that the interracial movement had a history of applying pressure on the northern Church to integrate Catholic schools, hospitals, and seminaries, but that LaFarge was "more successful at improving the church's image than in changing the church's behavior."[9]

LaFarge had greatly refined and simplified his theology of racial justice by 1956, when he published *The Catholic Viewpoint on Race Relations*. This work, which was published near the end of his life, proposed that growing economic security for blacks depended on the social attitudes of whites toward African Americans. For LaFarge, there was little that blacks could do to improve or contribute to the betterment of their own situation. LaFarge cited African Americans from time to time, but not as inspiration for his thought; instead, their writings served as proof-texts for his own preconceived notions. In a subtle jab at the policies of the FCC before he and Markoe took over the organization, he stated that "the more repeatedly the demands [for justice] were uttered, the less attention and interest did they create."[10] He considered the black empowerment presence in the FCC to be a form of separatism that made its members' calls for integration hypocritical. He believed that after being properly educated, whites would destroy the idol of racism they were worshipping. An emphasis on white agency and clerical leadership was necessary because "although the Negro is the victim of discrimination, he does not necessarily know the answer or the cure."[11] Such a sentiment left scant room for appreciating either African American sources or black agency. Essentially, LaFarge's thought did not extend beyond the theology found in the papal encyclicals on labor, such as *Rerum novarum*. The papal social encyclical tradition does not advocate that the oppressed should confront their oppressors, but rather promotes the use of moral suasion to convince those in power to act properly.[12]

---

8. LaFarge, *Interracial Justice*, 179–87.
9. Southern, *John LaFarge*, 358.
10. LaFarge, *Catholic Viewpoint on Race Relations*, 31, 64.
11. Ibid., 71–73.
12. Southern, *John LaFarge*, 366. For more information on moral suasion in the papal encyclical tradition, see Berrera, "The Evolution of Social Ethics"; Brady, Goodpaster, and Kennedy, "*Rerum Novarum* and the Modern Corporation"; and Francoeur, "In Pursuit of a Living Wage."

U.S. Bishops' Statements

Discrimination and the Christian Conscience

In 1958, the U.S. bishops issued their first major post-World War II document on racism—*Discrimination and the Christian Conscience*. In the wake of *Brown v. Board of Education of Topeka* (1954), twenty-one documents decrying segregation had been published by various Protestant denominations before the issuance of the U.S. bishops' document. This document, authored by Fr. John Cronin, S.S. (1908–1994), was published only after the death of a prominent opponent bishop, Cardinal Edward Mooney, who had anticipated that the document would divide the bishops. Even a cable from Pope Pius XII, on the day before his death, directing that the document be published immediately, was ignored by leading bishops on the grounds that it lacked the papal seal and was, therefore, unofficial. Nevertheless, when the document was finally brought before the bishops, they approved the statement with only four bishops dissenting.[13] *Discrimination and the Christian Conscience* grounded its theology of racial justice primarily in two doctrines: (1) the universal Fatherhood of God and (2) Jesus Christ's salvific death for all peoples. It also utilized the Catholic natural law teaching on the basic equality of all human persons and each person's right to life and justice. Despite this strong doctrinal grounding, the bishops urged a "method of quiet conciliation," which they saw as a middle path between "gradualism" and "rash impetuosity" in combating the unacceptable practice of mandated segregation.[14]

Although the document called for movement toward a society more clearly marked by equality, there was no clear set of goals or specific mechanisms to execute any plan. Essentially, the document offered vague generalities concerning the manner in which to address the problem of racism. In the end, the document lacked any mention of African American sources or black agency, and called for "responsible and sober-minded Americans of all religious faiths . . . [to] seize the mantle of leadership from the agitator and the racist."[15] The bishops did not clarify if an African American demanding his or her rights could be anything but an agitator.

---

13. Cronin, "Religion and Race," 472; McGreevy, *Parish Boundaries*, 90–91.
14. National Catholic Welfare Conference, *Discrimination and the Christian Conscience*, 192.
15. Ibid.

The National Race Crisis

In 1968, the U.S. bishops released another statement on race: *The National Race Crisis*. The writing and publication of this document was swift compared to that of the previous statement. Massingale cites four reasons for its hastened publication: (1) the race riots of 1967; (2) the release of the Kerner Commission's report, which blamed the recent race riots and racial segregation on the racism of whites; (3) the assassination of Martin Luther King Jr.; and (4) the inaugural meeting of the National Black Catholic Clergy Caucus (NBCCC), in which African American clergy were extremely critical of the Catholic Church.[16] *The National Race Crisis* was issued a mere three weeks after the assassination of King—a far cry from the four years between *Brown v. Board of Education of Topeka* and the 1958 document. Also, unlike *Discrimination and the Christian Conscience*, it stressed the necessity for solutions that addressed the structural aspects of racism by employing the Kerner Report. *The National Race Crisis* moved beyond the moral suasion present in *Discrimination and the Christian Conscience* and clearly stated that recent events made immediate changes necessary: "There is no place for complacency and inertia. The hour is late and the need is critical." In addition, it explicitly recognized the fault of Catholics for the present problem.[17]

Although *The National Race Crisis* referenced King's "Poor Man's Bill of Rights," it can be difficult at first glance to ascertain the source of the bishops' proposed solutions.[18] The bishops' document asked for "special attention" to be paid to the following areas: (1) education, (2) jobs, (3) housing, and (4) welfare. All four areas were named in the Kerner Report, but they were also important to King and the Poor People's Campaign. Michael K. Honey writes that in the Poor People's Campaign, King wanted "to abolish poverty directly through government redistribution that allowed poor people enough money to pay for their own housing, education, and other

---

16. Massingale, *Racial Justice*, 56–58; *Report of the National Advisory Committee*, 91–93. The Kerner Report was the popular name for the *Report of the National Advisory Commission on Civil Disorders*, which President Lyndon B. Johnson requested of a blue-ribbon citizen commission in the wake of dozens of riots in the summer of 1967. The two largest riots were in Detroit and Newark. All together, the riots resulted in close to $100 million in damage and eighty-four deaths.

17. National Conference of Catholic Bishops, *National Race Crisis*, 175, 178.

18. Ibid., 176.

necessities."[19] The current economic benefits possessed by the wealthy were due to the slave labor and cheap wage labor of African Americans and the poor of all racial backgrounds. Additionally, King noted, "So often in America, we have socialism for the rich, and rugged, free enterprise capitalism for the poor."[20] Unlike the authors of the Kerner Report and *The National Race Crisis*, King commented on the need to significantly decrease funding to the military. King contended that the cost of the Vietnam War, if left unabated, would limit the resources necessary to abolish poverty in the United States.[21] So although one could argue that the bishops made partial use of King as a source, they did not specifically cite King with regard to their four focus areas or utilize his claim that poverty and racism could not be properly addressed as long as America's financial resources were dedicated to a war in Vietnam.

Furthermore, *The National Race Crisis* left no role for black agency. Three particular agents are mentioned for enacting needed change: (1) an interreligious Urban Task Force, for the creation of church programs throughout the United States; (2) the business community, particularly for the creation of jobs; and (3) the government, for intervention to complement the actions of the first two agents.[22] In contrast, King wanted to coordinate a massive mobilization of poor people from all racial backgrounds in Washington, DC, to nonviolently agitate the government into spending billions of dollars to solve the problem of poverty in the United States.[23]

Even though the document prescribed the formation of the Urban Task Force, nothing substantial occurred in the organizing of this entity for over a year. A large part of the reason for this was because John McCarthy, the primary author of *The National Race Crisis* and a member of the Catholic Committee on Urban Ministry, "had no experience of community organization," as he himself admitted.[24] McCarthy, who was elevated to bishop of Austin, Texas, in 1979 (and is now retired), "helped forge the idea [of the Urban Task Force] that would grow into the Catholic Campaign

---

19. Honey, *Going Down Jericho Road*, 175; *Report of the National Advisory Committee*, 229–65.

20. King, quoted in Honey, *Going Down Jericho Road*, 186–87.

21. Honey, *Going Down Jericho Road*, 175.

22. Engel, "The Influence of Saul Alinsky," 651; *National Race Crisis*, 176–78; Honey, *Going Down Jericho Road*, 186.

23. Honey, *Going Down Jericho Road*, 186.

24. John McCarthy, quoted in Engel, "Influence of Saul Alinsky," 651.

for Human Development."²⁵ McCarthy also wrote a "supporting technical paper" that explored in more detail the need for the empowerment and self-determination of blacks: "Political, organizational and economic independence were important elements in earlier rapid integration of immigrant ethnic groups into the American society. The church must now support the black community in its efforts to achieve the organizational, political and economic power so necessary to break down existing patterns of dependence and frustration."²⁶

The bishops approved McCarthy's supporting paper "in substance," as a guide for the bishops themselves, but it would not be issued to the public.²⁷ Despite the high ideals put forth in the supporting document for fostering the self-empowerment of African Americans, Massingale points out that the bishops budgeted only $28,000 for the Urban Task Force while they allocated several hundred thousand dollars for a study of clerical celibacy during the same period.²⁸ The Urban Task Force quickly morphed into the Campaign for Human Development, for which the bishops would raise $8.5 million in 1970 alone, but that program focused more on eliminating poverty than addressing racism. This change of emphasis from race to poverty ignored the issue of racism and would quickly negate McCarthy's call for black agency and empowerment under the more generic guise of empowering the poor.²⁹

Brothers and Sisters to Us

In 1979, the U.S. bishops issued *Brothers and Sisters to Us*. As the document itself states, it was written for two reasons: (1) an appeal for a new document on racism was requested at the 1976 Call to Action conference on social justice, which the bishops convened to consult with the laity as a way to celebrate America's bicentennial and to give a greater voice to the laity, as envisioned by the Second Vatican Council; and (2) racism was just as pernicious as it had been ten years previous, though the "external appearances"

---

25. "Bishop John E. McCarthy," Diocese of Austin Website.

26. McCarthy, quoted in Jennings, *Daring to Seek Justice*, 4–5.

27. Jennings, *Daring to Seek Justice*, 5. I contacted both the Catholic University of America and an archivist with the United States Conference of Catholic Bishops, but neither could locate the supporting document.

28. Massingale, *Racial Justice*, 60.

29. Jennings, *Daring to Seek Justice*, 8–78.

had changed and become more "subtle."[30] This document, in a vein similar to LaFarge's writings and the bishops' previous statements, grounded the sin of racism in a denial of (1) the universal Fatherhood of God and (2) the Incarnation, in which Jesus became the brother of all, with the intention of offering salvation to all humanity. Unlike previous statements, it affirmed that minorities have something "rich" to bring to our nation and that "each [racial group] is a source of internal strength for our nation."[31] The document admitted that the Church was experienced by many as a "racist institution," and called for the Church to be an exemplar of racial justice in its employment practices, in the fostering of vocations, in calling for racial justice in the structures of greater society, and in supporting the poor, especially through providing "spiritual and financial support" for Catholic associations organized by minority groups.[32]

Also in contradistinction to the previous two statements on racism, which were composed solely by whites, *Brothers and Sisters to Us* had considerable input from a black Catholic. Cyprian Davis, an African American Benedictine monk and Church historian, was asked by then Auxiliary Bishop Joseph A. Francis (d. 1997) of Newark, the chair of the committee working on the document, to rewrite a draft of the statement. Davis believes that the most significant idea he added to the document was a systemic notion of racism.[33] In addition, the document admits that the civil rights movement of the 1960s supported by Catholics and others received "much of its initiative and inspiration within the black Protestant Churches," which acknowledges that black agency and black sources have led to concrete Catholic involvement in racial justice.[34]

As Massingale writes, *Brothers and Sisters to Us* was "more concrete and detailed" in its plans to address racism than previous documents and it did lead to more African Americans entering the priesthood as well as broader liturgical inculturation.[35] This analysis corresponds with Davis's memory: when he was solicited by the bishops to rewrite the document, he was asked to

---

30. National Conference of Catholic Bishops, *Brothers and Sisters to Us*, 1–2, 14. Bryan Massingale notes that black Catholics played an "integral part" in Call to Action and raised awareness concerning racism to their fellow Catholics. Massingale, *Racial Justice*, 63.

31. *Brothers and Sisters to Us*, 3, 5.

32. Ibid., 8, 11–14.

33. Davis, interview by author.

34. *Brothers and Sisters to Us*, 11.

35. Massingale, *Racial Justice*, 66–67.

add "strong language" and "definite" plans to the document. Massingale also asserts, however, that the document appears to be written by white Catholics for white Catholics. Davis agrees with this assessment: at the time, he believed that he was supposed to maintain the writing style of the bishops, who were overwhelmingly white, making heavy use of hierarchical sources. He further points out that this is why "*What We Have Seen and Heard*," a 1984 document on evangelization published by the African American Catholic bishops, is an important sequel. Davis observes that in the latter document, in which he also had a significant authorial role, the black bishops spoke as black bishops. Therefore, Davis felt at liberty to contribute to it as a black Catholic.[36] Although *Brothers and Sisters to Us* acknowledges the importance of African American sources and black agency during the civil rights movement, and even suggests that Catholics cooperate with black Protestant churches in the pursuit of racial justice, the document is implicitly addressed to white Catholics and does not offer any direction or encouragement for Catholics belonging to any racial minority group.[37]

"What We Have Seen and Heard"

In contrast to the implicit white orientation of *Brothers and Sisters to Us*, "What We Have Seen and Heard" is explicitly addressed "To Our Black Catholic Brothers and Sisters in the United States."[38] This document could properly be placed in the latter section of this chapter because of its emphasis on black agency and African American sources, but it will be kept in the present section to reflect Cyprian Davis's belief that it is a sequel to *Brothers and Sisters to Us*. "What We Have Seen and Heard" is inundated with black sources and African American spirituality. The African American bishops wanted to bring to the Church the gifts present in black spirituality: (1) spontaneous contemplation; (2) a holistic faith that brings together "intellect and emotion, spirit and body, action and contemplation, individual and community, sacred and secular"; (3) joyful celebration; (4) a stress on community; and (5) the importance of the extended family. The document perceived a role for African American men and women in transforming

---

36. Davis, interview by author; Massingale, *Racial Justice*, 75; Black Bishops of the United States, "*What We Have Seen and Heard*." References to this document refer to the page numbers.

37. *Brothers and Sisters to Us*, 11–13.

38. "*What We Have Seen and Heard*", 1.

society based on what was particular to them, including roles within their families and in ecumenical efforts with different denominations within the greater "Black Church." The bishops encouraged black men to be responsible fathers and caring husbands despite the economic hardships of a society that often makes gainful employment for black men extremely difficult. Black women were called to complement the role of black men with service to the black community and the Church. For their task, black women have role models in Harriet Tubman, Mary McLeod Bethune, Mother Theodore Williams, Elizabeth Lange, and Henriette Delille, who all worked tirelessly for the betterment of the African American community.[39]

"*What We Have Seen and Heard*" is predominately a letter on evangelization, with the second half of the letter focusing on the requirement that blacks take an active role in this endeavor. The greatest hindrance to African American Catholics sharing their faith with others was racism within the Catholic Church itself. Therefore, African American Catholics must "demand" recognition and leadership roles in order to seriously carry out the work of evangelization. In addition, the black bishops observe the need for more African American vocations to the priesthood and religious life, the lack of which has been complicated by racism. Black leadership should also be fostered in the promotion of the permanent deaconate, a trained and empowered black laity, opportunities for child education, inculturation in the areas of liturgy, the Rite of Christian Initiation, and dedication to work for racial and social justice.[40]

Moreover, the document was partially informed by the input of African Americans in the United States. Feedback from listening sessions held in Catholic churches with predominantly black congregations was incorporated into the document. This may account for the emphases on the gifts that African American spirituality can bring to the Catholic Church as well as the perceived roles for black men and women in transforming society.[41]

---

39. Ibid., 8–16. Harriet Tubman (d. 1913) is most famous for aiding dozens of slaves to freedom after escaping slavery herself. Mary McLeod Bethune (d. 1955) was a prominent educator and businesswoman from Florida who founded the National Council of Negro Women in 1932. Mother Theodore Williams (d. 1931) established the Franciscan Handmaids of the Most Pure Heart of Mary in 1917, an African American religious order with the purpose of providing education for black children. Elizabeth Lange (d. 1882) was the founder and first superior of the first order of African American women in history, the Oblate Sisters of Providence. Henriette Delille will be covered below during the discussion of Shawn Copeland's writings.

40. "*What We Have Seen and Heard*", 20–34.

41. Massingale, interview by author.

In the conclusion, the African American bishops called upon all people in the Catholic Church, in their respective roles, to foster a climate conducive to evangelization among African Americans, and they specifically asked black Catholic lay leadership "to help implement the actions called for in this letter" on the local and national level.[42] This document is a stunning example of how valuable and practical a document can be that is informed by the African American experience and encourages black agency.

Individual Bishops' Statements

In a set of twenty-one statements from individual bishops and bishops' conferences from 1990 to 2000 analyzed by Massingale, only three utilize "What We Have Seen and Heard." Otherwise, African American sources are completely absent from these bishops' statements.[43] Since 2000, four American bishops have issued documents on racism: Cardinal Francis George of Chicago, Bishop Dale J. Melczek of Gary, Archbishop Harry J. Flynn of Saint Paul and Minneapolis, and Archbishop Alfred Hughes of New Orleans. I will very briefly examine these documents in chronological order, though the use of African American sources and the notion of black agency vary widely from document to document. Although I will be largely critical of these documents, these bishops should be commended for prioritizing racial justice.

In 2001, Cardinal Francis George of the Archdiocese of Chicago published *Dwell in My Love: A Pastoral Letter on Racism*, with aid from Bishop Joseph N. Perry and Sr. Jamie Phelps.[44] Perry, an auxiliary bishop in Chicago, and Phelps, a Dominican sister and systematic theologian, are both African American. Their names are the first two mentioned on a list of four researchers and writers. At face value, the document appears to have had significant input from the black Catholic experience. Nevertheless, it does not significantly address the role of black agency. Despite writing of the need for schools to "celebrate" the contributions of minorities to our society, the only role that blacks appear to be given in the document is that of "forgiving those who have offended them," and even this sentence is not race specific.[45] The conclusion offers many concrete structural changes

---

42. "What We Have Seen and Heard", 34–36.
43. Massingale, "James Cone," 724.
44. George, *Dwell in My Love*, Acknowledgments. This page is not numbered.
45. Ibid., 14–15.

that can and should occur on the parish, archdiocesan, educational, and societal levels, but there is not any specific role or mechanism for African Americans in ensuring that these changes take place.[46] Without a doubt, the absence of any significant role for African Americans in pursuing racial justice is the greatest weakness of this document. In addition, because this document does not relate narratives of black empowerment, the notion of black agency is not even implicit.

In August 2003, Bishop Dale Melczek of the Diocese of Gary issued *Created in God's Image: A Pastoral Letter on the Sin of Racism and a Call to Conversion*, which states that its sources are scripture, Church teaching, and the social sciences. For Melczek, racism is a sin that permeates society on an individual, cultural, and institutional level. The proper response to racism is threefold: (1) to analyze racism, (2) to convert Christian hearts to a more inclusive vision, and (3) for whites and people of color to work toward racial justice in solidarity. His concrete steps for confronting racism stress bringing whites and people of color together under various circumstances to nurture dialogue. Melczek does not make explicit use of the African American experience, utilize black sources, or put forth a coherent role for African American Catholics to address racism apart from collaboration with whites. His explicit use of black resources is limited to a generic citation from the African American philosopher Cornel West and an acknowledgement that a black priest and black bishop gave him feedback on a draft of the document.[47]

In addition, a recent dissertation that evaluated the Diocese of Gary's initiative to end racism states, "Although the Bishop referred to some of the history of the various ethnic groups in his Pastoral Letter, and individuals were able to tell their story within the context of Listening Sessions, a comprehensive history of white supremacy and racism in this region of Northwest Indiana and the Church's response was absent."[48] The dissertation also mentions that even though people of color have been present on the anti-racism committee for the diocese, the "primary architects of the Initiative were white."[49] Despite the genuine attempt of Melczek to confront the problem of racism in his diocese, both the use of black sources and the promotion of black agency are noticeably absent.

---

46. Ibid., 23–27.
47. Melczek, *Created in God's Image*, Opening Letter, 1–2, 27–28, 29–34, 41.
48. Fredal, "A Catholic Diocese's Initiative to End Racism," 188.
49. Ibid., 187.

In September 2003, Archbishop Harry Flynn of the Archdiocese of Saint Paul and Minneapolis (retired in 2008) promulgated *In God's Image: Pastoral Letter on Racism*. Flynn clearly states that the "demands of the Gospel" require that the Church take concrete actions to address the personal and social manifestation of racism. He views racism not only as a personal reality, but one in which the "dominant culture" negatively impacts people of color for its own benefit—often without knowing it. His proposed responses to racism include personal and structural strategies. Regarding the ecclesial realm, he recommends that African Americans be given leadership positions and play a role in decision-making. Although Flynn does not single out a particular role for African Americans in correcting racism, he does ask the "white community [to] work in solidarity with people of color."[50] This type of advice indicates that white persons require the input and collaboration of African Americans if they want to adequately address racism.

In 2006, Archbishop Alfred Hughes of the Archdiocese of New Orleans (retired in 2009) published *"Made in the Image and Likeness of God": A Pastoral Letter on Racial Harmony*. Near the beginning of the letter, he relates his belief that the continued existence of African American parishes is important for "the development of black Catholic identity, community, leadership, liturgy, and spirituality."[51] Hughes's belief may be a result of his experience of deciding to merge St. Augustine Parish with a neighboring parish. News of the merger resulted in a sit-in from some parishioners, community activists, and aid workers. St. Augustine refers to itself as the oldest African American Catholic parish in the United States and the protestors felt the archbishop had not properly consulted with the parishioners. Hughes reconsidered his decision, especially in light of the black population of the parish, and the parish remained open.[52]

For Hughes, racism is "both a personal sin and a social disorder."[53] He grounds his understanding of racial justice in Vatican II, other Vatican documents, and the documents of the United States Conference of Catholic

---

50. Flynn, *In God's Image*, no paragraph or page numbers.

51. Hughes, *"Made in the Image of God,"* 4.

52. Ibid., 5; St. Augustine's website is: http://www.staugustinecatholicchurch-neworleans.org/. Regarding this event, see also, Peter Finney, Jr., "Archbishop Reopens New Orleans Church After Dispute is Resolved," *Catholic News Service*, 10 April 2006, http://www.catholicnews.com/data/stories/cns/0602073.htm; Associated Press, "New Orleans Black Parish Faces Uncertain Future," *MSNBC.com*, 13 March 2006, http://www.msnbc.msn.com/id/11811002/ns/us_news-life/.

53. Hughes, *"Made in the Image of God,"* 5.

Bishops, as well as the heroic witness of black Catholics from the Archdiocese of New Orleans. Chief among these witnesses is Henriette Delille, a free black woman who dedicated her life to educating the enslaved.[54] In addition, Hughes references Homer Plessy, who lost the Supreme Court case *Plessy v. Ferguson*; A. P. Tureaud, who has been called the dean of the New Orleans black civil rights attorneys; and others. Hughes notes that those who worked for racial justice, whether black or white, often suffered severe consequences.[55]

Hughes develops the ideas of beauty and harmony to illustrate the importance of recognizing racial diversity in the Catholic Church. He also conveys the need to address the problem of white privilege in relation to the disadvantages faced by people of color. In the end, however, he does not assign any significant role for black Catholics.[56] This is surprising, since earlier in the document he raises up examples of black Catholics who performed acts of agitation, including those at one of his own churches. Ultimately, there is a disconnect in the document between the great black Catholic witnesses of the Archdiocese of New Orleans and the proposed solutions to contemporary manifestations of racism.

Vatican Documents

Within the last thirty years, the Vatican's Pontifical Council for Justice and Peace has published two documents dealing with racism: *The Church and Racism: Toward a More Fraternal Society* and *Contribution to the World Conference against Racial Discrimination, Xenophobia, and Related Intolerance*. *The Church and Racism*, issued in 1988, is similar to most American thought on racism, as it grounds its teaching against racism in the belief that every person is created in God's image and every person is offered redemption through the Paschal Mystery.[57] The document conveys the strong institutional aspect of racism and the complicity of Church members at certain times. It also introduces an image that is not present in American

---

54. In 1988, the cause for sainthood began for Delille. In March 2010, Pope Benedict declared that she had lived a life of "heroic virtues," which is one step before beatification and two steps before sainthood can be declared. She could very well become the first African American saint.

55. Hughes, "Made in the Image of God", 7–9, 13–16.

56. Ibid., 12, 18, 22–28.

57. Pontifical Council for Justice and Peace, *The Church and Racism*, 1,9, 22.

documents—Pentecost. Unexpectedly, instead of employing the Pentecost event as an opportunity to express the gift that diversity could bring to the Church, the document cites this event as a call to regard all "ethnic, cultural, national, social, and other divisions . . . [as] obsolete."[58] Later on, the document does point out "the diversity and complementarity of one another's cultural riches and moral qualities," but this is not grounded doctrinally.[59] The Pontifical Council for Justice and Peace describes racism as a type of blasphemy that must be addressed by educational and structural changes on all levels of society that will promote equality for all minority groups and respect for one another's "cultural and religious characteristics."[60] The document stresses that racism exists in every society and lists two specific instances of racism on the globe: (1) the American situation with African Americans, and (2) South African apartheid, which still existed in 1988. As a document written for a global context that encompasses countless situations of racism, it cannot be critiqued in the same manner as the American documents. Nevertheless, it is worth noting that the statement does not emphasize the importance of a theology from the oppressed or recognize that the oppressed have any sustained role in confronting racism. The recognized agents in society to confront racism are seen primarily as the Church and the state.[61]

The *Contribution to the World Conference against Racial Discrimination, Xenophobia, and Related Intolerance* was issued for the United Nations conference of the same name in Durban, South Africa, in late summer 2001. The document begins by citing the rise in ethnic violence since 1988, as well as the increasing gap between rich and poor. It asks for a "purification of memory," in which the oppressed are to be "guided by the spirit of forgiveness and reconciliation," while at the same time making sure that the past is not covered up, but revealed.[62] In other words, this is not a case of "forgive and forget," but rather a case of being keenly aware of what actions and responsible parties are being forgiven so that deficient structural realities can be repaired. Following this line of thought, the document supports the options of reparations and affirmative action as tools to correct past

---

58. Ibid., 22.

59. Ibid., 23.

60. Ibid., 24–30.

61. Ibid., 24–33.

62. Pontifical Council for Justice and Peace, *Contribution to World Conference Against Racism*, 3, 8–11.

injustices to the greatest extent possible. The document also recommends the proper role for the Church, state, and media in aiding the poor and protecting basic human rights, with a stress on access to education and material needs.[63] Although the document clearly denounces the evil of racism, it does not address the gifts that the oppressed can bring to a discussion of racism or the rich diversity that their cultural backgrounds can bring to the world. In addition, it does not allot any significant role to the oppressed in working toward their liberation other than forgiveness. Although a spirit of forgiveness and reconciliation is an essential aspect of a society trying to heal past injustices, this spirit will not prevent current or future injustices. Regarding how the oppressed should address current injustices, the document is silent.

Summary of the First Section

If *"What We Have Seen and Heard"* is removed from the first section, the result is a rather monolithic response to racism. The authors in this section ground their theology of racial justice not only in traditional European Catholic doctrines, but also a traditional European understanding of these doctrines, and thus all state that the most important action that one can perform in the cause of racial justice is moral suasion. With the publication of *The National Race Crisis* in 1968, there was room for structural responses to racism, but these always took on a secondary role—particularly in practice. Although *The National Race Crisis* mentioned Dr. Martin Luther King Jr., it was not informed by his thought. The inclusion of African American Catholic sources began with *Brothers and Sisters to Us*, but the document lacks any substantial role for African Americans and implicitly assumes white Catholics to be its primary audience. These deficiencies could be attributed to an almost exclusive use of hierarchical sources as well as Catholic social teaching's almost exclusive reliance on moral suasion for the resolution of injustices and emphasis on substantial change proceeding from those in power instead of from those being oppressed. The limiting of sources to hierarchical statements prevents innovation when searching for a solution to an injustice that Catholic social teaching has not been able to adequately address.

---

63. Ibid., 12–18. This document uses the terms affirmative action and positive discrimination interchangeably.

On the other hand, *"What We Have Seen and Heard"* was informed by African American Catholic sources, with final editorial control in the hands of the African American Catholic bishops. Black Catholics were its target audience, for whom the bishops saw a meaningful role in the field of racial justice and evangelization. Additionally, it asserted that African American spirituality had significant value that could augment traditional European Catholic thought. As the letter's primary purpose was evangelization, its analysis of racism itself was not in-depth. Nevertheless, *"What We Have Seen and Heard"* displayed a pronounced break with the traditional paradigm found in Catholic racial justice and is more representative of what will be found in the second section.

THE SUSTAINED USE OF BLACK AGENCY AND EXPERIENCE

James H. Cone

Almost every current Catholic theologian who writes about racial justice is deeply influenced by the work of James H. Cone, who professes a need and urgency for African American sources and black agency. Cone is considered to be the founder of black liberation theology and his thought is still prominent today. Cone's *Black Theology and Black Power* was the first book in the world published on liberation theology in 1969, and his thought has continued to develop over the past forty years.[64] The section will begin with Cone's critique of white churches and Eurocentric theology, followed by his thesis on the necessity of African American sources and black agency within a theological framework of racial justice.

In 2000, Cone was invited by *Theological Studies*, the flagship journal of U.S. Catholic theology, to write an article about racism and the Catholic Church. As Shawn Copeland observed, this was only the second time in twenty-five years that an entire issue of *Theological Studies* was dedicated to a "specific paradigm shift in theology"; the previous instance was a 1975 issue of the journal devoted to feminist theory.[65] At the beginning of the article, Cone frankly states that white Protestant churches, along with the Catholic Church in America, are "racist institutions whose priests, ministers, and theologians seem to think that White supremacy offers no serious contradic-

---

64. Hopkins, "Introduction," 3–4.
65. Copeland, "Guest Editorial," 603.

tion to their understanding of the Christian faith."[66] He perceives a reality that he also detected when he wrote an article about Catholic racism almost twenty years earlier—that white Catholic theologians are "virtually silent" about the issue of racism and its permeation of society.[67] This omission in white theology, Cone contends, illustrates the disdain that white theologians have for black thought and weakens all subsequent theological conclusions to a level that is racist and irrelevant.[68] White theology's silence regarding racism and its omission of black voices results in the dehumanization of blacks. Furthermore, Cone remarks that it is difficult for African Americans to take the many excellent social justice teachings of the Catholic Church seriously when those teachings are so neglectful of racism. He specifically comments on the "contradiction" required of black Catholics in order to remain in a racist Church. Black Catholics who want to affirm their blackness must "refuse to accept European values as the exclusive definition of the Catholic Church," even though those values have been and still are the *modus operandi* for constructing Catholic belief and practice.[69]

In light of the poor track record of white churches with eliminating racism, Cone insists that whites have no role to play in deciding if the elimination of racism has been suitably addressed. That role is reserved for blacks, who endure the evil of racism. Another problem with white European theology is its assumed objectivity and universalism. Cone argues that Jesus was not a universal human being, but an oppressed Jew.[70] Cone maintains that Jesus did not come to be everything for everybody, but primarily as a liberator for the oppressed. To illustrate this point, Cone frequently cites Luke 4:18–19,[71] in which Jesus unrolls a scroll from the prophet Isaiah in his home synagogue in Nazareth, stating, "The Spirit of the Lord is upon me, because he has anointed me to bring glad tidings to the poor. He has sent me to proclaim liberty to captives and recovery of sight to the blind, to let the oppressed go free, and to proclaim a year acceptable to the Lord."[72]

66. Cone, "Black Liberation Theology and Black Catholics," 731.
67. Ibid.; Cone, *Speaking the Truth*, 52.
68. Cone, "Black Liberation Theology and Black Catholics," 737.
69. Cone, *Speaking the Truth*, 55–57, 60.
70. Cone, *Black Theology of Liberation*, 13, 91. This book was first published in 1970 and, as Cone notes, the only changes he made to the book are a few stylistic changes and the omission of sexist language (p. xx).
71. Cone, *Black Theology of Liberation*, 3; *Speaking the Truth*, v, 123; *God of the Oppressed*, 69, 159–60.
72. All scripture citations are from the New American Bible.

Essentially, Jesus is bad news for the rich, because the kingdom of God is for "the poor *alone*."[73]

Notwithstanding the myriad problems associated with a Eurocentric theology and white churches, Cone believes there is a role for whites in black liberation. For instance, Cone commends white abolitionists for their work to end slavery, but he is critical of their omission of black sources and the perception that black freedom could be secured through legal means alone. These weaknesses need to be rectified. Cone believes that white theologians can have a role to play in black liberation, if they are willing to reorder their theological priorities according to an African American cultural viewpoint.[74]

The history of African American churches is an integral source for Cone's black theology, and the original reasons that African Americans separated from white churches are still pertinent today. Blacks separated from white churches during the age of slavery because of the unwillingness of white churches to condemn slavery as well as the outright support that was often shown for this terrible institution. In contrast, black churches were almost unanimous in their stance against slavery. Separation from white churches was concretized in the 1787 in Philadelphia, when Richard Allen, Absalom Jones, and other blacks walked out of St. George Methodist Church. In 1816, Richard Allen became the first bishop for the African Methodist Episcopal Church. In the South, blacks often met in underground churches to discuss their dignity and the struggle for liberation as found in Jesus Christ. In the 1770s, the first Baptist church organized by slaves was founded in Silver Bluff, South Carolina. These churches, along with other African American churches, were important institutions in working for the freedom of blacks before and after the dissolution of slavery.[75] Cone asserts

---

73. Cone, *God of the Oppressed*, 71–72. Emphasis in the original.

74. Ibid., 45–46. It appears that this is the white theologian's way of "becoming *black* with God," which requires that one share the oppression of African Americans and engage in the work of liberation. Cone, *Black Theology of Liberation*, 69.

75. Cone, *God of the Oppressed*, 141; Cone, *Speaking the Truth*, 91–96, 130–37. Unfortunately, Cone does not give sources for his historical retelling. It seems that he has internalized this history from various sources. As an ordained minister in the African Methodist Episcopal Church, Cone initially became familiar with the basic origins of African American churches in America through pastors in his own church. It seems that at some point after his ordination he took time to familiarize himself with this history at a much deeper level. This personal study was also necessary because he believed his formal education was too exclusively grounded in Eurocentric theology. Cone, "Preface to the 1989 Edition," *Black Theology and Black Power*, xi–xii; Cone, *My Soul Looks Back*, 71–72, 80, 84–85.

that the black church narrative has proven that integrated churches, during slavery and since, were essentially white churches that limited the work of liberation for African Americans and led blacks into a place of compromise. Additionally, Cone concludes that contemporary integrated churches continue to exhibit an inability to confront white supremacy by their lack of black sources and their virtual silence on the issue of racism.[76]

In 1970, Cone proclaimed that white theology, which is informed from a place of privilege, is inadequate to define theology. Talk about God's work in the world can only be known from the experience, writings, and freedom struggles found among blacks.[77] Cone's argument has not changed significantly between 1970 and today, although he recently stated that his stance had softened slightly because he had received additional insights on gender and class and become more aware of the broader scope of the Bible. Despite this softening, Cone still firmly believes that "the God of biblical faith and black religion is partial toward the weak."[78] According to this perspective, black Christians must start not with the Bible but with the black experience, which Cone designates as "a black tradition of struggle." The Bible is an indispensable source for Christian thought, but it is secondary to the black experience of oppression. It is only through the lens of oppression that the Bible can meaningfully speak to the liberation that God is enacting in contemporary situations.[79] Theology that does not have its starting point in the poor can be only a close-minded ideology.[80]

For well over forty years, Cone has persistently stated that African American sources and black agency are essential for achieving racial justice within societal and ecclesial realms. Any Christian theology that lacks these two ingredients cannot properly be called theology since it does not take seriously God's central work of liberation in the United States in the twenty-first century. Whites can play a role in liberation if they are willing to give preference to African American sources and the notion of black agency in their theologies. The theologians below, whether black or white, have all been influenced by Cone's call to make black theology a priority.

---

76. Cone, *God of the Oppressed*, 141, 221; *Speaking the Truth*, 91–96, 130–37; "Black Liberation Theology and Black Catholics," 731–47.

77. Cone, *Black Theology of Liberation*, 129–30.

78. Cone, "Preface to the 1997 Edition," *God of the Oppressed*, xi.

79. Ibid., xi–xii.

80. Cone, *God of the Oppressed*, 87.

M. Shawn Copeland

M. Shawn Copeland, unlike the other Catholic theologians I am examining, is a systematic theologian, as opposed to a moral theologian. As such, her emphasis is on formulating a coherent framework of the Catholic faith that accounts for racism, as opposed to proposing a theology of racism along with adequate responses. She retrieves the stories of black men and women for the purpose of putting forth a more accurate synthesis of Christian belief and practice. For Copeland, who is African American, the reality of Jesus Christ in the flesh paved the way for making use of black bodies as a theological resource. The embodied spirituality of Jesus has anthropological ramifications that can be further identified in the suffering of others.[81] Not being an ethicist, she rarely examines either the structural or systemic underpinnings of racism, though she is cognizant of this aspect of racism. Her understanding of racial justice is grounded in the doctrines of the Trinity and the *imago Dei*: "The creativity of the Triune God is manifested in differences of gender, race, and sexuality."[82] Racism, and particularly the enslavement of black women, is "the attempt to degrade the *imago Dei* . . . through commodifying, objectifying, and sexually violating black women's bodies."[83] The tortured and mutilated body of Jesus Christ on the cross, which has eerie similarities to the lynching tree, should jolt Christians out of their stupor and awake them to the plight of African Americans.[84]

Copeland submits two requisite steps to address racism and oppression: (1) *anamnesis*, or remembering the stories of the oppressed, and (2) solidarity. Through the mindful knowing of the oppressed, Christians will realize how the situation contradicts the Christian message and be moved to compassion. This compassion should elicit concrete acts of solidarity, which she defines as taking on "responsibility" for the oppressed at a personal risk. Actions of solidarity are a meaningful *modus operandi* for following and imitating Christ. In other words, "a praxis of solidarity for human liberation . . . make[s] the mystical body of Christ publicly visible in our situation."[85] For Copeland, the mystical body of Christ has inter-

---

81. Copeland, *Enfleshing Freedom*, 55–84. As she also states, the oppressed "body of Jesus of Nazareth impels us to place the bodies of the victims of history at the center of theological anthropology, to turn to 'other' subjects." Copeland, *Enfleshing Freedom*, 84.

82. Copeland, *Enfleshing Freedom*, 2, 109–10.

83. Ibid., 4, 23–29.

84. Ibid., 121–24.

85. Ibid., 100–101, 105. It is unclear how solidarity is practiced by women of color.

personal, ecclesial, and soteriological implications that she believes speak doctrinally to her notion of solidarity.[86]

Copeland is the author of a short book on the life and vision of Henriette Delille (1812–1862), which she originally delivered as the 2007 Madeleva Lecture in Spirituality. Delille, who could very well become the first American-born black saint, was the founder of a religious order for black women, the Sisters of the Holy Family, around 1842 (they were originally known as the Sisters of the Presentation).[87] Copeland's introduction to Delille occurred in 2004, when Archbishop Hughes of New Orleans appointed Copeland to sit on a theological commission to evaluate Delille's writings. She found in Delille an example of a black woman "acting as a moral agent, who, through discernment and prayer, intellectual and moral acumen, resourcefulness and, often, resistance, exercises her essential freedom in order to realize the integrity of her life."[88] As a free black woman in New Orleans, Delille was expected to participate in the extralegal system of plaçage, in which free black women became mistresses of white men of means. Instead, she "exposed the timidity of the church" by founding a religious order that dedicated itself to the education of free black people and slaves.[89] In Delille, Copeland recognizes a black woman who did not "submit to ecclesiastical indifference . . . [but rather] exercised her intelligence, creativity, and moral agency in a preferential option for despised enslaved blacks, the poor, aged, and infirm . . . [following] the path took [by] Jesus of Nazareth to the outcast, marginalized, and poor."[90]

Copeland pieces together a theological portrait of Delille by combining her few writings with her lived "praxis."[91] Delille wrote of her desire to "live and die for God"; according to Copeland, religious life provided Delille with the "liberative" avenue to avoid plaçage and dedicate her life to God as well as to free and enslaved people of color.[92] Copeland argues

---

Copeland's description of practicing solidarity seems to assume that one is not a woman of color.

86. Ibid., 101–05.

87. Copeland, *Subversive Power of Love*, 30, 58; Glatz, "Pope Brings African-American Foundress One Step Closer to Sainthood."

88. Copeland, *Subversive Power of Love*, 2, 8.

89. Ibid., 33.

90. Ibid., 66.

91. Ibid., 2.

92. Delille, quoted in Copeland, *Subversive Power of Love*, 27–28; Copeland, *Subversive Power of Love*, 10–11.

that religion was the impetus for a "crucial mediation of black personal and communal transformation," leading Delille "to the possibilities of self-transcendence in the midst of the direst circumstances."[93] By choosing religious life, Delille chose a degree of autonomy and self-determination over her own body for the purpose of giving priority to her spiritual life. For Copeland, the experiences of Delille point to the reality that "Christian witness demands an engagement with bodies, not their denial; a struggle with history, not surrender to it."[94] Within this context, she expands the definition of experience to include "the differentiated range and interconnections of black women's religious, racial, cultural, sexual, legal, and social (i.e., political and economic) experience."[95] Copeland's book on Delille has similarities to this book, but her project was more focused on the aim of demonstrating the contribution that Delille could make to systematic theology instead of Christian ethics.

Retrieval of African American sources is integral to Copeland's theological project as well as her analysis of white supremacy and privilege. She argues that only by exposing the ugly reality of racism to the light of day will Christians be moved to adequately realize the evil of racism and be provoked to oppose it. Within her theology of racial justice, she utilizes the horrific, inspiring, and faithful lives of African Americans—particularly women—to inform and expand the understanding of many traditional Catholic doctrines. Although she offers no explicit role for African Americans in confronting racism today, it was not the purpose of her project to suggest specific responses to racism for whites or blacks. Instead, she remembers the stories of many brave African American women from the past in order to inspire all Catholics to acknowledge and reflect on racial injustice in their own context and to follow the example of Christ in living a practice of active solidarity.

Bryan N. Massingale

Bryan N. Massingale, who is the only black Catholic ethicist that I will examine, has published multiple articles on racism, and in 2010 he published a comprehensive book on the issue, *Racial Justice and the Catholic Church*. Massingale wrote his dissertation on the social dimensions of sin

93. Copeland, *Subversive Power of Love*, 8.
94. Ibid., 55, 57.
95. Ibid., 8.

and reconciliation in the theology of James Cone and Gustavo Gutiérrez. He believes that "there is a valuable and essential contribution that the black experience—the experience of creating meaning and possibility in the midst of the crushing ordinariness of American racism—can make to Catholic faith and theology."[96] Since racism is in some manner connected to practically every justice issue in the United States and is still largely ignored by Catholic theologians, Catholic theology regarding justice has been decisively compromised and, by default, rendered inadequate.[97] In a 1997 article, Massingale examined *Theological Studies* and the *Proceedings from the Catholic Theological Society of America* dating from the 1940s to the present. He observed the absence of interest regarding racial justice in their regular summaries on important trends and publications in moral theology. As he poignantly pointed out, one would not be aware of the civil rights movement from these sources. When racism was addressed in the theological realm, blacks were often treated as objects of white study, analysis, and charity. In other words, African Americans were rarely seen as agents capable of independent action to better their own situation.[98]

Massingale's understanding of racism is largely informed by Bernard Lonergan's theory of culture. According to Lonergan, "a culture is simply a set of meanings and values that inform the way of life of a community."[99] For Massingale, racism refers to a set of meanings and values "attached to skin color," and "a way of interpreting skin color differences that pervades the collective convictions, conventions, and practices of American life."[100] Understanding racism as a cultural phenomenon is a key component of Massingale's thought and is viewed as a necessary way in which to understand racism if one hopes to confront it effectively. As Lonergan stated, "Culture stands to social order as soul to body."[101] Massingale, after incorporating the work of Lonergan, regards culture as a shared group reality that is learned, shapes the identity of a community, and is expressed symbolically.[102]

96. Massingale, *Racial Justice*, ix.

97. Ibid., x.

98. Massingale, "The African American Experience," 79–101.

99. Bernard Lonergan, quoted in Massingale, *Racial Justice*, 16. This quote is from Lonergan, *A Second Collection*, 232.

100. Massingale, *Racial Justice*, 1–2.

101. Lonergan, quoted in Massingale, *Racial Justice*, 16. This quote is from Lonergan, *A Second Collection*, 102.

102. Massingale, *Racial Justice*, 16–17.

Massingale asserts that culture manifests itself in the structural realities of a society. As a result, the American culture of racism and white privilege has produced such atrocities as slavery, *Plessy v. Ferguson* (1896), and the exclusion of domestic and agricultural workers (mostly non-white) from the Social Security Act of 1935. These structural manifestations of racism prevented African Americans from acquiring wealth and security in old age, which whites were able to obtain and pass on to their posterity. Consequently, the inequalities of the distant and recent past continue to affect the lives of blacks today. For there to be any reasonable expectation of legitimate redress, American Catholic ethical reflection must espouse structural and systemic approaches to challenge racism. Since culture pervades our society, racism will be eradicated from our culture only when it is seen as "contrary or foreign" to a deeper and more important "cultural ethos."[103] Massingale posits that authentic religious faith can provide a more foundational cultural ethos that can overcome the cultural bedrock on which structural forms of racism are grounded. Racial reconciliation, which is the objective of racial justice, should not result in "the elimination of racial differences, but rather the elimination of the stigma and privilege associated with race."[104]

In *Racial Justice and the Catholic Church*, Massingale presents two aspects of African American culture that can augment Catholic social teaching's concept of distributive justice: the welcome table and the beloved community. These images champion freedom and justice for all persons and all peoples, and offer a formidable threat to the problems of racism, war, and poverty.[105] These images are both biblical and require less extrapolation than the regularly used doctrines to promote racial justice: the Fatherhood of God and the Paschal Mystery.

In his 2010 presidential address to the Catholic Theological Society of America, Massingale enlisted Malcolm X as a resource for Catholic theological reflection on racism. Bringing Malcolm into dialogue with Catholic ethics permits Massingale to create an ethical system that is both "authentically black and truly Catholic."[106] One aspect of Malcolm's thought that Massingale believes still needs to be addressed today is "a profound

---

103. Ibid., 34, 37–42.
104. Ibid., 85, 90.
105. Ibid., 137–43.
106. Massingale, "*Vox Victimarum Vox Dei*," 63.

inner wounding" and demoralization that plagues African Americans.[107] This wounding requires healing through "cultural recovery and celebration," which is often absent in American society and in white churches. Additionally, Massingale incorporates Malcolm in order to illustrate the benefit of bringing African American thought into Catholic ethical dialogue—even that of African Americans who are not always "considered tame or acceptable"(i.e., activists more controversial than Martin Luther King Jr.).[108]

Essentially, Massingale attests to the need for U.S. Catholic ethicists to "adopt a more structural and systemic approach to racism, one that views this evil primarily as a cultural phenomenon, a culture of White advantage, privilege, and dominance that has derivative personal, interpersonal, and institutional manifestations."[109] The Catholic community can play an integral role in promoting structural changes while at the same time integrating African American practices into its liturgical life, which can address the foundational cultural elements of racism. For Massingale, the retrieval of black sources and the inclusion of the black experience are necessary as a corrective for Catholic racial justice. Although specific recommendations for black agency are more implied than spelled out in his publications, Massingale's dialogue with African American spirituality and the thought of Malcolm X, as well as his own work to combat racism, evidence the role of black agency in his ethical system.

Jon Nilson

Jon Nilson is arguably the white Catholic theologian most interested in retrieval of black sources and the concept of black agency. His book *Hearing past the Pain* begins by contrasting the insightful theology of a group of illiterate black slaves during the nineteenth century with that of a scholarly bishop who promoted slavery. The example illustrates for Nilson that all the rich learning and tradition found in the Roman Catholic faith has not prevented the Catholic Church in America from being a racist institution. Nilson avows that the problem with white Catholic theologians is their blindness to contemporary forms of racism and white privilege. He ponders how this can be the case when many of these same theologians have

---

107. Ibid., 67–68.
108. Ibid., 71, 81.
109. Massingale, "James Cone and Recent Catholic Episcopal Teaching," 730.

no problem noticing and addressing anti-Semitism, sexism, and classism, even when they are not members of the groups most directly affected. According to Nilson, the racism of white Catholic theologians has taken two forms: (1) ignoring the issue of racism "as a fundamental contradiction of the gospel," and (2) "marginalizing black theology."[110] Catholic thought on racism must be inclusive of African American thought because no theology is universal or relatively adequate for all times, places, and issues. Nilson takes his own advice to heart by ensuring that his book is imbued with the thought of African Americans, whether they are Catholic or non-Catholic. His black sources include James Baldwin, the black bishops of the United States, Stephen L. Carter, James Cone, Shawn Copeland, Ellis Cose, Cyprian Davis, W. E. B. Du Bois, James H. Evans, Diana L. Hayes, Dwight N. Hopkins, Bryan Massingale, Stephanie Y. Mitchem, Jamie T. Phelps, Cornel West, and Gayraud S. Wilmore. I provide this incomplete list of his African American sources to show that Nilson's inclusion of black sources is not superficial. Incorporating black thought is particularly important for Nilson, since "most of us [white] Catholic theologians have some vision problems that need correction before we can find the common ground necessary for engagement with black theologians."[111] In a previous article, entitled "Confessions of a White Catholic Racist Theologian," Nilson stated, "I am a racist insofar as I rarely read and never cited any black theologians in my own publications."[112] Obviously, Nilson has changed his scholarly practices.

Taking his cue from Cone, Nilson wants to underscore that racism should be viewed not as a type of sin, but as a heresy: "Sin does not threaten the integrity of the church, as heresy does."[113] Viewing racism as heretical shines a light on the incompatibility of racism with Christianity as well as the lack of tolerance that it deserves—unlike many sins for which we are asked to be patient with the sinner. Nilson sympathizes with his heretical peers, noting his belief that "Catholic theologians' horizons are limited not by bad will or a deliberate turning away from light, but from a lack of development in authenticity."[114] Nevertheless, without the aid of black sources, Catholic theology is lacking from the start. In other words: "Black theology is not a luxury or a hobby for white Catholic theologians. It is indispensable

110. Ibid., 1–5, 9.
111. Ibid., 45, 66.
112. Nilson, "Confessions of a White Catholic," 18.
113. Nilson, *Hearing past the Pain*, 68–69.
114. Ibid., 68–69, 73.

to their vocation and identity."[115] Employing a liberationist ethic, Nilson insists that theology must begin with those who are considered non-persons in society.[116] Nilson relays a quote from Cone at the end of his book, which puts the above sentiment into action: "One of the most important things whites can do in fighting white supremacy is to support black empowerment in the society, church and theology."[117]

In a 2010 article, Nilson used Martin Luther King Jr.'s image of the Beloved Community to write about the Church's role in confronting racism. Nilson understands this notion in King as pointing to "both the fulfillment of the American dream and the actualization of the Kingdom of God, a society where all live lives that befit their dignity as children of God; a society where everyone is accepted, everyone belongs."[118] Nilson then provides concrete examples of how the Beloved Community is not being actualized in American society or the Catholic Church. Across the United States, it is the norm to see the closing of diocesan offices dedicated to black Catholics. If anything, resources need to be rededicated to confronting racism on the diocesan and parish level. In order to take King's image seriously, Nilson wishes there were diocesan plans that "intentionally fostered interracial communities and neighborhoods."[119]

Without a doubt, Nilson's work is permeated with the thoughts and ideas of African American intellectuals and theologians. He is well read in black sources and familiar with the history of slavery, Jim Crow, racism, and black theology in the United States. That said, while his thought offers advice and admonitions to white theologians and Catholics, it rarely provides any proper role for African Americans in securing their own liberation. Nevertheless, Nilson's omission here is certainly due to humility and not to an accidental oversight. As someone who considers himself an apprentice to African American thinkers, Nilson does not deem himself qualified to give advice to blacks. This is why he quotes Cone's advice to white Catholics, telling them that their best role in fighting racism is to be supportive of black empowerment.[120]

---

115. Ibid., 74–75, 79.

116. Ibid., 83.

117. Cone, quoted in Nilson, *Hearing Past the Pain*, 94. The quote is originally from Cone, "Theology's Great Sin," 13.

118. Nilson, "Towards the 'Beloved Community,'" 84.

119. Ibid., 90.

120. Nilson, *Hearing past the Pain*, 94; "Confessions of a White Catholic," 33.

Summary of the Second Section

All the theologians I've discussed in the second half of this chapter are imbued with a sense that black agency and the use of African American sources are essential for any racial justice project. In addition, Cone plays a critical role in the thought of all the Catholic theologians, and it is difficult to imagine what their theology would look like without the inspiration they have received from Cone. Nevertheless, while Cone is suspicious of any interracial project, his Catholic peers, black and white alike, cannot comprehend a Catholic racial justice framework that is not interracial. In other words, while Cone is not at all troubled by the prospect of leaving whites behind who are roadblocks on the path to racial justice, the Catholic theologians never consider this as an option in their writings. For example, Massingale clearly laments and agonizes over the racist attitudes entrenched in the mindset of much of the Catholic laity and even among the American bishops, but he continues to dialogue with and challenge white Catholics.[121]

Placing an importance on African American sources and the black experience in the United States means that examinations of racism must begin with the suffering that is experienced by blacks. This experience, which is usually augmented with data from the social sciences, converses with traditional theological doctrines in order to permit fresh and relevant theological insights into the problem of racism.[122] The theology in the second section is almost as much a historical project as an ethical project. Moreover, the inclusion of historical scholarship demonstrates the benefit and necessity of black agency. The stories of black struggle and survival brought to light by these theologians illustrate the powerful role that African Americans can and must play in their own liberation.

CONCLUSION

The contrast between the first and second sections of this chapter reveals the necessity and practicality of creating a racial justice framework that embraces African American sources and promotes black agency. The theological framework of the second half of the chapter began with racial injustice as its

---

121. Massingale, *Racial Justice*, 78–82.

122. Cf. Copeland, "Foundations for Catholic Theology," 137–39; Copeland, lecture at the Institute for Black Catholic Studies, summer 1994, quoted in Massingale, "Cyprian Davis," 76.

starting point in order to properly diagnose the evil. The theological framework of the first section of the chapter was more theoretical, less concrete, and less relevant to the all too common injustices that are faced by African Americans. Therefore, the solutions for addressing racism—such as calls for state and Church intervention, for patience and forgiveness to be practiced by African Americans, and for whites to be more kind and intentional in their actions toward blacks—were often theoretical and impractical.

Even if it could be argued that the decades of writings by LaFarge and the issuance in 1958 of *Discrimination and the Christian Conscience* laid the groundwork for Catholic involvement in the civil rights movement, it was the witness and actions of African Americans that inspired white Catholics to support or join the movement. The American bishops admit in *Brothers and Sisters to Us* that Catholic involvement in the civil rights movement had its impetus in African American thought and action.[123]

Cone is also very frank in his belief that black liberation can brought about only by African Americans. Cone's historical narrative of black and white churches illustrates how white churches have repeatedly compromised their Christian values in regard to white supremacy. Even the African American bishops of the United States candidly wrote that black Catholics must "demand" recognition and leadership roles to aid the Catholic Church in eradicating racism.[124] Copeland's retrieval of Henriette Delille, a figure who shamed the greater society and the local Catholic Church of her time period with her aid to fellow blacks, is another reminder of the constant failure of white clerics and laity to address white supremacy in the United States.

In the writings of the theologians of the second section, there is an emphasis on the positive—and integral—role that black retrieval can have in deepening our comprehension of the mysteries of the Christian faith as well as in producing efficacious ethical formulations based on these mysteries. The profound experience of suffering and injustice that plagues the African American experience is invaluable as a resource for understanding hope in dire circumstances as well as the Christian necessity to reject any notion that racial injustice is willed by God. The very use of the black experience affirms the dignity and respect that the authors have for African Americans. This respect is completely absent in LaFarge. At best, LaFarge's omission of black sources represents his lack of creativity; at worst, it represents a form of racism that does not deem the black experience as worthy of retrieval or

---

123. *Brothers and Sisters to Us*, 11.
124. "What We Have Seen and Heard", 20.

having anything important to offer. Massingale's emphasis on the elimination of racial stigma and racial privilege instead of racial differences is very different from the viewpoint offered by LaFarge, which focused solely on the ontological equality of the races and dismissed any type of cultural equality.

The survey performed in this chapter on the state of Catholic social thought regarding racial justice in the twentieth and early twenty-first centuries clearly indicates the necessity for continued retrieval of African American narratives to aid the Church in more adequately confronting white supremacy. In addition, Cone asserts that white theologians, like me, can play a role in black freedom if they are willing to reorder their theological priorities according to an African American cultural viewpoint.[125] As a forgotten black Catholic who dedicated his life to fighting racial injustice, Dr. Arthur G. Falls is an indispensable resource for those wishing to improve on contemporary Catholic racial thought. Therefore, the next chapter will narrate the life of Falls, and chapter 3 will critique his writings.

---

125. Cone, *God of the Oppressed*, 46.

2 The Life of Dr. Arthur G. Falls

THIS CHAPTER WILL EXAMINE the life of Dr. Arthur G. Falls, highlighting segments that exhibit his work for racial justice. It will provide a historical context for his writings, which I will focus on in the following chapter. I begin with an overview of his background and childhood, followed by an introduction to his medical career and the start of his own family. This will set the stage for his work with the Chicago Urban League, the Federated Colored Catholics, and the Catholic Worker movement, as well as his correspondence with Cardinal Samuel Stritch, his integration into the upper-class white suburb of Western Springs, and his later work for hospital integration.

Remembering and listening to historical black Catholic figures is important. As Bryan Massingale asserts, "Thinking about the Catholic tradition's pluralism, ambiguity, and contradictions through serious, responsible, careful, and disciplined scholarship—while also being attentive to the dynamics of exclusion, silence, and repression of certain voices in that tradition—strikes me as an essential dimension of the vocation of Catholic theologians today, and especially so for U.S. Catholic scholars of African descent."[1]

Although I am not of African descent, I view my attentiveness to Falls as an affirmative response to Massingale regarding his vision of the Catholic ethicist.

GROWING UP AND THE RIOT OF 1919

Falls was born in Chicago on Christmas Day 1901, in his family's home at 3801 S. Dearborn Street. He was the descendant of Creole Catholics from

---

1. Massingale, "Cyprian Davis," 74.

Louisiana and the surrounding area.² His father, William Arthur Falls, was a postal worker, and his mother, Santalia Angelica (née de Grand Pré), was a dressmaker.³ His father had converted to Catholicism as an adult, but his mother's side of the family had been Catholic for generations, going back to their French ancestry.⁴

Falls could never remember a time that being African American did not signify "a certain handicap." As a child, his parents would often remind him and his siblings that they had only one person to fear—God. His parents also taught the children that all people shared in a common humanity, reinforcing this with the warning "that if we ever attacked another child because he happened to be white, we would get a licking when we got home."⁵

Falls's parents sent him to a public school because the only Catholic school he could be admitted to was St. Elizabeth's, which was designated for blacks and known to be inferior to the other Catholic schools. In addition, Falls noted that the North Central Association did not accredit St. Elizabeth High School and its students therefore could not attend Crane Junior College.⁶ Essentially, receiving a Catholic education would have meant that Falls could not have become a medical doctor.

Early on, Falls's parents stressed the importance of religious tolerance, and he credited his family's befriending of the Jewish family next door as the main reason he did not have anti-Semitic feelings growing up. It should

---

2. AGF, Box 1, Folder 1, p. 1. According to family lore, when his extended family entered the bedroom to see the newborn Falls, his mother presented him, saying, "Meet Dr. Falls." AGF, Box 1, Folder 1, p. 1. Falls would be baptized within a couple weeks at St. Monica parish. Baptismal Records, St. Monica Church, 5 January 1902, AAC, Sacramental Registers, Microfilm Roll 179.

3. Unsworth, *Catholics on the Edge*, 130, 132; *Who's Who in Colored America*, "Falls, Arthur Grand Pre." AGF, Box 1, Folder 1, p. 2; Falls, Unpublished Autobiography, disc 11-side 2 p. 1 (also Box 1, Folder 6). In tracing his own family tree, Falls believed he had African, French, German, Spanish, and Choctaw Indian ancestry. AGF, Box 1, Folder 1, pp. 1–2.

4. AGF, Box 1, Folder 1, p. 7. William's baptismal record is available at Baptismal Records, St. Monica Church, 23 November 1900, ACC, Sacramental Registers, Microfilm Roll 179.

5. AGF, Box 1, Folder 1, p. 5, 21.

6. AGF, Box 1, Folder 12, disc 18-side 2, pp. 4–5. He discovered this when the daughter of a National Catholic Interracial Federation member was rejected from Crane Junior College until after she took evening courses at Englewood High School. Perhaps in response to this incident, St. Elizabeth's did receive accreditation from the University of Illinois in December 1933. It published this news in the local Archdiocesan newspaper. *Chicago New World*, "St. Elizabeth's H. S. Accredited."

be noted that the neighborhoods in which he grew up were mostly white.[7] During Falls's high school years, his father served many volunteer hours as the secretary for St. Monica's Order of Foresters. Without being specific, Falls recalled an instance in which "I saw my father stand and fight on principle. He was the only person fighting in a group of two hundred, and I saw him fight until he won. This left a lasting impression on me."[8] The influence of this event will be seen throughout the life of Falls.

After graduating from Englewood High School in 1918, he attended Crane Junior College. There he befriended a group of German Jews who told him that he should not associate with Slavic Jews, as they were inferior. Believing this to be "silly," he refused to follow their advice.[9] Later on, while he was involved with the Catholic Worker movement, he had opportunities to speak to white Catholic schoolchildren, among whom he found a great deal of anti-Semitism. It was his practice in these situations to ask how many of the girls were named Mary. Many of the children would proudly raise their hands and tell him that the name was holy because it was the name of "our Holy Mother." To this, he would respond: "Mary was a Jew. Christ was a Jew. And an Oriental Jew. Believe me, Oriental Jews are not blue-eyed blondes!" This line of reasoning usually made the kids think twice about their anti-Semitic comments.[10]

The summer of 1919 is often referred to as the Red Summer because there were over two dozen separate race riots in the United States, including one in Chicago.[11] While the black population had been steadily increasing in Chicago since the Civil War, it doubled in the three years before the riot. This led to very tense racial conditions in the job market following the end of World War I, with the return of white workers whose labor had been replaced by black men. Many of the whites felt that black workers should be fired to provide more jobs for whites.[12]

---

7. AGF, Box 1, Folder 2, pp. 43–44.

8. AGF, Box 1, Folder 1, pp. 39–40.

9. AGF, Box 1, Folder 2, pp. 60–61.

10. Falls, interview by Troester, DDCW, Series W-9, Box 4, Folder 12. On 2 April 1939, Falls was on a local radio station where he spoke against anti-Semitism from a Catholic perspective. He stated that he received many anonymous threats from Fr. Charles Coughlin supporters. AGF, Box 2, Folder 1, disc 24-side 1, p. 8.

11. For further information on this riot, see Abu-Lughud, *Race, Space, and Riots in Chicago, New York, and Los Angeles*; Tuttle Jr., *Race Riot: Chicago in the Red Summer of 1919*.

12. Avella, *This Confident Church*, 250; Tuttle, *Race Riot*, 18, 66, 83–84. At the time

The riot in Chicago lasted from 27 July to 3 August. On the second day of the riot, several white gangs stopped streetcars to pull off blacks, beat them, and in some cases, kill them. One gang attacked the streetcar one of Falls's brother was riding on his way home from work. A white man on the streetcar hid Falls's brother under his seat, saving him from being discovered.

On the third day of the riot, not realizing the situation was still dangerous, the eighteen-year-old Falls and his father decided to go to their jobs at the post office. They were attacked by a gang of whites on a street that was brimming with many other people going to work. After initially fighting back, Falls ran off, hoping to take most of the gang with him, which he did. Being young, fast, and athletic, he outran them and made it to the post office. His father arrived an hour later, with six white men who had surrounded him and protected him from the remaining members of the gang. They later discovered that a black man by the name of Robert Williams had been killed less than an hour earlier on the very corner where they had been attacked.[13]

Falls and his father did not bother trying to go to work the rest of the week. For the next few nights, they stayed alert in their home and listened to the rioting that, fortunately, did not come to their doorstep. The family did not own a gun. When they finally went back to work, the African Americans from his neighborhood traveled in groups of five or more, and Falls and his father armed themselves with knives.[14]

Falls had felt helpless as the rioting occurred outside his parents' home, since they had little with which to protect themselves. Although Falls was never a proponent of violence in the struggle for racial justice, he never wavered in his belief in the right to self-defense.

MEDICAL CAREER

Falls attended the prestigious Northwestern University Medical School and earned his bachelor of arts and doctor of medicine degrees in 1925.[15]

---

of the riots, black workers amounted to twenty-five percent of the labor force in the stockyards. Tuttle, *Race Riot*, 124–25, 160.

13. AGF, Box 1, Folder 2, pp. 74, 79–85; Box 1, Folder 3, p. 86. *Chicago Defender*, "List of Slain," 1.

14. AGF, Box 1, Folder 3, p. 88–94.

15. AGF, Box 1, Folder 2, 69–70. Falls was probably the last black person to graduate

Healing the Racial Divide

Though it was not required of most medical students at the time, Falls did an internship at Kansas City General Hospital the year before he graduated.[16] This was his first experience of a city that was deeply segregated in all respects. Despite episodes of racial prejudice and violence in Chicago, he was accustomed to walking into any shop he pleased. In Kansas City, he was not allowed into most stores or restaurants because of his skin color. Even at church, he encountered racism: often, a white person would genuflect before entering Falls's pew, but then notice that he was black and go to a different pew. He frequently "wondered why such people bothered to come to church at all." These experiences in Kansas City gave him "a sense of being contaminated by the bigotry and discrimination," and he temporarily developed a hate for white people that scared him. He was very glad to return to Chicago.[17]

Immediately after graduation, Falls opened his own office.[18] At the time, newly minted physicians were expected to begin general practices of their own and to accumulate some experience before hospitals would even consider hiring them. In March 1926, Falls applied with a number of other blacks to the Chicago Medical Society. Out of that group, he was the only one to regularly write, call, and stop in the society's office to see what was happening with his application, to which he was always told he would receive a response soon. He was finally notified of his admittance to the society in March 1927. None of the other African American doctors were admitted. Falls believed that the other men were not admitted because "they were not willing to fight."[19]

From 1926 to 1930, Falls also worked as a junior surgeon from time to time at Wilson Hospital in Chicago. From 1932 onward, he worked more

---

from Northwestern. A younger friend of Falls, Dr. Quentin Young, a white physician, who also graduated from Northwestern, was always in disbelief that Falls graduated from Northwestern, since he knew first hand the racism present there. Young, interview by author.

16. AGF, Box 1, Folder 2, p. 70. In the early twentieth century, most medical degrees, like Arthur's program at Northwestern University, were granted in four years without an extra year as an internship. Graduates were then expected to begin their own practice and perhaps later work their way into a hospital. For more information concerning medical training during this era, see O'Shea, "Becoming a Surgeon in the Early 20th Century," 236–41.

17. AGF, Box 1, Folder 3, pp. 156–58; Box 1, Folder 5, pp. 173–75.

18. AGF, Box 1, Folder 4, p. 176.

19. Falls, Unpublished Autobiography, disc 11-side 2 pp. 4, 7–9. (also AGF, Box 1, Folder 6)

and more regularly at Provident Hospital in Chicago, initially as a junior surgeon, then as an attending surgeon, and for a time as the chief of staff.[20] In his memoir, Falls pointed out that Provident was known as "the colored hospital" in Chicago, and a fellow physician noted its standing as a "second-rate" hospital, but it was one of the very few places that would hire Falls.[21]

During his time as a doctor, Falls wrote a number of articles in medical journals regarding the use of different treatments for various ailments.[22] In 1929, he wrote an article for doctors just beginning in the medical profession entitled "As a Beginner Figures It Out," [23] in which he lamented the constant difficulty in collecting bills. He began by using moral suasion—explaining to clients that he expected prompt payment in return for his full attention to their needs. This method was not successful, and he found that almost 25 percent of his patients were delinquent in their bills. In response, he sent a letter to all his delinquent patients, in which he clearly stated that all payments would be expected at the time of service, with emergency patients given an extra two weeks to pay. If he was to perform a surgery, 30 percent was due at the consultation, with the balance due at the time of the operation.

20. *The American Catholic Who's Who*, "Falls, Arthur Grand Pre." Falls, "The Search for Negro Medical Students," 15; "Re-Elect Dr. Falls Head of Staff," Unknown newspaper clipping, 10 January 1957, WSHS, Folder: Dr. Arthur G. Falls.

21. AGF, Box 1, Folder 3, p. 161. Young, interview by author. It was Young who referred to it as a "second-rate" hospital from personal experience. It is unclear when he stopped working as a surgeon, but he stated that he worked as a doctor in general practice until he was eighty-eight years old. Falls, interview by Troester. Sykes, interview by author. Dr. Sykes is the granddaughter of Arthur Falls. In a letter that Lillian wrote to her sister, Muriel, when Falls was eighty, Lillian mentioned that "Art has several patients [today]." Lillian Proctor Falls to Muriel Proctor Holcombe, 11 October 1982, Henry Hugh Proctor and Adeline L. Davis Papers 1989 Addendum, 1919–1984, Amistad Research Center, Tulane University, New Orleans, LA, Unprocessed.

22. Falls, "Protein (Milk) Therapy," (1928) 117–21; "Management of Pulmonary Tuberculosis," (1955) 399–402; "Ammonium Chloride and Novasurol," (1927): 65–67, 72–73.

23. Falls, "As a Beginner Figures It Out," (1929):16–18, 65, 67.

Dr. Falls at his office desk. Chicago Illinois: 1941.
Courtesy of the Library of Congress, LC-USF34–038835-D.

When Falls wrote the article, he was also prosecuting two delinquent cases in court. The following year, his delinquent accounts only amounted to 6.92 percent of his clients. Falls concluded, "Every individual has certain hobbies; one of mine has been 'figuring.'" He continued, "It seems to me that the sooner a practitioner establishes a reputation for demanding the same conscientious co-operation from his patients that they demand from him the sooner his collections will increase."[24] Falls applied the knowledge that "personal appeals alone" do not work to his future confrontations with racism.[25]

MARRIAGE AND FAMILY

Arthur met his wife, Lillian Steele Proctor,[26] on 18 April 1921, while he was a nineteen-year-old medical student at Northwestern. She was from Atlanta and had graduated *summa cum laude* from Fisk University. She was studying

---

24. Ibid., 65, 67. Although this method improved his financial position momentarily, the worsening depression eventually made many of his patients uncollectible. AGF, Box 1, Folder 9, p. 458, 463; Folder 10, p. 524; Folder 11, p. 572.

25. Falls, "As a Beginner Figures It Out," 67.

26. There does not appear to be any relation between Lillian Proctor and Samuel DeWitt Proctor (1921–1997), who was best-known for his active role in civil rights during the 1950s and 1960s as well as being a mentor and friend to Martin Luther King Jr.

for her master's degree in the School of Social Service Administration at the University of Chicago, with a fellowship from the Urban League.[27]

Lillian was instrumental in changing Arthur's attitude toward the role of women in marriage and society. He had initially thought that a woman should stay at home and raise the kids, but Lillian would not tolerate such a viewpoint since she planned on having a career in social work.[28] The year before they married, Arthur purposefully read books on sociology and psychology "to understand more thoroughly the work that Lillian was doing and to establish a closer rapport with her."[29] Before, he had almost exclusively read medical texts, and his interest in her studies undoubtedly gave him a foundation in the social sciences.[30]

They dated for seven and a half years, with prolonged periods of separation usually pertaining to her schooling, before they married on 6 December 1928 in New York City in the living room of her parents' house. The Congregationalist minister who witnessed their marriage was Dr. William D. Berry, an old Proctor family friend.[31] In August 1929, Lillian received her master's degree from the University of Chicago. Her thesis, "A Case Study of Thirty Superior Colored Children in Washington, DC," studied the potential of black children in particular social and cultural settings.[32]

The Fallses had one son, Arthur Falls Jr., who was born on 19 October 1929 and baptized in the Catholic Church on 1 December. Later that December, they had a Catholic wedding in the rectory of a Catholic Church.[33]

---

27. AGF, Box 1, Folder 3, pp. 121, 127.

28. AGF, Box 1, Folder 5, p. 166. When Arthur and Lillian first met, she said that she had no plans to marry. This was very likely grounded in the reality that most men at the time would expect their wives to stop working when they got married. AGF, Box 1, Folder 5, pp. 165, 169–70; Folder 8, pp. 399–400.

29. AGF, Box 1, Folder 5, p. 208.

30. Ibid., p. 208.

31. AGF, Box 1, Folder 8, pp. 413–14. Lillian's family was Congregationalist and was not happy with her marrying a Catholic. Arthur and Lillian had originally planned on having a Congregationalist and Catholic ceremony in New York, but Lillian could not agree to an aspect of the Catholic ceremony, which Falls left unnamed, and so they only had the Congregationalist ceremony in New York with hopes of having a Catholic ceremony in Chicago in the near future.

32. AGF, Box 1, Folder 9, pp. 443–44.

33. AGF, Box 1, Folder 9, pp. 418, 446–47. The details concerning the reason for two marriage ceremonies by a Congregationalist minister and a year later by a Catholic priest are unclear. They were probably married at Our Lady of Solace, but Falls does not name the church and sacramental records for this time period are not yet open to the public.

It was an all too common practice during that time period for Catholics marrying non-Catholics to have the wedding in the rectory. It was not considered proper to celebrate a "mixed" wedding in the church building itself.

On 29 March 1929, Arthur's father died unexpectedly. As members of Our Lady of Solace Catholic Church, his family wanted to have the funeral there. Since the riot of 1919 ten years earlier, however, there had been increased discrimination and segregation in Chicago, and St. Elizabeth's had been deemed the church where funeral services were held for blacks. It was also the parish that many white Catholics believed was the only proper parish for black Catholics to attend. Therefore, Fr. Joseph Eckert, S.V.D., who was serving at St. Elizabeth's, had announced to the congregation that the funeral would be at St. Elizabeth's. The family had protested that William Falls would be "buried from his local parish or he would not be buried from a Catholic church at all." The parish relented and on 1 April, Fr. MacDowell celebrated the funeral mass for William at Our Lady of Solace.[34]

Arthur Falls never understood why African Americans often segregated themselves. He had been raised not to segregate himself from whites, and he was well aware that better resources existed for whites. As such, the Fallses would go to the "white beaches" in Chicago because they knew that those beaches were superior. Realizing that this could become a dangerous situation if some whites decided they did not like the family being there, they always went to the beach with a loaded revolver. Fortunately, they never felt compelled to use it.[35]

CHICAGO URBAN LEAGUE

By early 1928, Falls had joined Albon L. Foster (d. 1968), executive secretary of the Chicago Urban League, in forming a local men's division, which called itself the De Saible Club.[36] The Chicago Urban League is an interracial organization that was founded in 1916 as the black population was rapidly increasing in Chicago. Representing a wide range of people and groups in the field of race relations, it promoted the social and economic advancement of blacks in the Chicago area. Arthur's mother had always had an interest in community organizations like the League, and

34. Ibid., pp. 431–33.
35. AGF, Box 1, Folder 13, pp. 19-2-7/8.
36. Falls, Unpublished Autobiography, disc 12-side 1 p. 9. (Also see AGF, Box 1, Folder 7.)

it was she who piqued Arthur's interest in it.[37] Another reason he became involved with the Chicago Urban League was because it "gave me a better opportunity of knowing social work in which Lillian was interested."[38] Most of all, though, he felt obligated to work with the group because "it gave me added opportunity to follow the promise that I had made as a child that as I lived I would fight discrimination and segregation."[39] When Arthur became involved with the Chicago Urban League, he was not aware of any Catholic group, such as the Federated Colored Catholics, that was interested in race issues.[40]

The De Saible Club hosted a number of speakers who provided an in-depth education for Falls concerning the plight of blacks in America and abroad, with the first speaker being W. E. B. Du Bois.[41] From these speakers, who were often significant people in the field of race relations, Falls was "learning something of their attitudes and activities, all of which helped to provide a framework for the activity with which I would be engaged in the future."[42] The group also served the purpose of actively addressing issues in "industry, housing, health, discrimination and civic improvement."[43]

In April 1928, this newly organized group was the first to make contact with the Chicago World's Fair leadership about paying respect to Jean Baptiste Pointe du Sable.[44] Du Sable was the first settler in Chicago as well as a black Catholic. As Falls succinctly stated in 1968, "The first white man

---

37. AGF, Box 1, Folder 6, disc 11-side 2, p. 1. Santalia Falls was also involved with the League of Women Voters.

38. Ibid., disc 12-side 1, p. 10.

39. Ibid., disc 12-side 1, p. 10.

40. Falls, "The Chicago Letter," December 1935, p. 8; Falls, Unpublished Autobiography, disc 12-side 1, p. 17. (Also see AGF, Box 1, Folder 7.) In the cited autobiography, Falls wrote that black Catholics in Chicago during the early 1930s would be "in constant contact with almost every group except their own religious groups [sic]." In other words, if black Catholics wanted to work for racial justice in the early 1930s, most had to work with non-Catholic groups because most white Catholics did not work for racial justice.

41. Falls, Unpublished Autobiography, disc 12-side 1, p. 17. (Also see AGF, Box 1, Folder 7.)

42. AGF, Box 1, Folder 8, p. 379.

43. Chicago Urban League, "Inter Racial Good Will Through Social Service: Twelfth Annual Report of the Chicago Urban League," 31 October 1928, CUL, Series I, Box 1, Folder 8.

44. Reed, "In the Shadow of Fort Dearborn." There were a number of spellings for Jean-Baptiste Pointe du Sable in common usage during the 1920s and 1930s.

to settle in Chicago was black."[45] Other groups soon added their voices to those of the De Saible Club, and a replica of du Sable's cabin would be exhibited at the fair when it opened in 1933.[46]

In February 1932, Falls was elected to the executive board of the Chicago Urban League and asked to organize its Interracial Commission. The commission was to examine race relations in the Chicago area and to be a coordinating point for the various groups working on racial justice.[47] On 29 April, the commission met with Mayor Anton Cermak (1873–1933) to urge the appointment of African Americans to the school board, to ensure that there was a black voice to address problems related to racism. Cermak told them that the decisions had been already made for the term in question, but that he would strongly consider their suggestion next time.[48] In February 1933, the mayor did not follow through with appointing an African American to the school board, although he did appoint Earl Dickerson, a black lawyer, as Assistant Attorney General of Illinois.[49] Falls and the commission resumed pressuring the mayor about the school board, but Cermak was shot on 15 February while shaking hands with President Franklin D. Roosevelt and died on 6 March.[50]

---

45. Falls, quoted in Schueler, "W. Springs Doctor," WSHS, Folder: Dr. Arthur G. Falls.

46. Reed, "In the Shadow of Fort Dearborn," 402–11. This article does an excellent job of documenting the struggle that black groups faced in obtaining permission to build a replica of du Sable's cabin. Although Falls was aware that du Sable was Catholic, this was not a point that the De Saible Club pushed. They were not a Catholic organization and wanted du Sable recognized at the fair because he was black.

47. AGF, Box 1, Folder 10, p. 540. Falls, "Interracial Cooperation in Chicago," (May 1935) 74–75. In the just cited *Interracial Review* article, Falls noted that the Interracial Commission began in the fall of 1931, but was ineffective until he took control in February 1932 and created a Committee on Organization and Development. When the De Saible Club first formed, Falls was the secretary for group. In February 1930, he was elected president of the club, but it is uncertain for how long he was president or even how long the club continued. The Chicago Urban League archives at the University of Chicago at Chicago has scant information on the De Saible Club. AGF, Box 1, Folder 9, p. 454–55.

48. AGF, Box 1, Folder 10, p. 540. During this time period, school board members were appointed, not elected.

49. AGF, Box 1, Folder 11, pp. 592–93; *Chicago Daily Tribune*, "First Colored Democrat Named to State Law Post," 11. The newspaper article states that Dickerson was appointed by Attorney General Otto Kerner, Sr., but Falls was certain that the appointment was made possible because of the influence of Mayor Cermak.

50. AGF, Box 1, Folder 11, pp. 592–93.

On 3 April 1933, the commission met with the new mayor, Edward J. Kelly, but in May, Kelly appointed five white men who had no experience in education, with the obvious intention of pleasing his financial backers.[51] In January 1938, Falls and the Interracial Commission were still asking the mayor to appoint an African American to the school board.[52] It would not happen until late October 1939, when Dr. Midian O. Bousfield, a black physician, was appointed to the Chicago School Board by Mayor Kelly, although the exact reasoning and timing for the appointment are unclear.[53]

As the head of the Interracial Commission, Falls helped with the formation of an interracial group for the residents of Morgan Park and Beverly Hills. These were two adjacent areas of Chicago, with Morgan Park being almost completely black and Beverly Hills being completely white except for servants who lived there. Certain white residents in Beverly Hills were "disturbed" by the obvious segregation and asked the Interracial Commission to help them make some positive steps toward breaking down racial prejudice. In May 1932, Falls met with some of the residents to begin planning how best to organize such an association. Falls recommended waiting until October for a formal gathering, with smaller groups meeting in their respective communities in the interim. These groups were given a reading list that placed heavy emphasis on understanding the black experience through the social sciences.[54]

In October, at Bethany Union Church, Falls explained that the entire group would meet for the next six weeks to hear speakers on various race issues, with plenty of time for discussion. As chair of the Interracial Commission, he was in contact with various organizations, which he utilized in obtaining a number of expert speakers. Based on responses from the audience, he noted that between the first and last sessions, the attitude of

---

51. AGF, Box 1, Folder 12, pp. 602–3. *Chicago Daily Tribune*, "5 New School Trustees," 13.

52. AGF, Box 1, Folder 14, disc 23-side 1, p. 8.

53. *Chicago Defender*, "Dr. Bousfield on School Board," 1–2; Bethea, letter to the editor, 12. Dr. Bousfield (1885–1948) was the vice president and medical director of Supreme Liberty Life Insurance Company and must have known Falls because Bousfield also served time as director of Provident Hospital and president of the Chicago Urban League. *Chicago Daily Tribune*, "Dr. Midian O. Bousfield," 21.

54. AGF, Box 1, Folder 10, pp. 540–41–44. The three books that Falls recommended were Young, ed., *The American Negro*; Johnson, *The Negro in American Civilization*; and Seligmann, *The Negro Faces America*.

many white people about blacks had undergone "some modification," while blacks "still had [a] very deep-seated distrust" of whites.[55]

The following August, when Falls's brother Leo moved into his Morgan Park home, the house was stoned. Falls used this as an opportunity to call a special meeting of the Morgan Park–Beverly Hills Interracial Group, to hold "very frank discussions which resulted in the organization taking a determined stand in terms of equal opportunities for all people."[56]

As chair of the Interracial Commission, Falls performed a similar function in helping to form the Lower North Interracial Group on the Lower North Side of Chicago, where there was "increasing friction between Italian and Colored boys."[57] This situation was different from that between Beverly Hills and Morgan Park because the Italian and African American residents were not segregated. Beginning in December 1932, Falls arranged with the residents to have a number of speakers come and talk to them on race relations. In addition, a survey indicated that larger recreational facilities were needed so that the Italian and black children would not feel compelled to fight over the current resources, which were very limited.[58]

Within the context of forming and sustaining each of these interracial groups, Falls strongly emphasized teaching and listening. His two-pronged approach of assessing each group's needs while communicating the latest scientific information on race undoubtedly had its source in Lillian with her expert knowledge of the social sciences.

Taking advantage of the Chicago World's Fair, the Interracial Commission held a national conference on 20 June 1933 in the Illinois Host Building of the fairgrounds. Falls viewed this conference, which brought together experts in the field of race relations from all over the country, as "an outstanding success."[59] Noted personalities at the conference included Eugene Kinckle Jones (1885–1954) from New York, who was the first executive secretary of the National Urban League, and Mary McLeod Bethune (1875–1955) of Florida, a prominent educator and businesswoman who founded the National Council of Negro Women in 1932.[60]

---

55. AGF, Box 1, Folder 10, pp. 544–49. *Chicago Daily Tribune*, "Interrace Group Opens Weekly Forum Series," p. F4.

56. AGF, Box 1, Folder 11, pp. 624–25.

57. Ibid., pp. 574–75.

58. Ibid., pp. 575–77.

59. Ibid., pp. 609–10.

60. Ibid., p. 610; Young, "Race Relations Parley," p. WC 11.

On 15 July 1934, Falls decided to observe how the police would react to an organized interracial group of swimmers at Jackson Park Beach. A week before, the police had arrested eighteen swimmers at the beach who were promoting integration. This time, the police marched toward the interracial group in double columns and arrested eleven of the white swimmers. Falls believed that the intention of the police was to enforce segregation and scare interracial groups from attempting another event at the beach. The Interracial Commission met with the superintendent of the South Park System and a representative of the South Park police. After a two-hour discussion, the police agreed to change their tactics of enforcing segregation. They did in fact stop harassing interracial swimming groups, and there were no more disturbances at Chicago beaches that year.[61]

By May 1935, the commission had developed affiliations with about one hundred organizations and thousands of individuals.[62] Nonetheless, it appears that after 1936, Falls involvement with the Urban League lessened, though he would carry the spirit of active struggle that was present in the league to his activities in the Catholic Worker movement.[63] Unfortunately, Falls was not often forthcoming about his declining participation with any group. A plausible explanation in this case is that he thought the Catholic Worker would be a better avenue for racial integration and racial justice. Even though his involvement with the Chicago Urban League would be minimal by the late 1930s, he did rejoin its board of directors for a short period during the second half of the 1940s.[64]

---

61. AGF, Box 1, Folder 13, disc 19-side 2, pp. 8–12.

62. Falls, "Interracial Cooperation in Chicago," (May 1935) 75.

63. Chicago Urban League, "Two Decades of Service: 1916:1936," 1936, CUL, Series I, Box 1, Folder 12.

64. See, Chicago Urban League, "Chicago Urban League," 1946 Annual Report, CUL, Series I, Box 1, Folder 17; Chicago Urban League, "Annual Report of the Chicago Urban League: 1916–1947," 1947, CUL, Series I, Box 1, Folder 19; Chicago Urban League, "Freedom from Want . . . Freedom from Fear . . . Security . . . A Human Aspiration: 33rd Annual Report of Chicago Urban League: Jan. 1 to Dec. 31, 1949," CUL, Series I, Box 1, Folder 21. The exact reason for Falls rejoining the board of directors is unknown, but as the following example illustrates, he still believed it was a useful organization. In October 1947, Falls was delayed while traveling with Lillian in South America and missed a Chicago Urban League meeting. He sent a letter, notifying the League and letting them know that "all of these countries certainly could use such an agency as the Urban League." Falls, to Mr. Sidney Williams, 6 October 1947, CUL, Series I, Box 50, Folder 556.

FEDERATED COLORED CATHOLICS

Before addressing Falls's involvement with the Federated Colored Catholics, I will describe the situation of African American Catholics in the Chicago Archdiocese, including the personal experience of Falls. After the Chicago race riot of 1919, not only were more public places segregated, but Cardinal George Mundelein ordered that only blacks be served at St. Monica's Catholic Church. This action, whether intentional or not, resulted in the almost complete segregation of the archdiocese's parishes and schools. In fact, two years before the riots, the cardinal had brought in the missionary order of the Divine Word Fathers (S.V.D.) to St. Monica's to pastor to blacks. When St. Monica's burned down in 1924, Mundelein had that congregation join St. Elizabeth's.

As the black population grew, Mundelein dedicated more churches for ministry to the African American population.[65] Beginning in the early 1930s, some of the parishes that found themselves in neighborhoods with a growing black population and only a remnant of white parishioners decided to open their schools to black students in order to become black Catholic parishes. This led to the resurgence of St. Anselm and Corpus Christi in the early 1930s and St. Malachy in 1938.[66]

Falls was keenly aware that no diocesan priest advocated the cause of desegregation. While he was growing up, it had become clear to him that black Catholics were not viewed as legitimate Catholics; they were viewed as a "missionary problem."[67] Believing St. Monica's to be composed mostly of blacks who had been Catholic for generations, he did not understand why they needed to be served by missionary priests.

When he was six years old, his family had moved to Holy Angels, an almost completely white parish. At that time, his mother had tried to enroll him in the parish school, but she was unable to because he was a "problem." Thirty years later, Falls was unable to enroll his son at Our Lady of Solace

---

65. Avella, *This Confident Church*, 252, 258. Karen Johnson, "The Universal Church in the Segregated City," 43–51. It should be noted that the arguments for Mundelein's segregation of black Catholics in Chicago are more complicated than can be accounted for here. For a more nuanced view of segregation of blacks in the parish and school system of the Chicago Archdiocese, see the just cited Johnson, "The Universal Church in the Segregated City," 43–51.

66. Avella, *This Confident Church*, 252–53, 284–85.

67. Falls, interview by Troester. In the opinion of Falls, the Archdiocese of Chicago did not stop treating African Americans as a missionary problem until the 1950s. AGF, Box 1, Folder 1, p. 7.

grade school for the same reason.[68] His favorite niece was likewise excluded from St. Margaret of Scotland Catholic Church in Chicago in 1933 as a child of six years. Since the family had a very light complexion, Vilma's mother was told by the mother superior that if she stated that Vilma was white, Vilma would be accepted into the school. Vilma's mother could not in good conscience deny her race, and the school refused admission.[69]

In mixed parishes, blacks were discriminated against not only in the schools, but also in the Church's sacramental system. Black children, for example, had their confessions heard only after the white children were finished. Falls explained, "We had to keep going to the back of the line. Each parish had its way of telling you that you didn't belong."[70] At some point, he came to the conclusion that the Church's preaching at the time about the necessity of its schools and other activities that blacks were often barred from meant "either that someone was lying about the necessity of these aids, or else the priest and the mother superior were saying to col-

---

68. Falls, interview by Troester. According to Arthur's granddaughter, Arthur Jr. was accepted as a student at St. Raphael, a German parish that was not much further away than Our Lady of Solace (Sykes, interview by author). Arthur Falls Jr. went to Upsala College in East Orange, New Jersey and married Muriel Bryant. They had one child, Michelle Falls Sykes. The family remained in New Jersey and Falls Jr. was a social worker. In 1997, he died from complications related to cancer and a stroke (Sykes, interview by author).

69. *Chicago Defender*, "Catholic School Joins Jim Crow Crowd," 12. The article also states that shortly after the refusal to accept Vilma, a gas bomb was thrown into the family's home while they slept. The events were not assumed to be related. The school situation would not improve very quickly either. In a report presented at the 1960 Chicago Catholic clergy conference on race relations, it was related that "practically all Negro high school students in Chicago are receiving a secular education [because of] a definite policy of exclusion on the part of many religious who staff our Catholic high schools." It continued: "Many religious teachers use every subterfuge to keep Negro pupils out of the Catholic high schools even in areas almost entirely surrounded by Negroes." See, "The Catholic Church and the Negro in the Archdiocese of Chicago," pp. 14–15, September 20–21, 1960, Cardinal Albert Meyer Papers, AAC, Box 43809.01, Folder: Clergy Conference–Apostolate for the Colored." Hereafter, referred to as "Negro in the Archdiocese." During the 1990s, Vilma shared this story with Unsworth, as well as telling him that her parents had to bring her to four parishes before they could find a priest who would baptize her. Vilma Childs, quoted in Unsworth, *Catholics on the Edge*, 130–31.

70. Falls, quoted in Unsworth, "Lonely Prophet Falls in Chicago." James Cone and Cyprian Davis both document examples of African Americans waiting last for communion in churches in the South. Cone, *Speaking the Truth*, 145; Davis, "Reclaiming the Spirit?," 46. In the early 1990s, Falls also related to a group on retreat how he remembered being spat on as a child by white children in the choir loft above him. Bright, interview by author.

ored Catholics 'You can go to hell.'"[71] This attitude reminded him of a joke that was prominent among African Americans: "Two colored men are sitting looking at a TV show and they hear a Representative of Congress . . . expostulating about the rights of the citizen, and about the principles of democracy, and the needs of the people; and when the program is all over, one colored man turns to the other and says, 'And he don't mean you.'"[72] In similar fashion, Falls was aware that "Catholic" meant "universal" and that the Catholic Church was supposed to include everybody, "but 'universal' didn't mean us."[73]

Dr. Thomas Wyatt Turner (1877–1978), a lay black Catholic, founded the Federated Colored Catholics (FCC) in 1924 with the purpose of uniting black Catholics and ensuring greater racial justice within the Catholic Church.[74] In early September 1931, Falls attended the FCC conference in St. Louis. At the conference he gave talk entitled "Industrial and Social Problems." He was pleased with the interracial nature of the group and attended a Mass on 6 September celebrated by Fr. Stephen L. Theobald of the Archdiocese of St. Paul, the first American-trained diocesan black priest. Falls believed that this was the first time he had seen a black priest.[75] Shortly after his return to Chicago, Falls organized a local chapter of the FCC for his parish, Our Lady of Solace, and became its president.[76] The chapter's purpose was "the stimulation of inter-racial co-operation in all parish activities."[77] Shortly after the group formed, they began selling the FCC's national journal, the *Chronicle*, in front of the parish, with the parish having recognized and approved the publication.[78] Falls lamented that his parish chapter of the FCC was completely African American and that he was not able to integrate the group, especially since he was aware of its integrated character on the national level. It was at this time that Falls

---

71. AGF, Box 1, Folder 2, pp. 45–46.

72. Ibid., p. 45.

73. Falls, quoted in Unsworth, *Catholics on the Edge*, 130.

74. Nickels, *Black Catholic Protest*, 2–4; Davis, *History of Black Catholics*, 220. For more information about the history of the Federated Colored Catholics and the disagreements among the major players, see the just cited Nickels, *Black Catholic*.

75. AGF, Box 1, Folder 10, pp. 510–12.

76. Ibid., pp. 513–15. When Falls founded his chapter, there were fifteen other chapters in Chicago. Johnston, "Chicago, ILL," 15.

77. Falls, "Our Lady of Solace Chapter Formed," (1932) 15.

78. Falls, "Colored Churches," 27.

was appointed associate editor of the FCC's national publication.[79] Regarding this time period and the self-empowerment felt by the black Catholics in the FCC, Falls wrote, "To many of the clergy, the hierarchy was 'The Church,' but some of us felt that we also were the church and we certainly were sustained in this position by the actual teachings of the church itself."[80]

In January 1932, Falls was one of the organizers of the Grievance Committee of the Federated Colored Catholics for the Chicago area. This committee was composed of members from various Chicago parish chapters of the FCC. On 5 February, this committee met with Auxiliary Bishop Bernard James Sheil. Although Bishop Sheil listened to their complaints and was sympathetic, Falls doubted that anything would change.[81] On 5 June 1933, the Grievance Committee met with Mundelein's secretary, Msgr. Robert C. Maguire, who "gave evidence of knowing very little about the basic factors involved in human relations and caring even less."[82] Falls wrote that this was the first in a series of meetings of the Grievance Committee at the chancery, but as no other meetings are noted in his memoir, they must have been uneventful.[83]

It was probably experiences like this that made Falls believe that the acts of racism by priests and laity in the Catholic Church were "an

---

79. AGF, Box 1, Folder 10, pp. 511–12, 515. He would stay on as an associate editor until William Markoe left his position as editor of the journal in September 1934. *Interracial Review*, "New Editorial Board," 118.

80. AGF, Box 1, Folder 10, p. 521. Falls also commented that he felt that many clerics thought that the empowerment of the laity in the United States would lead to the anticlericalism that existed in parts of Europe. As a result, Falls thought many priests "went overboard in fighting any type of organization of Catholic laity and certainly of Catholic Negroes." AGF, Box 1, Folder 10, pp. 521–22. One must consider that Falls wrote this in 1962 and was possibly informed from the strong emphasis on the laity being considered during the Second Vatican Council. Nevertheless, this emphasis existed prior to the Council and one can see it even in the 1820s in the Trustee Controversy and the Black Catholic Congresses of the late nineteenth century. In addition, Arthur's struggle for racial justice, dating back to the late 1920s, justifies the opinion that Falls always had a strong sense of lay empowerment. Arthur's other writings from the 1930s clearly exhibit a sense of lay empowerment. The discussion of the mystical body of Christ in the next chapter will explore the notion of lay empowerment during this time period more in-depth. For more on the lay trustee controversy, see Carey, *People, Priests, and Prelates*.

81. AGF, Box 1, Folder 10, pp. 527–28.

82. AGF, Box 1, Folder 11, pp. 607–08.

83. AGF, Box 1, Folder 10, p. 527. The *Chicago Defender* did record another disappointing meeting that Falls and the grievance committee had with Msgr. Maguire that occurred in 1935. *Chicago Defender*, "See Catholics Planning Jim Crow Church," 12.

organized act of intolerance ... [and] that the very structure of the Catholic Church made the discrimination an almost built-in part of this structure and almost prevented any correction by the laity."[84] Unfortunately, he never expanded on this thought of how he believed the structure of the Church could reinforce racial discrimination. During the 1990s, Falls would still insist that racism is "not just a way of life or a cultural thing. Those who were responsible for it always knew what they were doing. And that included church leaders."[85]

In Falls's encounters with the chancery, he would never receive a response that he recognized as adequate. At one point during the 1930s, he told his mother, who had been afraid that he might leave the Catholic Church, "It is very fortunate that I was born into the Roman Catholic Church because under no stretch of [the] imagination could I conceive that I ever voluntarily would have joined it because of the discrimination and segregation which existed."[86] At the time, Falls believed that the FCC could effect some change in the Church's practices.

The national conference for the FCC in September 1932 was a pivotal turning point in the organization's history. It would signal a change in leadership and style. It was at this meeting in New York City that LaFarge and Markoe took control of the organization out of the hands of its black leadership—particularly out of the hands of Turner. The strategy that the two white priests employed to enact this course of events was a proposal to change the name of the FCC.[87]

Because of finances, Falls was unable to attend the national conference, but Chicago did send some delegates. Falls urged the delegates to push for the name change being proposed by the white priests because he felt the present name excluded the goal of integration for the organization. At the conference, the organization's name was indeed changed to the National Catholic Federation for the Promotion of Better Race Relations; it would also be referred to as the National Catholic Interracial Federation. Falls stated that Turner "refused to recognize the decision of the group and insisted that the name remain the Federated Colored Catholics and made an attack on Father Markoe of St. Louis which was very difficult to

---

84. AGF, Box 1, Folder 10, pp. 506–07.
85. Falls, quoted in Unsworth, *Catholics on the Edge*, 125.
86. AGF, Box 1, Folder 10, pp. 506–07.
87. Nickels, *Black Catholic Protest*, 16–18, 96–135; Davis, *The History of Black Catholics*, 226–29.

understand."[88] Turner's resignation soon followed, which Falls saw as a "satisfactory" development.[89]

I do not think that Falls was completely aware of the intentions of Markoe and LaFarge. Markoe was paternalistic and did not believe that African Americans or laypersons should be leaders in Church movements. LaFarge thought that the issue of race relations could be solved almost solely by education. Their leadership kept the organization in the hands of white priests and prevented the gifts of black lay Catholics from growing or flourishing.[90] Falls had talked to Markoe and was obviously impressed with him. It was Markoe who had invited Falls to speak at the St. Louis convention of the FCC.[91] Shortly after the controversial meeting, Markoe and LaFarge visited the Chicago FCC. In recalling this October 1932 meeting, Falls stated, "To me, the opportunity of meeting men like Father Garvy, Father LaFarge, and Father Markoe was a very heartening experience because I had no such experience with the clergy in Chicago itself."[92] Falls was obviously taken by their interest in race issues and their willingness to engage with black Catholics. Nevertheless, in his memoir, Falls recalled a disagreement he had with Garvy in 1931 over the priest's belief in the ability of education alone to address racial prejudice in the Catholic Church. In addition, Falls did not have much respect for Fr. Eckert at St. Elizabeth's because he "never thought of colored people as the equals of white people nor did he ever think that lay people should have anything at all to say

---

88. AGF, Box 1, Folder 11, pp. 577–80. The proposal sent by the Chicago Group is available at: Federated Colored Catholics of Chicago, "Recommendations of the Federated Colored Catholics of Chicago. Changes in the Revised Constitution Submitted by the Committee on the Revision of the Constitution," Thomas Wyatt Turner Papers, Howard University Moorland-Springarn Research Center, Washington, DC, Series E, Box 153–13, Folder 25. Thank you to Karen Johnson for sharing this document with me. Even in the 1990s, Falls felt the name of the FCC was too exclusive to the purpose of integration. Falls, quoted in Unsworth, *Catholics on the Edge*, 126.

89. AGF, Box 1, Folder 12, p. 604; disc 18-side 2 p. 4.

90. For further discussion on the views of Markoe and LaFarge on the issue of black leadership, see McGreevy, *Parish Boundaries*, 38–47; Nickels, *Black Catholic Protest*, 199–201; Nilson, "Confessions of a White Catholic," 25–26; Southern, *John LaFarge*, 105–46, 186–213, 357–75.

91. AGF, Box 1, Folder 10, p. 510.

92. AGF, Box 1, Folder 11, pp. 582–83. Fr. Garvy refers to Rev. Arnold J. Garvy, S.J., who oversaw the St. Joseph Colored Mission at Holy Family Catholic Church in Chicago during the 1930s and early 1940s. Avella, *This Confident Church*, 253, 258; Holy Family Parish, "Newsroom."

about what the Catholic Church did."[93] If Falls had had as much contact with LaFarge and Markoe as he did with Garvy and Eckert, whose views of race relations were almost identical to LaFarge's and Markoe's, I believe his high opinion of them might have waned. Falls wanted an integrated group with integrated leadership; he did not want the leadership to change from lay black to clerical white. Lastly, it should be noted that there is no evidence that Falls ever met Dr. Thomas Wyatt Turner. Perhaps the perspective of Falls would have been different if he had ever personally engaged Dr. Turner.

During the latter half of 1932, Falls's parish, Our Lady of Solace Catholic Church, denied the child of a black couple entry into the parish school. Falls talked extensively with the parish priest, the mother superior, and the superintendent of the school board. The FCC chapter sent letters to the archdiocese, but to no avail. Mundelein, by his refusal to intervene in the refusal of many white Catholic schools to admit blacks, had given the priests of each parish the final say over the admittance or denial of black children. Consequently, as was the case in many such instances across the archdiocese, the parish priest at Our Lady of Solace refused admittance to this couple's child.[94]

In early 1933, Falls was appointed chair for a new committee of the Chicago branch of the National Catholic Interracial Federation. This committee adopted a new constitution that brought all the Chicago chapters together as the Chicago branch of the federation. It was hoped that the unification of the chapters would result in better coordination of activity with more expedient results for racial justice in the Chicago Archdiocese.[95] On 8 May 1933, Falls was appointed to the executive board of the federation, and on 7 June, he was elected president of the Chicago branch. His first action as president was to work on reorganizing the group by outlining a new constitution and by-laws.[96] In 1934, as the president of the Our Lady of Solace chapter, he sent a letter to Bishop John F. Noll (later archbishop) of Fort Wayne, Indiana, to critique an article in *Our Sunday Visitor*, a paper

---

93. AGF, Box 1, Folder 10, pp. 504–06.

94. Brantley, "Our Lady of Solace Chapter," 229.

95. Falls, "Chicago Further Organizes," (April 1933) 70.

96. AGF, Box 1, Folder 12, p. 604; disc 18-side 2, p. 4. At this point it might seem that Falls was simply interested in collecting titles. To illustrate that this was not the case, Falls did turn down a position on the Chicago Civil Liberties Committee because he was too busy. AGF, Box 1, Folder 12, disc 18-side 2, p. 18. It is unknown how long he was on the executive board or how involved he was with the organization on this level.

Noll had founded. Noll, who at the time was also the chair of the Action Department of the National Catholic Welfare Conference, the predecessor of the United States Conference of Catholic Bishops, had written about the future of America, concerned with its aging population and the "*Negro predominance*" that could occur to the detriment "of a homogenous population," which was ideal.[97] Falls told Noll that his statement was an "appeal to race-prejudice" that was representative of the "lack of consistency between the doctrine and the practice of our Catholic groups."[98] Bishop Noll responded to Falls, explaining that the article was a copy of a speech he had given to the National Council of Catholic Women in Washington, but he had not actually said "Negro predominance." And in any case, the phrase had "no greater significance than if I had said 'Slav predominance,' which is often referred to."[99] Noll went on to insist that "the Negro has no better friend than the Catholic Hierarchy," that the color line had been created by Protestants, and that a greater Catholic influence would dissolve the color line. Noll finished by writing, "I can appreciate why you should be sensitive, but I am certain that your conclusions, if they relate to the Bishops of the United States, must often be wrong."[100] Falls sent Noll a final letter in which he stated his continued disagreement and reminded him that some bishops are indeed "hostile" to blacks and that the Catholic Church is viewed as the "bitter enemy" by most blacks in the United States.[101]

In 1935, even though the National Catholic Interracial Federation had changed focus, Falls lamented that only a few whites had joined the Chicago branch.[102] A year later, he wrote to a friend that the group still had potential because its national organizational structure was still intact, but it was currently ineffective because of "insufficient good leadership and good 'followship.'"[103] In other words, the group contained only followers of

---

97. Falls to Bishop J.F. Noll, 16 November 1934, Carbon copy by Falls to New York Catholic Worker, DDCW, Series W-2.1, Box 3, Folder 1. Emphasis in Arthur's letter. Quoted from Noll, "Objectives for Catholic Action," 8.

98. Falls to Bishop J.F. Noll, 16 November 1934.

99. Noll to Falls, 24 November 1934, Carbon copy by Falls to New York Catholic Worker, DDCW, Series W-2.1, Box 3, Folder 1.

100. Ibid.

101. Falls to Noll, 28 November 1934, Carbon copy to New York Catholic Worker, DDCW, Series W-2.1, Box 3, Folder 1.

102. Falls, "Interracial Cooperation in Chicago," (August 1935) 123.

103. Falls to Mr. Priest, 14 March 1936, DDCW, Series W-2.1, Box 3, Folder 1.

ecclesiastical leadership and lacked innovative leaders who were willing to take the militant steps necessary to bring about racial justice.

In early 1937, he bemoaned the federation's lack of any type of "definitive program."[104] Additionally, he was disappointed because of the organization's insistence on working "within the framework of clerical leadership."[105] He believed that the group was too eager to please Archbishop John T. McNicholas of Cincinnati. Falls considered this overt association with clergy to be compromising the group's mission. Interestingly, he did not see LaFarge as having any involvement in this situation. It was his opinion that "precisely because the Catholic Worker Group did not operate in such a manner that it proved to be much more effective."[106]

Because the Chicago branch refused "to take decisive stands in the problems which confronted us," Falls planned to officially withdraw from it in 1939, but was persuaded not to by the president of the National Catholic Interracial Federation, George W. B. Conrad. At this point, however, Falls viewed the federation as defunct. Therefore, he decided to start a separate Catholic interracial group that would meet at his home. This first Chicago Catholic Interracial Council, which first met on 7 December 1938, was largely made up of Catholic Workers who were interested in having a group that focused solely on race relations. They decided to keep the group small to allow for the possibility of direct action.[107]

THE CATHOLIC WORKER

Peter Maurin (1877–1949) and Dorothy Day (1897–1980) founded the Catholic Worker on 1 May 1933. On that day, they began selling the *Catholic Worker* newspaper on the streets of New York City; soon afterward, they started providing food and shelter to the poor in New York. Others followed their example and opened Catholic Worker houses of hospitality in various cities across America.[108]

---

104. AGF, Box 1, Folder 14, disc 22-side 1, p. 8.
105. Ibid.
106. Ibid., pp. 8–9.
107. AGF, Box 2, Folder 1, disc 24-side 1, pp. 7–8.
108. The Catholic Worker movement is far more complex than what can be mentioned here. In addition to the works of mercy for the poor and a dedication to peace issues, the Catholic Worker movement has a social theory largely informed by the notion of distributism. For further information about the Catholic Worker movement,

Right from the start, the newspaper reported on the issue of racism. In October 1933, a friend of Falls gave him a copy of the *Catholic Worker*. A month later, he wrote Dorothy Day and complimented her on the paper and its coverage of problems facing both white and black workers. In this same letter, he wrote, "It also would be interesting to see one of the workmen at the top of your front page shown to be a colored workman."[109] Immediately after this letter to Day, the masthead was changed to feature a white and black worker instead of two white workers.[110]

The *Catholic Worker* changed one of the white workers to a black worker at the suggestion of Falls. Courtesy of Marquette University Archives.

After reading the newspaper, Falls wanted to start a Catholic Worker school in Chicago. The school was the part of the Catholic Worker program that focused on bringing various groups of people together to discuss the issues of the day. Unfortunately, most priests were against the idea, and Falls received a lukewarm response from laypersons. In 1934, in a letter to Day regarding some negative clerical response, he commented that "some clergy ... [seem to have a] distinct superiority complex as concerns the laity (I already knew they had as concerns racial groups)."[111] Beginning in April 1934, he became a regular contributor to the *Catholic Worker* newspaper—almost always writing about race issues—and would remain so for the rest

---

McKanan, *The Catholic Worker after Dorothy*; Miller, *Dorothy Day*; Piehl, *Breaking Bread*; Troester, *Voices from the Catholic Worker*.

109. Falls to Dorothy Day, 3 November 1933, DDCW, Series W-2.1, Box 3, Folder 1.

110. *New York Catholic Worker*, December 1933, p. 1; AGF, Box 1, Folder 12, disc 18-side 2, p. 19.

111. Falls to Day, 16 June 1934, DDCW Series W-2.1, Box 3, Folder 1.

of the decade.[112] Despite a strained budget, he visited the Catholic Worker in New York in August 1934 and shared his opinion about the evils of segregated Catholic schools. Shortly afterward, the *New York Catholic Worker* wrote an article about the visit and the need to integrate Catholic schools as a way to "build up the understanding of the dogma of the Mystical Body."[113] As will become even more apparent in the following chapter, living out the dogmas of the Church was extremely important to Falls.

At this point, Falls was still chair of the Interracial Commission for the Chicago Urban League, which had the purpose of coordinating and bringing together varied groups interested in interracial justice. Believing the Catholic Worker to be a vehicle for furthering these goals, he advertised a speaker and discussion series being sponsored by the National Association for the Advancement of Colored People (NAACP) in the June 1935 issue of the *Catholic Worker*. In the same article, he announced an upcoming regional meeting for the National Catholic Interracial Federation in St. Louis, as well as an interracial retreat and other opportunities for interracial learning and cooperation. It was his hope that this list of opportunities "will give to our [Chicago] Catholics information on some lines of approach."[114] In another example of promoting collaboration in race relations, Falls hosted a group of Catholics and non-Catholics in his home that June to hear a talk given by Fr. John LaFarge.[115] Falls believed that contact with people from disparate backgrounds would permit Catholics to mature in their "understanding of social and economic problems and of the application of Christian doctrine to those problems."[116]

Falls also used the *Catholic Worker* newspaper as an opportunity to publicize both good and bad examples of Catholics regarding interracialism in the Chicago area. During the summer of 1935, he lauded the administration and the professors at Rosary College in River Forest, Illinois for not only beginning to accept African American students, but also implementing an

112. Arthur's first article was Falls, "The Communist Says: 'Welcome, Negro Brother!'" April 1934, pp. 1, 8.

113. *New York Catholic Worker*, "Interracial," 4. Falls also recounted this visit in his memoir. AGF, Box 1, Folder 13, disc 19-side 2, p. 16.

114. Falls, "Chicago Letter," June 1935, 8.

115. Falls, "Rosary College Will Welcome Negro Students," July-August 1935, p. 3. For other examples of Falls promoting the work of various racial justice groups, see also Falls, "Chicago Fights Racial Prejudice," September 1935, 2, 6; Falls, "The Chicago Letter," December 1935, p. 8; Falls, "The Chicago Letter," April 1936, 7.

116. Falls, "The Chicago Letter," January 1937, 6.

entire curriculum concerning race relations from a Catholic perspective. He took the opportunity to remind readers that blacks were already welcome at Loyola in Chicago, but not at DePaul or Mundelein.[117]

In June 1936, Falls wrote an article for the *Catholic Worker* that documented the case of an African American student being admitted to a white Catholic high school after students protested the decision of the school's faculty to deny the student's admittance. Falls attributed this action for justice on the part of the student body "in no small part to the increasing circulation of THE CATHOLIC WORKER and to the appearance of Dorothy Day and Peter Maurin in this area." This belief renewed his desire to start a Catholic Worker group in Chicago.[118] Falls orchestrated a visit by Peter Maurin in late spring 1936 at St. Ignatius College on Roosevelt Road. Falls remembered that when he stood up to explain the outline for the program, a woman also rose and "said just because she was a Catholic didn't mean she had to associate with niggers. And walked out [of] the church."[119] Nevertheless, Maurin's visit produced enough excitement about the Catholic Worker for Falls to coordinate a weekly gathering in the basement of St. Patrick's Church to discuss the issues of the day.[120] The attendance at the clarifications of thought eventually included diocesan priests, Benedictines, Jesuits, Dominicans, Society of the Divine Word priests, lay Catholics, and non-Catholics, as well as people from the city and from the suburbs.[121] Some of the non-Catholics "offered a distinct challenge to Catholic thought on social and economic problems."[122] One of the speakers, Fr. John Hayes (later monsignor; d. 2002), a teacher at Archbishop Quigley Preparatory Seminary in downtown Chicago, discussed the doctrines of the Catholic Church in "clear-cut descriptions . . . which, otherwise, might

117. Falls, "Rosary College Will Welcome Negro Students," 3.

118. Falls, "The Chicago Letter," June 1936, 3.

119. Falls, interview by Troester. Falls also shared this story over a decade earlier with Francis Sicius, Falls, interview by Sicius, 16 June 1976; *Chicago Daily Tribune*, "Peter Maurin," p. NW8.

120. Falls to Priest, 5 May 1936, DDCW, Series W-2.1, Box 3, Folder 1.

121. Clarification of thought is a technical term referring to the first part of the Catholic Worker program, which hopes to bring an eclectic group of people together to discuss important issues of the day and see where a consensus can be reached. The other two parts include the creation of houses of hospitality for performing the works of mercy and farming communes to foster community and address unemployment. For more information on Maurin's three point program, which he referred to as the Green Revolution, see Stocking, "When the Irish were Irish."

122. Falls, "Chicago Letter," August 1936, 3.

be lost in the maze of theological terms." Falls was particularly impressed with his explanation of the mystical body of Christ.[123]

By November, the Catholic Worker group in Chicago had organized itself into four primary committees, each with a chair: labor, cooperatives, Church, and schools. The organizational scheme was most likely at the behest of Falls. Each committee performed its separate work and also organized a "Sunday Forum" once a month, which meant that there was a public discussion every Sunday on a different topic. Falls believed that this style of organization provided an opportunity for personal responsibility and activity by each member of the group;[124] nevertheless, the committee style probably bothered Dorothy Day, who believed in a less organized *modus operandi* for the Catholic Worker.[125]

The Sunday before Thanksgiving 1936, the Chicago Catholic Worker group procured a storefront at 1841 Taylor Street, for which Falls paid the rent.[126] At this address, people like the sociologist Fr. Paul Hanly Furfey (1896–1992), the Catholic philosopher Jacques Maritain (1882–1973), and the liturgical reformer Virgil Michel, O. S. B. (1890–1938), spoke during clarifications of thought.[127] Falls became friends with Michel, and when the Falls family traveled through the northwestern United States and Canada

---

123. Falls, "The Chicago Letter," September 1936, 3. In 1940, Fr. John Hayes, later Monsignor Hayes, worked on the Social Action Committee of the National Catholic Welfare Conference until he contracted tuberculosis in the 1944. His work on that committee included immigration, race, and labor issues. Epiphany Catholic Church, "Monsignor John Hayes." In September 1937, he even led a retreat for the Chicago group. *New York Catholic Worker*, "Chi CW Holds Retreat," 2. At this point, he officially became their spiritual director. Farrell, "Chicago," January 1938, 6; Farrell, "Chicago Catholic Worker," November 1937, 3.

124. Falls, "Chicago Letter," November 1936, 7. Falls was the chairman of the school committee.

125. Day's recently published letters document a disagreement between her and Friendship House founder, Catherine de Hueck. Upon visiting the New York Catholic Worker in February 1936, de Hueck wrote to Day of the need for cleanliness, a rule for the community, more organization with a stress on hierarchy. Day disagreed. Day and du Hueck, in *All the Way to Heaven: The Selected Letters of Dorothy Day*, 86–87. In contrast, Falls believed that Day did not take advantage of having a national organization. See Falls, interview by Sicius.

126. Falls, "Chicago Letter," January 1937, 6. Unsworth, *Catholics on the Edge*, 128.

127. Falls, "Chicago Letter," February 1937, 2; Sicius, *Word Made Flesh*, 30, 36–37. After meeting Falls at the Chicago Catholic Worker, Furfey invited Falls to give a presentation at the New Social Catholicism Colloquium at the Catholic University of America in Washington, DC at the end of March 1937. AGF, Box 1, Folder 14, disc 22-side 2, p. 1.

in late August and early September 1937, they visited Michel at St. John University in Collegeville, Minnesota, and stayed a short while. At the invitation of Michel, Falls gave a number of presentations to the nuns and seminarians who were situated around the campus. The family then drove Michel to the Chippewa Reservation and the Red Lake Reservation, where Falls gave presentations to the groups of nuns ministering at each place. On 26 November 1938, Virgil Michel died unexpectedly after a catching pneumonia. For Falls, his death was a tragedy. Michel was "one of the few persons who had commanded my utter respect and devotion."[128]

Although Falls had convinced his pastor at Our Lady of Solace to host an FCC group in 1931, he could not persuade the priest to let him discuss the Catholic Worker with the parish's Holy Name Society. Falls indicated that, by and large, most priests and lay persons in the Chicago area were still reticent about the Catholic Worker movement. The pastor initially told him he could not speak to the Holy Name Society because the purpose of the society was entertainment. When Falls reminded him that the subject of the last meeting had been narcotics control, the priest "became frustrated and said, 'I am not going to have you coming in to stir up my men to do something.'"[129]

The Chicago Catholic Worker started a library that focused on such issues as labor, race, and cooperatives, to be accessible to the "man in the street." It also began giving out children's clothes, and would soon use the storefront as a soup kitchen on a regular basis. Although providing food and clothing to those in need was important, it was "only part of our job." The most important part was to awaken Catholics from their apathy regarding the important social issues of the day, to which they could properly apply their vital Christian doctrines.[130]

The Catholic Worker was the first opportunity Falls had to bring white and black Catholics together as well as Catholics and non-Catholics. "Black people didn't call upon me because I was an anomaly—being a member of such a racist Church. So that when I first became aware of the Catholic Worker movement, I said, 'Well, here's an opportunity!'" He brought rabbis, Protestant ministers, social workers, doctors, and lawyers to the weekly

---

128. AGF, Box 1, Folder 14, disc 22-side 2, pp. 1. 3, 6; Twomey, *Seventy-Five Years of Grace*, 15. The safe use of antibiotics that could have treated his pneumonia did not come into use until 1945.

129. AGF, Box 1, Folder 14, disc 22-side 2, p. 3.

130. Falls, "Chicago Letter," January 1937, 6.

Catholic Worker meetings. For some Catholics, these Catholic Worker meetings were the first time they knowingly interacted with non-Catholics.[131] The organizers not only invited groups to meet at Taylor Street, they also sent people from the Chicago Catholic Worker to give talks at YMCAs and other clubs for young people, as well as at Catholic and Protestant churches.[132] Although Falls was able to bring such a diverse group of people together, he lamented that he was unable to get very many African Americans interested in the Chicago Catholic Worker.[133]

In 1937, John Cogley (1916–1976), who would go on to serve as executive editor at *Commonweal* and religion editor at the *New York Times*, went with a friend to check out the Chicago Catholic Worker. He was "surprised to learn" that the leader at the house was African American: "It was unheard of that black people should have positions of leadership in a general Roman Catholic undertaking."[134] As Cogley recalled, everyone else during his first visit to the Catholic Worker was white, and the group included "veteran leaders of the German social movement . . . as well as a number of middle-aged men and women of the kind one might find at almost any parish gathering."[135] The German social movement was the *Central Verein*, which was an organization made up of German Catholic immigrants with an emphasis on social reform.[136]

During the time that Falls ran the school, there were regular meetings, and everyone who wanted to be involved was assigned to a committee. In addition to attending the clarifications of thought, the group regularly came together to recite Compline. And, at least for a period of time, the group agreed that one person would be praying in adoration at every hour of every day.[137] All the members of the group were sacrificing time from

131. Falls, interview by Troester.
132. Falls, "Chicago Letter," January 1937, 6.
133. AGF, Box 1, Folder 14, disc 22-side 1, pp. 9–10.
134. Cogley, *Canterbury Tale*, 8.
135. Ibid., 9.

136. For more information on the *Cental Verein*, see Brophy, "The Social Thought of the German Roman Catholic Central Verien"; Gleason, "The Central-Verein, 1900–1917"; Alphonse, "Father Virgil and the Social Institute," 135–38. Tom Sullivan also confirmed that there was a number of *Central Verein* at the meetings, particularly from St. Alphonsus Catholic Church at 1429 W. Wellington. Sullivan, interview by Sicius, 24 June 1976, transcript. DDCW, Series W-9, Box C-8.

137. Cogley, *Canterbury Tale*, 10; Falls, "Chicago Letter," *New York Catholic Worker*, January 1937, p. 6.

their busy schedules. According to Falls, each member of the group was "either working or in school."[138]

Falls encouraged members of the group to interact with other organizations in Chicago. Because of his insistence, Fr. John Hayes, who acted as a spiritual director for the group, attended a meeting of the board of directors of the Chicago Urban League. This was the first time a Catholic priest had attended one of their meetings. Falls found himself successfully coordinating a degree of interaction with the Chicago Catholic Worker school, the Chicago Urban League, and the local cooperative movement.[139]

Cogley, who associated the Catholic Worker more with voluntary poverty and houses of hospitality, stated: "There was little or no emphasis on the themes of the *Catholic Worker* itself."[140] Cogley admitted that "people did remain interested," but Dorothy Day "was obviously not happy about the way things were going on Taylor Street."[141] By May 1937, committee meetings and public talks were occurring at Taylor Street every day of the week, with sometimes more than one program happening on a given day.[142] The group had also started a credit union with a state charter, with Falls on its board of directors. The credit union's services were available to anyone involved with the Catholic Worker movement, regardless of religion, race, or nationality. It began making loans right after opening.[143] The credit union would continue until 1948, when those with immediate control of it had made too many loans to people who could not honor them. At that point, Falls reimbursed everyone who had lost money and officially closed the credit union.[144]

138. Falls, "Chicago Letter," April 1937, 7.
139. AGF, Box 1, Folder 14, disc 22-side 1, pp. 9–10.
140. Cogley, *Canterbury Tale*, 10.
141. Ibid., 11.
142. Falls, "Chicago Letter," January 1937, 6; "Chicago Letter," May 1937, 2.
143. Falls, "Chicago Letter," March 1937, 2; "Chicago Letter," April 1937, 7. Falls, interview by Sicius.
144. Falls, interview by Sicius; Sicius, *Word Made Flesh*, 30. Falls would go on to be on the board of directors of the Peoples Co-Op Credit Union in Chicago and serve as its president from 1945 until at least 1958. This credit union would become the largest credit union in America that was primarily owned and operated by African Americans. "Falls Is Re-Elected Head of Credit Union," Unknown newspaper clipping, 21 February 1957, WSHS, Folder: Dr. Arthur G. Falls; *Jet*, "Masses of Negroes Learn Thrift," 24. During 1957, the Peoples Co-Op Credit Union grew in membership from 85 members to almost 2,500 and was providing over $5,000,000 in financing for its members. *Chicago Defender*, "Co-Op Hits $1 Million in Assets," 9. Perhaps trying to learn from mistakes made by

Healing the Racial Divide

In May 1937, while Day was visiting Chicago, she rented an apartment near St. Elizabeth's parish, and upon leaving town, gave the keys to Cogley and Paul Byrne, a Loyola sophomore, with instructions to open a Catholic Worker house of hospitality. Day did this without consulting anyone at Taylor Street. Although the apartment she had rented did not work out as a Catholic Worker, a hospitality house did open shortly afterward a few blocks away on Blue Island Avenue. The main players of the Blue Island house—John Cogley, Ed Marciniak, Tom Sullivan, and Al Reser—also founded the *Chicago Catholic Worker* newspaper.[145] Msgr. Hayes pointed out that there were two reasons for the additional house. First and foremost, "Bowers was a very difficult man to work with. He was abrasive and caustic in his comments." John Bowers (d. 1950), whom I have not mentioned yet, would become the face of the Taylor Street Catholic Worker within a couple years. In 1937, he was a minor figure who was particularly interested in working with the neighborhood children. Many at Taylor Street did not want to work with Bowers, who made his insulting attitude his "trademark." Second, many wanted to provide hospitality for homeless men, and even if the rest of the group at Taylor had been willing, the size of the Taylor Street storefront could not accommodate large-scale hospitality.[146] No one in the Blue Island group ever mentioned Falls as the reason for starting another house, and there was no apparent animosity between them and Falls. Nevertheless, Falls thought that the opening of a second house

---

the Catholic Worker credit union, Peoples had a reputation for building a relationship with all the members. In addition, if a member was denied a loan, they made clear to the member what was needed to rectify the situation. Credit Union Bridge, "Talking to Members," newsletter of the Credit Union National Association (CUNA), February 1957, pp. 10–13, available upon request from CUNA Archives in Madison, WI, (608) 2321-4104.

145. Sicius, *Word Made Flesh*, 36–39; Cogley, *Canterbury* Tale, 8–14; Sullivan, interview by Sicius; AGF, Box 1, Folder 14, disc 23-side 1, p. 8. The new house originally opened at 4105 S. Wabash Ave. *New York Catholic Worker*, "New Branch of C.W. Opens in Chicago," 2.

146. John Hayes, interview by Francis Sicius, 14 June 1976, Cassette, DDCW, Series W-9.1, Box C-3. Falls, in his interview with Sicius, stated that he disagreed with Bowers regarding "methods of procedure," but that they remained good friends. Falls, interview by Sicius. Even before the split, John Bowers had focused on making the storefront more of a daycare center to better the lives of the neighborhood children. Sicius, *Word Made Flesh*, 36–39. Hayes, interview by Sicius. Tom Sullivan, who was a member at both the Chicago and New York Catholic Workers during his lifetime, also confirmed Hayes opinion that Bowers, with his caustic attitude, drove a number of people away. Sullivan, interview by Sicius.

with a focus on hospitality would detract from what he believed was a more effective means of improving the situation of black Chicagoans.

Also during 1937, Falls began regularly meeting with a group of about thirty seminarians at different individuals' homes on the topic of race relations.[147] These meetings continued, though after a while less regularly, through 1942.[148] Fall took pride in the positive influence he believed that he had on these future priests, which included Martin William Farrell,[149] Howard Matthias Hoffman,[150] and John Egan.[151]

In early 1938, Day was admitted to Little Company of Mary Hospital in Evergreen Park, Illinois, a suburb of Chicago. In her column, she simply wrote, "Dr. Arthur Falls visited me daily and operated on my abscessed

---

147. AGF, Box 1, Folder 14, disc 22-side 2, p. 7; Falls, interview by Troester. In addition, during this time period, Falls chaired the Civic Committee, which had the purpose of disseminating the thought of the Catholic Worker throughout the city of Chicago. Farrell, "Chicago Catholic Worker," 3.

148. AGF, Box 2, Folder 3, disc 28-side 1, p. 9; Falls, interview by Troester.

149. Rev. Martin "Doc" William Farrell (1910–1991) was ordained in 1938 and was immediately assigned to St. Malachy's, with newly assigned pastor, Fr. John F. Brown. With Brown and Farrell, St. Malachy "took on new life as a Negro parish." They would be the first diocesan priests to serve the black community since Mundelein brought in the Divine Word Fathers. He was known for his organizing to prevent mistreatment of the African American community. Farrell was closely associated with The Woodlawn Community in the early 1960s as it fought against attempts by the University of Chicago to remove African Americans from the neighborhood. Koenig, *History of the Parishes*, 553; Kirby, "Rev. Martin W. Farrell"; Msgr. Daniel Cantwell, interview by Rev. Steven Avella, 14 December 1983, Transcript, ACC, Box 43615.05, Folder Msgr. Daniel Cantwell.

150. Rev. Howard Matthias Hoffman (d. 2004) was ordained in 1940 and is the least well known of this group of priests. He taught at Chicago's Quigley Preparatory Seminary from 1944 to 1960 and at St. Mary on the Lake Junior College for the entirety of its existence, from 1961–1967. From 1966 to 1979, he was the pastor at St. Teresa of Avila Parish, where he diligently pastored to the Spanish-speaking community, which had just recently moved into the neighborhood. Archdiocese of Chicago, "Fr. Matthias Hoffman"; Koenig, *History of the Parishes*, 916–17. AGF, Box 1, Folder 14, disc 23-side 2, p. 1; Box 2, Folder 2, disc 25-side 2 pp. 7–8.

151. Rev. John "Jack" J. Egan (1916–2001), who was ordained in 1943, is the most well known of this group of priests. From 1958 to 1969, he headed the Archdiocesan Office of Urban Affairs, which addressed issues of segregation and urban renewal projects that were often intended to drive African Americans out of desirable neighborhoods. In 1965, he marched in Selma, Alabama with Rev. Martin Luther King Jr. During the 1960s he worked with Saul Alinsky in community organizing and did similar work with Peggy Roach at Notre Dame during the 1970s. Steinfels, "John J. Egan," Section C, p. 18. For more information on Egan, see McGreevy, *Parish Boundaries*; Frisbie, *An Alley in Chicago*; Satter, *Family Properties*.

throat." She could not read or speak for a week.[152] Falls, in a 1991 interview, shared more details. After Day was admitted to the hospital, the staff asked her if she had a private physician. She replied that Dr. Falls was her physician and he was called to the emergency room. There was a frantic discussion by a group of nuns in charge just after he arrived because no Catholic hospital allowed black doctors to practice medicine in the Chicago Archdiocese. The nuns finally allowed Falls to operate on Day and treat her, though Day had to be officially admitted to the hospital by a white doctor. Not too long after this incident, Falls applied for staff status at the hospital, which would have allowed him to refer and treat patients there, but he was turned down.[153] The mother superior, however, assured Falls "that they did admit colored physicians to their hospitals in Africa."[154]

**Dr. Falls preparing for surgery. Chicago Illinois: 1941.
Courtesy of the Library of Congress, LC-USF34-038656-D.**

152. Day, "More Houses of Hospitality Needed," 1.
153. Unsworth, "Lonely Prophet Falls in Chicago," 18.
154. AGF, Box 1, Folder 14, disc 23-side 1, p. 10.

At the end of December 1938, Falls and a number of his fellow Catholic Workers attended the first annual conference of the American Catholic Sociological Society. Falls was interested in a "sociological discussion and exploration on the basis of Catholic doctrine." He and his fellow Workers believed that they could add to the discussion at the conference based on their practical experience in addressing social problems in Chicago.[155]

In 1938, the Chicago Catholic Worker also started hosting folk dances and musical appreciation programs that incorporated the music of various ethnic groups. Additionally, they performed humorous skits written by Falls about the field of race relations. These programs were very popular and Falls was hopeful that they all—particularly an appreciation for another culture's music—could be another helpful tool in promoting interracial cooperation.[156]

At the end of 1940, the Chicago Catholic Interracial Council that Falls had formed was still active and, as noted above, largely made up of Catholic Workers. On the evening of 30 November 1940, Arthur and Lillian, along with Al Reser and others from the group, attended a dance sponsored by the Illinois Club for Catholic Women at the Drake Hotel. The presence of an interracial group in attendance was shocking for many of the members and the Interracial Council was asked to leave. They rejected this request and decided to have a pleasant evening.[157]

Falls left an indelible mark on many Catholics he met at that time. John Cogley was strongly anti-racist during and after his time at the Chicago Worker.[158] Ed Marciniak would become regularly involved in race relations in Chicago. Shortly after the *Chicago Catholic Worker* ceased publication, Marciniak founded the labor newspaper *Work*, which he published until the end of 1961. He was also a founding member of the archdiocesan Catholic Interracial Council during the 1940s, and he would work for the City of Chicago as the executive director of the Chicago Commission on Human Relations during the 1960s. In this capacity, he stated that one of his priori-

---

155. Ibid., pp. 10-11. The American Catholic Sociological Society still exists today, but is now known as the Association for the Sociology of Religion. Falls would be a member of the society until at least 1943. American Catholic Sociological Society, "Roster of the American Catholic Sociological Society," 220.

156. AGF, Box 1, Folder 14, disc 23-side 2, pp. 1-2.

157. AGF, Box 2, Folder 1, disc 24-side 2, p. 10.

158. For example, see Cogley, "Racial Prejudice is a Stupid Sin," 3; Cogley, "Negroes in Catholic Schools," 3; Cogley, "Archbishop Ousts Selma Priest," 13; Cogley, *Catholic America*, 132-34.

ties was to open up all hospitals in the Chicago area to black physicians. During a late 1980s interview, he stated that although they were working on the hospital issue from different vantage points, he kept in contact with Falls while Falls was suing the hospitals, which will be covered below.[159] No other Catholic Worker house from this time period can claim to have so many influential individuals come out of their ranks with a dedication to racial justice. And even though Cogley and Marciniak opened a house of hospitality separate from the house started by Falls, the next few decades of their lives would be dominated less by hospitality and more by their attempts to change the social sphere—the method of Falls. Falls alleged that "the Catholic Worker group may be credited with changing completely the stance of the Catholic Church in Chicago in terms of human relations."[160]

Since most Catholic Worker houses of the time provided shelter for the homeless or had a soup kitchen, Falls's focus almost solely on the roundtable discussions aspect of the Catholic Worker made the Chicago group an oddity. Falls himself wrote that the greater need in Chicago was for an avenue of "intellectual exploration and an avenue for bringing together white and colored Catholics for mutual enterprise," not housing and feeding the needy. According to Falls, the Catholic Worker group in Chicago never did focus "a great deal" on hospitality, and he "had the feeling that Dorothy Day was not particularly pleased" with the situation.[161] At the fiftieth anniversary

159. Edward Marciniak, interview by Rev. Martin Zielinski, [1987?], transcript, ACC, Unprocessed [therefore, no box number], Box "Rev. Martin Zielinski's Oral History Project," Folder "Mr. Ed Marciniak."

160. Falls, Chicago Catholic Worker 50th Anniversary Celebration, 5 December 1986, Cassette, DDCW, Series W-9.1, Box C-27. In this same talk, he also stated his belief that the Catholic Worker gave many non-Catholics in Chicago a much better attitude toward the Catholic Church. Additionally, Arthur's statement on race relations probably is meant to include the effect that that the Chicago Catholic Worker had on the many CISCA students who were involved. CISCA (Chicago Inter-Student Catholic Action) was a group of Catholic college students that were involved in the work of charity and social justice. They organized in 1927 at Loyola around Fr. Joseph Reinert, S. J., and continued into the 1960s. For more information on CISCA, see Bielakowski, "You are in the World."

161. AGF, Box 1, Folder 14, disc 23-side 1, p. 10. Falls disagreed with Day on a number of issues. For example, the Catholic Worker movement espoused voluntary poverty, something to which Falls never aspired. Nevertheless, Falls was obviously interested in certain Catholic Worker ideas, such as the cooperative movement and roundtable discussions.

celebration of the Catholic Worker in Chicago, he stated, "We didn't have a house of hospitality established, but we did a lot more."[162]

The Blue Island house closed at the beginning of the Second World War. Most of its members disagreed with Dorothy Day regarding her pacifist stance and joined the armed forces.[163] The closure of the house and the departure of the majority of its workers also marked the end of Falls's involvement with the Catholic Worker movement, except for the credit union. Falls did not participate in World War I or World War II, but not because he was a pacifist. World War I had ended before he was old enough to participate, and he refused to serve as a physician in the Second World War.[164] Regarding both wars, he wrote that he "was under no illusions" that his contribution would have made "the world safe for democracy because I recognized the fact that one of the most bigoted institutions in our country was the armed forces."[165] He noted that during both world wars, African Americans were segregated, given more menial work than white soldiers, and prevented from achieving higher ranks.[166]

As noted above, Falls's participation in the Catholic Worker movement left a profound impression on many white Catholics in the Chicago area. Although Falls had always preached an integrated solution for racial justice, the Chicago Catholic Worker allowed him his first extended foray into working with whites for racial justice that was on a level greater than moral suasion. During the remainder of his life, as we shall see, he would

162. Falls, "Chicago Catholic Worker 50th Anniversary Celebration."
163. Sicius, "The Chicago Catholic Worker," 349–52.
164. AGF, Box 2, Folder 2, disc 26-side 1, pp. 9–10. Falls believed that his experience with the riots of 1919 prevented him from ever entertaining the idea of pacifism. He thought that such violence had to be "opposed vigorously." AGF, Box 1, Folder 2, p. 62. Beginning in September 1941, Falls was regularly contacted by the Navy and asked to serve as a doctor and accept a commission as a lieutenant junior-grade. Other white doctors he knew, with less experience, were being offered positions as commanders and lieutenant commanders. They refused him higher rank and he refused to join. AGF, Box 2, Folder 2, disc 26-side 1, pp. 9–10.
165. AGF, Box 1, Folder 2, pp. 55–56. In another place, Falls stated: "I certainly was not going to volunteer to serve in the United States Jim Crow army." AGF, Box 1, Folder 14, disc 23-side 2, p. 9. He stated this again at AGF, Box 2, Folder 2, disc 25-side 1, p. 9. As World War II progressed and scandalous incidences of Jim Crow continued, Falls decided in July 1943 that if he were drafted, he "would accept non-military service or go to jail." Falls was never tested on this because soon afterward the U.S. government's War Manpower Commission determined that Falls medical service in Chicago was essential. AGF, Box 2, Folder 4, disc 29-side 2, p. 6.
166. AGF, Box 1, Folder 2, pp. 56–58, 67–68.

seek out coalitions consisting of both whites and blacks that were willing to use any moral means possible to attain racial justice.

THE FELLOWSHIP OF RECONCILIATION, THE CONGRESS OF RACIAL EQUALITY, AND FRIENDSHIP HOUSE

In October 1941, Falls accepted an invitation to join the Fellowship of Reconciliation's Program Planning Committee and their newly formed Race Relations Cell.[167] The Fellowship of Reconciliation (FOR) is an international interfaith group dedicated to justice through nonviolence that started in England in 1915. On 26 October, Falls took the Race Relations Cell on a field trip around Chicago to show them the housing problem faced by African Americans.[168]

Falls served the cell for a while in a mostly advisory capacity. Then, almost to a person, its members became founding members of the Congress of Racial Equality (CORE), a group dedicated solely to the elimination of racial discrimination. CORE's initial activities included confronting restaurant owners in the downtown area who were notorious for denying service to African Americans. It would talk to the owners, try to obtain service with interracial groups, and leaflet outside restaurants that continued to refuse service to blacks.[169] Eventually, CORE published a list of restaurants that served blacks as places worthy of patronizing.[170]

As with the FOR, Arthur and Lillian participated in a more advisory role.[171] Many of the men in CORE would be sent to the conscientious objector camp in Coshocoton, Ohio, in 1943. In February of that year, Arthur took a road trip to visit them. Later that year, Arthur sat on a couple of CORE committees and hosted the executive committee meetings at 4655 S. Michigan

---

167. AGF, Box 2, Folder 2, disc 26-side 2, pp. 8–9.

168. AGF, Box 2, Folder 2, disc 26-side 2, p. 9. For more information on the Fellowship of Reconciliation, see Deats, Introduction to *Peace is the Way*; Barton, "The Fellowship of Reconciliation."

169. AGF, Box 2, Folder 3, disc 28-side 1, pp. 5–7. For the first year, the group was known as the Committee of Racial Equality.

170. AGF, Box 2, Folder 4, disc 29-side 2, pp. 8–9.

171. AGF, Box 2, Folder 3, disc 28-side 1, p. 7. Arthur and Lillian attended their first CORE meeting on 12 July 1942. AGF, Box 2, Folder 3, disc 28-side 1, p. 5.

Boulevard, where his private practice was located.¹⁷² Although Arthur's involvement with CORE would stop at this point, CORE would go on to play a pivotal role in numerous civil rights campaigns during the 1960s.

On 2 July 1942, Baroness Catherine de Hueck (later Catherine Doherty) visited Falls to discuss the opening of a Friendship House in Chicago.¹⁷³ Friendship House was a Catholic interracial apostolate that de Hueck had founded in Toronto in the early 1930s. Based on the correspondence of its members, it appears that the group was happy to have the support of Falls; one member stated that Falls was well respected in the African American community and was known for refusing to compromise.¹⁷⁴ Although Falls was too busy to be active in another group, he did invite the Friendship House people to his home to meet others in the interracial movement about two weeks before Friendship House officially opened in Chicago on 5 November 1942.¹⁷⁵

CARDINAL STRITCH CORRESPONDENCE¹⁷⁶

Cardinal Samuel A. Stritch (1887–1958) was the Archbishop of Chicago from early 1940 until his death in May 1958. Stritch was born in Tennessee and would remain Southern in his accent and attitudes toward African Americans for the whole of his life. Although he would always strongly support efforts toward the evangelization of African Americans, he would remain apathetic on matters of racial justice.¹⁷⁷

---

172. AGF, Box 2, Folder 4, disc 29-side 2, pp. 7–8. Arthur's early interaction with CORE is confirmed by the listing of his name on two separate committees on a program for an Interracial Education Conference in Chicago in November 1943. "Conference on Interracial Education," 19 November 1943, Congress on Racial Equality Collection, Wisconsin Historical Society, Madison, WI, Series 3: Executive Secretary's File, Box 6, Folder 5.

173. AGF, Box 2, Folder 3, disc 28-side 2, p. 3. For information on Friendship House, see Sharum, "A Strange Fire Burning."

174. Ellen Tarry to Baroness Catherine de Hueck, 1942, Madonna House Archive, Combermere, Canada, Catherine de Hueck Doherty's Correspondence, Folder Ellen Tarry 1940–1942—1992 042-250. Thank you to Karen Johnson for sharing this document with me.

175. AGF, Box 2, Folder 3, disc 28-side 2, pp. 3–4.

176. It is likely that the cited correspondence between Stritch and Falls that is held at the ACC is all that was written between the two of them.

177. Avella, *This Confident Church*, 2, 254.

Falls first wrote Stritch shortly after he came to Chicago in August 1940 to commend him on the archdiocesan presence at the American Negro Exposition that had been recently held in Chicago.[178] To his credit, Stritch had sent a circular to all the priests of the archdiocese a few weeks earlier, asking the priests and their assemblies to attend the exposition, which commemorated the seventy-fifth anniversary of the emancipation of slavery. Stritch hoped that the friendly Catholic presence would give a better impression to African Americans of white Catholics and perhaps lay the groundwork for the winning of African American souls.[179]

Falls appreciated Stritch's "zeal" for the exposition, hearing of his effort from the moral theologian Fr. John A. Ryan (1865–1945), who was at the Catholic booth and whom Falls had "had the opportunity of working with . . . from the early days."[180] It appears that Stritch accomplished his goal. Falls remarked that many African Americans whom he knew to have an antagonistic view of the Catholic Church were now speaking of the Catholic Church with "respect and reverence." Falls offered Stritch his services in the field of racial justice and spoke of "a new note of hope in the hearts and minds especially of our Catholic Negroes."[181] Falls was apparently very hopeful that this early effort by Stritch to improve race relations in Chicago would be indicative of a strong archdiocesan stance on racial justice. In addition, Falls's memoir joyously recorded 19 September 1940 as the day Fr. Vincent Smith, S.V.D., became the assistant rector of St. Elizabeth Parish. Smith was the first African American priest assigned to a parish in the Archdiocese of Chicago in over forty years. This was a dramatic change in policy from that of Cardinal Mundelein, who Falls believed would not have allowed any black priests to serve in the Chicago Archdiocese.[182] This was, undoubtedly, the most pleased that Falls would be with Stritch during his tenure in Chicago.

178. Falls to Most Rev. Samuel A. Stritch, 9 August 1940, Chancery Correspondence, General Correspondence, Executive Records, ACC, Box 43848.01, Folder 14. Falls also covered this event in his memoir. AGF, Box 2, Folder 1, disc 24-side 2, pp. 7–8.

179. Stritch to Priests of the Archdiocese of Chicago, 17 July 1940, Chancery Correspondence, General Correspondence, Executive Records, ACC, Box 43848.05, Folder 7.

180. Falls to Stritch, 9 August 1940. Unfortunately, nothing is known of the "the early days." It is possible that Falls had contact with Ryan when the Chicago Catholic Worker was first forming. There is a large section of the memoir that is missing for that time period.

181. Ibid.

182. AGF, Box 2, Folder 1, disc 24-side 2, p. 8.

In December 1941, Falls wrote Stritch again, asking for the creation of a new Chicago Interracial Council, to be "developed under your auspices, consisting of representatives of clergy and of laity, of labor and capital, of the press and of such other groups as might be effective in this field."[183] Falls related to Stritch the "frustration and despair" among African Americans in Chicago; the vast resources of the Chicago Archdiocese, deployed in the guise of an interracial council, could accomplish much in the field of racial justice.[184] Stritch immediately wrote back, acknowledging Falls's frustration but ignoring his request for the council.[185] In 1943, the recently ordained Rev. Daniel M. Cantwell (d. 1996) also unsuccessfully asked for a Catholic Interracial Council. Nevertheless, in early 1945, Cantwell organized a group that included Illinois Appellate Court Judge Roger J. Kiley, Alderman George D. Kells, a couple of attorneys, and black labor leader John Yancey. In September 1945, the group officially asked the archdiocese to recognize it as the Catholic Interracial Council, presenting itself as pliant to the cardinal's authority. Stritch approved the group, but gave them a short leash.[186] Falls would never serve on this Catholic Interracial Council. It is safe to assume that Stritch would have considered Falls too volatile and confrontational for the group.[187]

In response to three days of race riots in Detroit in late June 1943, which ended only with the aid of federal troops, Mayor Edward J. Kelly of Chicago appointed a municipal Committee on Race Relations in July 1943.[188] In May 1944, the chair of this committee asked Falls to sit on its health subcommittee and he accepted.[189] It was probably Falls's involvement with this committee that led him to write Stritch again in December 1946, when he sent an urgent telegram pleading for Stritch to use his "lead-

183. Falls to Stritch, 26 December 1941, Chancery Correspondence, General Correspondence, Executive Records, ACC, Box 43849.04, Folder 5.

184. Falls to Stritch, 26 December 1941.

185. Stritch to Falls, 27 December 1941, Chancery Correspondence, General Correspondence, Executive Records, ACC, Box 43849.04, Folder 3.

186. Avella, *This Confident Church*, 290–92.

187. Edward Marciniak, in an interview that he gave in the 1980s about his involvement in the Catholic Interracial Council could not remember exactly why Falls was not a part of it, but speculated that "whites weren't ready" and would have viewed him as "too militant" at that time. Marciniak, interview by Zielinski.

188. Mayor's Committee on Race Relations, *Race Relations in Chicago*, 1, 26.

189. Edwin R. Embree to Falls, 10 May 1044, Julius Rosenwald Fund Records, Tulane University, New Orleans, LA, Box 179, Folder 3.

ership" to positively address the riot that had broken out at the Airport Homes.[190] The Airport Homes were a housing project for World War II veterans near what is now called Chicago Midway International Airport. A couple of African American families had attempted to move into the project while the white men were at work; a mob of mostly white women had attacked the black families as well as police and city officials. Though worse incidents would follow, it was at the time the worst outbreak of racial violence since the riot of 1919.[191] Falls indicated that he had been asked by the Chicago Housing Authority "to mobilize dynamic Catholic leadership" for support in this matter.[192] Stritch did not respond to Falls and remained completely silent on the subject.[193] Falls would not write to Stritch again for three years.

In December 1949, Falls wrote to Stritch once more about the continuing outbreak of riots. The impetus for Falls's letter was a pledge against "indecency as expressed in motion pictures and in theatrical productions" that Falls and his fellow parishioners had been asked to make the day before by the parish priest at Sunday Mass. Although Falls did not state that he had any problem with such a pledge, he could not understand why Catholics were not being asked to make a much more important "pledge of opposition to indecency as expressed in rioting and physical attacks on one's fellow-man, as so recently demonstrated in Visitation Parish," which is also, without doubt, "a mortal sin."[194] In Falls's opinion, Catholics were the most active group and even had leadership roles in the rioting and violence against African Americans. Falls pointed out, and other sources concur, that the unmitigated racism of the clerical and lay leadership at Visitation Parish was largely responsible for the November 1949 riot in the Englewood neighborhood of Chicago.[195] The Englewood riot had been triggered by a rumor that a black family might be moving into the neighborhood, after African Americans were seen through the living room window of a man's home; he was holding an informal union meeting. At one point,

190. Falls to Stritch, 6 December 1946, Chancery Correspondence, General Correspondence, Executive Records, ACC, Box 43863.02, Folder 3.

191. Hirsch, *Making the Second Ghetto*, 60, 76, 90, 187.

192. Falls to Stritch, 6 December 1946.

193. Falls to Stritch, 12 December 1949, Chancery Correspondence, General Correspondence, Executive Records, ACC, Box 43873.07, Folder 2.

194. Ibid.

195. Falls to Stritch, 12 December 1949; Hirsch, *Making the Second Ghetto*, 85–86; Avella, *This Confident Church*, 256–57.

ten thousand protesters surrounded his house, attacking Jews, blacks, and whites in the area whom they suspected of supporting integration.[196]

Falls communicated to Stritch that his silence was fostering an anti-Catholic sentiment among African Americans because his "silence [about the riot] is construed as sympathy with those responsible for the rioting." Falls suggested that a public denunciation as well as an "intercultural education" program on the parish level could curb future large-scale participation of white Catholics in race riots.[197] It does not appear that Stritch responded to Falls but, without any concrete direction, he ambiguously told his secretary, Msgr. John Fitzgerald, to eliminate racist activity at Visitation Parish.[198]

On a matter of lesser importance, in June 1951 Falls wrote to Stritch on behalf of Kappa Alpha Psi (a predominantly though not exclusively African American fraternity Falls had joined as a student at Northwestern), asking his opinion regarding the best way to publicize the October coming of the Boys' Town Choir, which was an interracial ensemble.[199] Stritch promptly responded that Falls should contact the editor of the archdiocesan newspaper, the *New World*.[200] A large advertisement with an interracial photograph and prices ran in the *New World* a couple of days before the choir sang at the Chicago Opera House.[201] There is one more known instance of correspondence between Falls and Stritch, which I will cover below in the section entitled "Hospital Integration."

INTEGRATING WESTERN SPRINGS

In the summer of 1952, Arthur and Lillian decided to integrate Western Springs, Illinois, a totally white suburb of Chicago, by purchasing land there with the intent of building their future home on it. This move may have been prompted in large part by their belief that the "core of the difficulties

---

196. Hirsch, *Making the Second Ghetto*, 55–56.
197. Falls to Stritch, 12 December 1949.
198. Avella, *This Confident Church*, 257.
199. Falls to Stritch, 18 June 1951, Chancery Correspondence, General Correspondence, Executive Records, ACC, Box 43878.02, Folder 10; AGF, Box 1, Folder 3, pp. 116–18.
200. Stritch to Falls, 20 June 1951, Chancery Correspondence, General Correspondence, Executive Records, ACC, Box 43878.02, Folder 10.
201. *Chicago New World*, "Father Flanagan's Boys Town Choir."

in race relations . . . lay in the matter of housing segregation."[202] The move to Western Springs was a direct assault on housing segregationists.

In early 1943, the Fallses had purchased their first home at 1412 West 61st Street in Chicago. They were the first African American family to move onto the block and they only had difficulty with one neighbor two houses down. This neighbor struck Arthur Jr., who was thirteen at the time. Falls had her arrested and placed on a peace bond. Peace bonds were court orders that required perpetrators to deposit an amount of money that they would lose if they continued to harass the victim. From this point on, the Falls family no longer faced any difficulties with the neighbors on 61st Street.[203]

In mid-September 1952, some residents in Western Springs became aware that the Fallses were African American.[204] Before the Fallses could even obtain a building permit for their home, they were required to perform "elaborate and expensive soil tests" and meet with members of the property owners' association. The purpose of this meeting was to dissuade the Fallses from building a home in Western Springs.[205]

During this period, a group of residents collected 1,267 signatures on a petition to the Park District of Western Springs, asking it to condemn the property for park land using eminent domain.[206] After the Fallses finally obtained a building permit, they were forced to endure a drawn-out legal battle with the Park District.[207] The Fallses hired two lawyers, Edward B. Toles and Sydney A. Jones Jr., to defend them. (Toles would become the

---

202. Deerfield Citizens for Human Rights, Short History of the Fallses' Purchase and Building of their Home in Western Springs, IL, December 1959, Archives, WSHS. Hereafter referred to as "Western Springs Situation." This paper was put together by the Deerfield Citizens for Human Rights and does not have a title. AGF, Box 2, Folder 3, disc 27-side 1, p. 3.

203. AGF, Box 2, Folder 4, disc 29-side 2, p. 4.

204. Western Springs Situation.

205. Western Springs Situation; Raulin B. Wight to Mr. George Smith, 7 November 1952, Western Springs Department of Community Development, Western Springs, IL, Folder: 4812 Fair Elms Avenue. This letter contains the bill for the soil sample tests. Falls, interview by Troester; Bogardus and Davis, "Experience in Interracial Living," 16.

206. Park & Development Committee of the Forest Hills Association to Mr. Frank E. McWethy, 6 November 1952, in Western Springs Park District v. Arthur Falls, et al., 52C 14741, 1 December 1952, Richard J. Daley Center–Archives Room 1113, Clerk of the Circuit Court of Cook County, Chicago. Hereafter referred to as "Park District v. Falls." The actual signed petitions are also in this court file.

207. Park District v. Falls.

first African American bankruptcy judge in Chicago in 1968, and Jones would become the first black alderman of the Sixth Ward, later serving as a municipal court judge for Chicago and a circuit court judge for Cook County.)[208] The Council Against Discrimination in Greater Chicago, declaring that "Dr. and Mrs. Falls are rendering a public service in resisting the pressure to prevent their moving into this suburb," offered "psychological and financial" support to the family and put out an action notice to all of its affiliates, urging them to attend the court proceedings.[209]

The circuit court met about sixteen times from early January to mid-June before the judge finally decided to dismiss the suit, citing the Park District's abuse of power in attempting to condemn a home with the primary purpose not of building a park, but keeping a black family out of the area.[210] An article in the national newspaper of Friendship House, the *Catholic Interracialist*, referred to the ruling as "probably the most important court decision upholding property rights since restrictive covenants were declared unconstitutional by the Supreme Court of the United States in 1948."[211] Judge Jacob Berkowitz was quoted as stating, "If this land were condemned . . . it would be a monument in that particular area to hate and intolerance . . . and I'm sure none of us would want our little children playing on it."[212] Berkowitz continued, "Dr. and Mrs. Falls can enjoy the fraternity of brotherhood not in five, fifty or a hundred years, but now."[213] The family's lawyers remarked that, to their knowledge, this was the first

---

208. Dan Baron, "Edward Toles," 23; Heise, "Judge," 15.

209. Council Against Discrimination of Greater Chicago, "Minutes of the Monthly Board Meeting of the Council Against Discrimination," CUL, Box 263, Folder 8; Council Against Discrimination to All Affiliates, 2 June 1953, CUL, Series I, Box 263, Folder 2630. The Council was founded in 1943 and originally called the Chicago Council Against Racial and Religious Discrimination. It was organized to "coordinate efforts to eliminate inter-group tensions by education, legislation, and direct action." Annetta Dieckmann to Mr. Sidney Williams, 1 January 1953, CUL, Series I, Box 263, Folder 2628. Falls served on the council's advisory board.

210. Park District v. Falls; Deerfield Citizens for Human Rights, Short History of the Fallses' Purchase; *Jet*, "Chicago Couple Win Court Fight," 8.

211. McCleary, "Vital Court Decision in Chicago," 1.

212. Berkowitz, quoted in Bogardus and Davis, "Experience in Interracial Living," 16–17; McCleary, "Vital Court Decision in Chicago," 1.

213. Berkowitz, quoted in Council Against Discrimination of Greater Chicago, *Newsletter*, June 1953, CUL, Series I, Box 263, Folder 2639.

time a court had refused to grant a government entity the right to condemn land on the basis of racial discrimination.[214]

Shortly after the dismissal of the suit, a referendum was brought before the citizens of Western Springs to authorize a bond sale for $116,000 for the purposes of funding an appeal, purchasing the Fallses' land, and turning that land into a park. On 10 July 1953, the village voted 1,037 to 896 against the bond issue, so the appeal of the court case was dropped and the Fallses moved into their new home that December.[215]

Though they received a number of threats, the only instance of violence they experienced after moving into their home was that of a brick thrown through a window, which almost hit a family friend in the head. For two weeks afterward, Arthur and Lillian often sat at the door with a shotgun. Word apparently got out that they were armed, and they were left alone. In telling this story, Arthur confessed his "one failing": "I have utter contempt for stupidity. I have a hard time [because I am] utterly contemptuous of stupid people. And of course this whole thing is so stupid."[216]

The outcome of *Park District v. Falls* had been by no means certain, and it did not lead to victory in later, similar cases. In 1959, the Progress Development Corporation bought land in Deerfield, Illinois, in order to build an integrated housing project: about ten of its fifty-one homes were to be sold to African American families. Falls was the chair of the corporation's board of directors. The village of Deerfield is a suburb of Chicago, although it resides in a separate county.[217] Unlike the village of Western Springs, the Deerfield community was more covert about its racist intentions, and its residents approved a $550,000 bond issue to cover court costs and additional expenses, succeeding in their quest to condemn the land

214. Jones and Toles, "Dr. Falls Will Build in All-White Suburb," 4.

215. Bogardus and Davis, "Experience in Interracial Living," 17; *Council Against Discrimination Newsletter*, July 1953, CUL, Series I, Box 263, Folder 2640; "Western Springs Situation." *Western Springs Times*, "Villagers Will Vote Next Friday," 1–2; *Western Springs Times*, "Drop Appeal," 1. The *Western Springs Times* can be obtained at the Thomas Ford Memorial Library, Western Springs, Illinois. Of the five precincts that voted regarding the bond issue, the only one that voted in favor of it was the one in which the disputed property resided. This village's vote was also covered by the *Chicago Defender*. *Chicago Defender*, "Voters Defeat Last Attempt," 5.

216. Falls, interview by Troester.

217. Schueler, "W. Springs Doctor"; *Chicago Daily Tribune*, "U. S. Enjoins Deerfield," A10. The extent of Arthur's involvement in the Deerfield situation is uncertain. For more information about the very complicated court cases and their appeals, see Rosen and Rosen, *But Not Next Door*; *Chicago Tribune*, "Builder Ask Rehearing," B17.

and build a park on it.[218] No doubt they based their tactics on the results of the Western Springs case a few years earlier.

Arthur and Lillian Falls won their assault against segregation in Western Springs, but they did not do it alone. They had the support of the Chicago Urban League, Friendship House, and many other organizations. During the trial, Lillian's Congregationalist minister took the stand in support of the Fallses, gave a discussion at church on the matter, and urged church members to go to the trial to support the family.

Arthur, who at the time belonged to St. Cletus Catholic Church, received no support from his priest, even though he was very active in the predominantly white parish and the trial was widely covered in the press.[219] Moreover, two of the main figures in the Western Springs property owners' association were trustees of a local white Congregationalist church. Once again, the retrieval of black voices, whether Catholic or Protestant, is of utmost importance in piecing together a racial justice framework. In this episode, both the white Catholic and white Protestant churches in the area placed their own immediate desires over the gospel of Jesus Christ.

HOSPITAL INTEGRATION

When Albert G. Meyer became Archbishop of Chicago in 1958, the Catholic hospital system was still thoroughly entrenched in racial discrimination. Despite clear documentation of this, Meyer testified before the U.S. Commission on Civil Rights in 1959 that African Americans were "performing operations in our hospitals."[220] A number of studies addressed the lack of integration by Catholic hospitals in Chicago. I will look at a selection of these reports and give an overview of Falls's previous activity in this arena to set the scene for his action of suing almost every Chicago-area hospital in February 1961, with a number of black physicians as fellow plaintiffs.

---

218. *Chicago Daily Tribune*, "U. S. Enjoins Deerfield," A10. The same article states that the bond issue referendum, which had the largest voter turnout in the village's history, won by a vote of 2,635 to 1,207.

219. Bogardus and Davis, "Experience in Interracial Living," 16–17; Falls, interview by Troester. The contrast here between Lillian's black church and white churches to which Falls and the Western Springs officials belonged confirm Cone's suspicion that white churches are too concerned with their own selfish interests to practice the gospel of liberation.

220. Meyer, quoted in LaFarge, *Catholic Viewpoint on Race Relations*, 152. By the word "our," it appears that Meyer is indicating secular as well as Catholic institutions.

Healing the Racial Divide

A report presented at the National Catholic Conference for Interracial Justice in 1958, which met in Chicago, stated, "Our consultants have provided more-than-sufficient evidence to indicate that many Catholic hospitals now practice policies of racial exclusion or segregation, a condition which we can only describe as scandalous."[221] Also in 1958, Dietrich C. Reitzes (1935–1988), a sociologist best known for chronicling the life of Chicago community organizer Saul Alinsky, published the book *Negroes and Medicine*. Reitzes had discovered that although in many large cities Catholic hospitals were leaders in integration, this was not the case in Chicago. He even found a white physician who went so far as to say that the Catholic hospitals, "with two notable exceptions, were the worst of all hospitals as far as facilities for Negroes were concerned."[222] Only one Chicago Catholic hospital in 1955 did not segregate patients.[223]

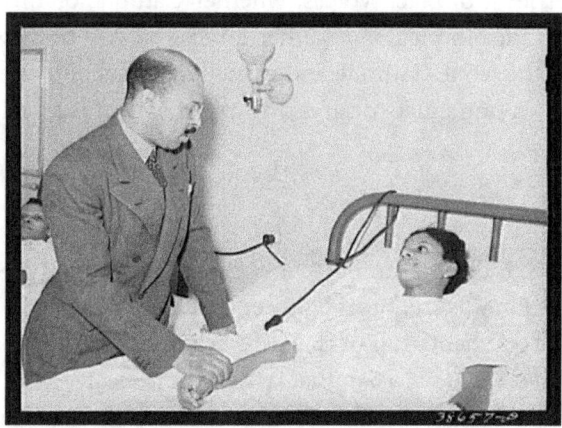

**Falls visiting a patient at Provident Hospital. Chicago Illinois: 1941.
Courtesy of the Library of Congress, LC-USF34- 038657-D.**

221. Commission on Parochial and Institutional Life, "Findings and Recommendations," 4. Cardinal Albert Meyer Papers, ACC. Box 43809.01, Folder Catholic Interracial Council (1/2).

222. Reitzes, *Negroes and Medicine*, 130. Reitzes cited a couple interviews he had with black Catholic physicians in his book, but he withholds all the names of interviewees. Based on the extensive research performed by Reitzes, it is highly probably that he interviewed Falls.

223. Avella, *This Confident Church*, 279. Avella noted that this information is from the Report on Discrimination in Catholic Hospitals, submitted by Chicago Friendship House, 30 September 1955. A copy of this report is in the Stritch Personal Papers, ACC. Unfortunately, since Avella did his research, the Archives of the Archdiocese of Chicago have completely renumbered their boxes and this report could not be located.

Reitzes had also ascertained that the number of black physicians in Chicago had actually decreased from 228 in 1938 to 226 in 1955. The only other major city to regress in its number of black physicians was Boston. In Chicago, only sixteen had affiliations with white hospitals, and these were largely because the doctors were personally connected to influential members of the hospitals. Only one affiliation had come about when the African American physician's first contact with the white hospital had been his application for the position. Additionally, in 1956, the physician-population ratio in Chicago was 1:587 for whites and 1:3,123 for African Americans. The denial of medical care to blacks by many white hospitals was obviously leaving an unmanageable burden for black doctors to contend with. At the time of the study, Cook County Hospital, Provident Hospital, and Michael Reese's Sarah Morris were notable as the only hospitals to admit African Americans or schedule them for physician appointments as a matter of course. Although some hospital personnel were forthright about their denial of care to African Americans, most "hesitated to discuss the situation with representatives of the survey, and the answers submitted on questionnaire schedules were ambiguous, unreliable, and frequently misleading."[224] Dr. Quentin Young, a physician who worked with Falls on hospital integration issues during the 1950s and 1960s, comments that tens of thousands of black union workers in Chicago had great health insurance through their union contracts, but were forced to receive substandard care at black hospitals because of discrimination.[225]

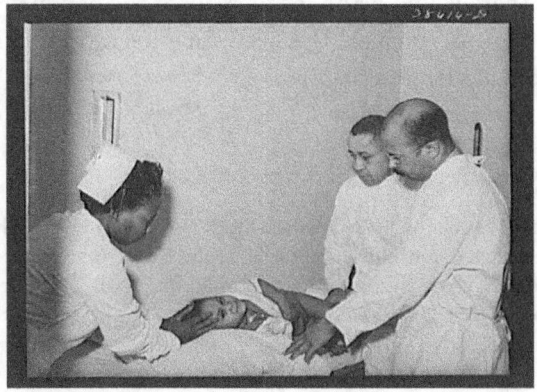

Dr. Falls examining a child at Provident Hospital. Chicago Illinois: 1941.
Courtesy of the Library of Congress, LC-USF34- 038616-D

224. Ibid., 103–5, 108, 132, 389.
225. Falls, in "Says Medical Bias" (1960) 3. Young, interview by author.

In *Negroes and Medicine*, Reitzes recognized the work of the Committee to End Discrimination in Chicago Medical Institutions (CED), of which Falls was a founding member. The CED was formed around 1952 by area physicians, educators, medical students, and other concerned parties for the purpose of eliminating "discrimination in the teaching and practice of medicine." Falls served as the CED's chair and co-chair at various times during its existence.[226] Its first action was to contact the deans of each of the five medical schools to inquire why so few African Americans were in their programs. Every dean clearly responded: "No quota, no discrimination, send us qualified applicants!"[227] Therefore, the CED turned its attention to the white private hospitals that discriminated against African Americans while benefiting from "tax exemption, government licensure, and community support."[228] Exploiting the information above, the CED successfully lobbied the state of Illinois and the city council in Chicago to pass ordinances, in 1955 and 1956 respectively, that were supposed to prevent the denial of care in any hospital because of "race, color, creed, national origin, or ancestry."[229] The difficulty of enforcing this measure and the lack of black doctors on staff made the ordinances ineffective.[230] These laws had little, if any, impact.

On 3 April 1956, after the state and city non-discriminatory bills had been passed, Falls (along with the co-chair of the CED, Dr. Alfred B. Stein, and the secretary of the banquet committee, Mrs. Walter Johnson) wrote to Cardinal Stritch, asking him to be an official sponsor for the group's banquet in June. There would be no fee to sponsor the banquet, which would be used as a tool to publicize the need for integration within Chicago's hospitals. The banquet was also going to honor two black medical doctors, William Montague Cobb and T. R. M. Howard, for their contributions

---

226. Falls, "The Search for Negro Medical Students," 15–16. Although the CED clearly remained in existence until the lawsuit against the Chicago hospitals was completed, it is unclear when the group ceased. Dr. Quentin Young, a white doctor who was also a founding member of this group, refers to Falls as "a very key person" in the CED. Young, interview by author.

227. Falls, "The Search for Negro Medical Students," 16.

228. Ibid., 17.

229. Reitzes, *Negroes and Medicine*, 131; National Medical Association, "Chicago Ordinance," 69; National Medical Association, "Chicago Enacts Hospital," 202; Falls, "The Search for Negro Medical Students," 17.

230. Reitzes, *Negroes and Medicine*, 131.

in fighting discrimination in the medical field.[231] Stritch promptly replied, stating that his position against racism within hospitals was well known thanks to a speech he had addressed to the Hospitals Conference of the Catholic Interracial Council of Chicago in October 1955.[232] Stritch added that he could not attend the banquet because of a previous engagement. To the probable dissatisfaction of Falls, there was no mention of the request for sponsorship.[233]

Falls would write to Stritch again a month later on banquet letterhead, which listed the sponsors down the left-hand side of the page (a list that did not include Stritch). Falls thanked him for his previous letter and asked him if he would send a priest as his representative to the banquet with the purpose of leading the opening prayer.[234] Stritch responded that Falls should contact Msgr. John Barrett, the director of hospitals for the Archdiocese of Chicago, who was "much interested in this matter."[235]

In September 1960, at a clergy conference in Chicago on race relations, a report was presented on the exclusion of African Americans in parishes, high schools, hospitals, and lay organizations.[236] A stunning paragraph from the report illustrated the nefarious situation:

> Chicago has the least degree of medical integration of any of the major northern cities. In this picture the Catholic hospitals are at least as bad as the white secular hospitals: Only six of our seventeen Catholic hospitals have Negro physicians on their staffs—ten

231. Falls et al. to Cardinal Samuel A. Stritch, 3 April 1956, Chancery Correspondence, General Correspondence, Executive Records, ACC, Box 43891.04, Folder 7.

232. An abridged version of his speech appeared in Stritch, "Interracial Justice in Hospitals," 185–86. In his speech, Stritch stated that there can be no "distinction of color" for Catholics and that even private hospitals have an obligation to serve the public good of all. In addition, he said that doctors need to be hired "without any respect to color" and asked, "How can we kneel before our blessed Savior on the Cross with His arms outstretched for all, and limit our charity and limit our ministration to any particular group?"

233. Stritch to Falls, 6 April 1956, Chancery Correspondence, General Correspondence, Executive Records, ACC, Box 43891.04, Folder 7.

234. Falls to Stritch, 4 May 1956, Chancery Correspondence, General Correspondence, Executive Records, ACC, Box 43891.04, Folder 7.

235. Stritch to Falls, 9 May 1956, Chancery Correspondence, General Correspondence, Executive Records, ACC, Box 43891.04, Folder 7.

236. See, "The Catholic Church and the Negro in the Archdiocese of Chicago," September 20–21, 1960, Cardinal Albert Meyer Papers, ACC, Box 43809.01, Folder: Clergy Conference–Apostolate for the Colored." Hereafter, referred to as "Negro in the Archdiocese."

physicians in all. If Lewis Maternity Hospital is excluded, our Catholic hospitals delivered only one-half per cent of all the Negro babies born in 1956. Colored adult patients are almost exceptional in many of our Catholic hospitals.[237]

The section on hospitals concluded that improvement would take place only when the archbishop gave clear orders prohibiting segregation and put in place an archdiocesan coordinator to implement the hiring of black doctors.[238] Reitzes had arrived at a similar conclusion in *Negroes and Medicine*. He believed that one needed to reach people in positions of power within hospitals in order to change the current practices of discrimination. His study, which covered fourteen communities, found that "when influential persons in a hospital were determined to have integration, integration took place without great difficulty."[239] Although such methods may have had success in other parts of the country, the Archbishop of Chicago possessed little control over Catholic hospitals run by religious orders, and the religious orders were not swayed by his appeals to eliminate their discriminatory practices.

After Falls and the CED realized that their actions were not procuring results, they heeded the words of Robert M. Cunningham Jr. (d. 1992), who at the time was the editor of the *Modern Hospital*: "Until Negro physicians are accepted as attending physicians on hospital staffs on the same basis as white physicians, the problem of discrimination will continue to exist."[240] In other words, until African American physicians were unreservedly appointed to white hospitals, there would not be a substantial increase in black patients at those hospitals. Falls was well aware of a "gentleman's agreement" between white hospitals and their doctors against admitting too many African American patients. Doctors who broke this agreement would be "dealt with quietly and effectively at the annual or biennial staff re-appointment date." Such a quota agreement would be difficult to en-

237. Negro in the Archdiocese, 18. At this same conference, Cardinal Albert Meyer gave a speech imploring priests to work for justice and equality for blacks based on their human dignity. This required that African Americans be integrated into the full life of the Catholic Church, including hospitals. Meyer, "The Mantle of Leadership," in *The Catholic Church and the Negro in the Archdiocese of Chicago: Clergy Conference*, by the Archdiocese of Chicago, 20–21 September 1960, pp. 22–32, see especially p. 29, Chicago Historical Society, call number: F548.9 N3 1960.

238. Negro in the Archdiocese, pp. 18–19.

239. Reitzes, *Negroes and Medicine*, 131, 335–38.

240. Cunningham, quoted in Falls, "The Search for Negro Medical Students," 17.

force with a black physician, since his patients would probably include a disproportionate number of African Americans.[241]

Therefore, in addition to pressuring the City Council of Chicago (which unanimously passed another law against racial discrimination in hospitals in 1960), Falls and nine other physicians filed a lawsuit in the U.S. District Court, Northern District of Illinois, Eastern Division, against fifty-two corporations; these corporations owned fifty-six hospitals, or roughly 75 percent of all available hospital beds in the Chicago area in February 1961. The physicians sued with the intent of gaining admission to these hospital staffs.

It is beyond the scope of this work to go into the complexity of this lawsuit, but a few words of explanation are necessary. Falls and his fellow doctors sued the hospitals using the two major anti-trust acts as their foundation: the Sherman Act of 1890 and the Clayton Act of 1914. The doctors alleged that the hospitals' monopoly over private and federal insurance programs led to "substantial losses of income and return on property, and of reputation, stature and development in their chosen occupation through loss of patients."[242] Immediately after the suit was filed, a nurse from one of the hospitals being sued wrote to the *Chicago Sun-Times* to proclaim that no such discrimination existed at her hospital because one black doctor served on its staff. The rest of the letter revealed her bias that African American physicians were inferior to white doctors. She concluded that "these [black] doctors appear to be so contentious as to think any Negro must be admitted to any hospital he chooses just because he has a medical degree."[243]

Falls and the CED believed that the lack of staff appointments available for black doctors in Chicago not only curbed the number of young African Americans interested in medicine, deterring them from pursuing careers in the field, it also dissuaded black doctors in other areas of the country from moving to Chicago. The suit never went to trial, but it did spur action on the part of the hospitals. Within two years of the suit being

---

241. Falls, "The Search for Negro Medical Students," 17. In my interview with him, Dr. Young corroborated the quota system that Falls wrote about. Young, interview by author.

242. Robert G. Morris Jr., M.D., et al. v. Chicago Hospital Council, et al., 61 C232, U.S. District Court, 1819–1999, Civil Case Files, 1938–1985, Record Group 21; National Archives Building, Chicago. Box 54, Folder 1, "Complaint," pp. 2, 17, 23–24. Hereafter, the court case and location will documented as "Court Documents." Falls, "The Search for Negro Medical Students," 17–18.

243. A.M.N., letter to the editor, *Chicago Sun-Times*, 16 February 1961.

filed, those same hospitals gave over one hundred staff appointments to African American doctors and nurses. By January 1964, almost three years (and dozens of court dates) after the initial filing, all but two of the hospitals had agreed to subject themselves to a commission that would handle any further complaints of discrimination.

This was the first lawsuit of its kind to procure positive results.[244] It could have had much wider implications had the Civil Rights Act not been enacted five months later, on 2 July 1964. The legislation barred discrimination in employment because of skin color; had its passage been delayed, the lawsuit by Falls and his fellow black doctors might have led to a flurry of similar lawsuits across the United States. The happy response of the plaintiffs was covered in a *Chicago Defender* article, in which Dr. Quentin Young made clear that the agreement would be meaningless unless a sufficient number of African American doctors subsequently chose to practice in Chicago.[245] The commission that was put in place never received a single complaint of racial prejudice, because during its first year not a single black doctor was denied admittance to a hospital. This led to a dramatic increase in the number of African American patients admitted to traditionally white hospitals almost overnight.[246]

In June 1963, almost two and a half years into the pretrial motions, Falls wrote an article about the lack of new African American physicians in the Chicago area for *Integrated Education*. Falls observed that while the African American population in Chicago had tripled over the past twenty-five years, the number of black physicians had decreased from 228 to 218. During the previous twelve years, the number of black students in Chicago's five medical schools had decreased from fourteen to ten and the median age of black doctors had continued to rise. Falls placed the primary responsibility for this situation with the Chicago Board of Education, whose segregated school system provided "an inferior education and has produced a graduate lacking in both motivation and qualification for higher education."[247] At the time the article was written, the CED had begun an unofficial program to "find, stimulate, and guide Negro children who are interested in pursuing

244. National Medical Association, "Chicago Physicians Sue," 198–99; Cobb, "Hospital Integration," 336; Falls, "The Search for Negro Medical Students," 18; National Medical Association, "Chicago Court Agreement," 205–06; Unsworth, *Catholics on the Edge*, 137. Court Documents, Folder 1, "Stipulation."

245. Young, quoted in *Chicago Daily Defender*, "Negro Doctors Pleased," 4.

246. Young, interview by author.

247. Falls, "The Search for Negro Medical Students," 15.

medical or medical related careers."[248] The program coordinated the efforts of principals, vocational counselors, teachers, and doctors to locate and mentor young African Americans with a propensity for medicine. In one high school, where a pilot version of the program was already underway, eight students in the graduating class had been "discovered." There were another fifteen high schools, each with a predominantly African American enrollment, that the group wanted to target. Although Falls hoped that the board of education would adopt the CED's program, there was an even greater obstacle to eliminating discrimination in medicine: "the ending of segregation in education."[249]

In response, the CED founded the Council for Biomedical Careers. This group, of which Falls was an early president, wanted to make medical careers available to anyone who was interested.[250] In February 1965, it obtained a $12,000 National Science Foundation grant, which funded twelve three-hour sessions held on alternate Saturdays for over one hundred students. They had been selected from seventeen high schools, and they received stipends to compensate them for lost wages; the inherent cost of participating in the program would otherwise have been prohibitive for most of the students.

The purpose of the sessions was to examine critical areas in the sciences for those interested in medicine. The sessions also covered how to apply to universities and succeed at the university level and provided hands-on experience for the top thirty-five students. The sessions were a success, with 125 students receiving diplomas for completing the program that September.[251] It appears that this program eventually morphed into the Cooperative Laboratory Program in September 1969, solidifying a relationship between Waller High School, which had a significant African American population, and Wesley Memorial Hospital. The program expanded in 1971 and 1972 to include additional schools and hospitals.[252]

---

248. Ibid., 15–16.

249. Ibid., 18–19.

250. Schueler, "W. Springs Doctor."

251. Seals, "Human Relations Beat," 5; *Chicago Defender*, "125 Science Students," 35.

252. "Proceeding of the Chicago Board of Education," vol. 3: Jan. 22-June 25, 1966, for meeting held on 25 June 1969, p. 3114; vol. 3: Jan. 27-June 30, 1971, for meeting held on 13 February 1971, pp. 2607–08; vol. 1: July 1-Dec. 22, 1971, for meeting held on 27 October 1971, pp. 880–81; vol. 4: April 26-June 24, 1972, for meeting held on 26 April 1972, pp. 3455–56, Archives-Chicago Board of Education, Chicago.

Healing the Racial Divide

By 1966, the CED decided to change its focus; it became the Chicago branch of the Medical Committee for Human Rights. The Chicago branch focused on the ways in which people in the medical field could aid the civil rights movement. For a while, Falls was on the governing board of the national organization, and he chaired its 1966 conference, which was held in Chicago.[253]

During 1965, the Medical Committee for Human Rights provided financial support for marchers in Selma, which included one of its own members. The campaign, which had been strategically organized by Dr. Martin Luther King Jr. and the Southern Christian Leadership Conference, successfully pressured Congress to pass the Voter Rights Act of 1965.[254] The committee gave money to help provide food for the marchers, and sent a letter to those on its mailing list to procure additional funds for transportation. In the letter, Falls and a fellow doctor wrote of how the people traveling to the South to join the marchers would be dropped off at a bus depot in a dangerous white area. The requested donations would pay for picking up these new marchers from the bus station in Volkswagen vans.[255]

ST. JOHN OF THE CROSS CATHOLIC CHURCH

St. John of the Cross Catholic Church was founded in Western Springs, Illinois, on 10 August 1960. Its parishioners would use their school building for worship for over a decade once it was ready, but they started out by using a large home as their temporary chapel and headquarters. They also used the South Campus Gymnasium of Lyons Township School.[256] Falls was one of the founding members of St. John of the Cross and his family was listed in the parish's inaugural booklet as one of the "pioneer families of St. John of the Cross."[257] In his later years, Falls told a fellow parishioner that he had

253. Young, interview by author; *Western Springs Villager*, "Dr. Falls Chairman of Nat'l Meeting at University of Chicago," 17 March 1966, clipping of article available at Western Springs Historical Society, Western Springs, IL, Folder: Dr. Arthur G. Falls.

254. Falls and Mark Lepper to Friends of Medical Committee for Human Rights, 1965, CUL, Series III, Box 14, Folder 177.

255. Falls and Lepper to Friends of Medical Committee for Human Rights, 1965.

256. Koenig, *A History of the Parishes*, 1611; "St. John of the Cross Solemn Blessing," commemoration booklet for the completion of the church building on 12 October 1961, stored at St. John of the Cross Catholic Church, Western Springs, IL. The booklet does not have any page numbers.

257. "St. John of the Cross Solemn Blessing"; Falls, interview by Troester.

not felt like he was part of a real Catholic parish until he joined St. John of the Cross.[258] In large part, this may have been due to the parish's involvement with race issues during the late 1960s. St. John of the Cross' Parish Committee of Community Life was a regular sponsor of speakers and videos concerning race relations and the proper Catholic response.[259] Because this committee's minutes and lists of members appear to be lost, the exact role that Falls played in this group is uncertain, though it would be hard to believe that he was not involved in some way.

The parish council was formed during the summer and fall of 1967.[260] Falls was an alternate on the parish council in February 1968 when he asked it to address "Operation Hospitality," a project associated with Cardinal John Cody (1907–1982).[261] Operation Hospitality was a program of the Chicago Catholic School Board that began in 1967 with the purpose of busing kids from all-black inner-city Catholic schools to affluent all-white suburban Catholic schools. The program was voluntary on the part of the suburban schools and began with 256 children from fourth to eighth grade. It was hoped that the program would eventually be a two-way program, but the plan to bus white suburban children to the inner city was never realized.[262] Though it appears that the parish had not been asked by the archdiocese to join the program, Falls proposed that "the Council go on record and give serious consideration to the conditions which cause busing to be introduced."[263] The parish council voted thirteen to five to discuss the issue, with councilman Edgar Wolfe commenting on how the council would be "a useless thing if it addressed itself only to stone and mortar matters . . . We have to be concerned with the totality of the parish, the people. I don't know how I feel about busing. I don't

---

258. Gougiel, interview by author.

259. This information is from the St. John of the Cross parish bulletins that are stored at St. John of the Cross Catholic Church, Western Springs, IL. They will be cited as "JCBulletins." In 1967, the group held events such as playing an audio recording of Martin Luther King Jr. for discussion and bringing in the Executive Director of the Chicago Urban League, the Director of Housing for the Chicago Conference on Religion and Race as well as a real-estate agent. JCBulletins, 23 April 1967, 28 May 1967, 23 March 1969.

260. JCBulletins, 18 June 1967, 9 July 1967, 17 September 1967; Falls, interview by Troester.

261. Ibid., 25 February 1968.

262. Gardner, Wright, and Dee, "The Effect of Busing," 4–5. Hereafter referred to as "The Effect of Busing." *Integrated Education*, "Chronicle of Race and Schools," 29.

263. Falls, quoted in JCBulletins, 25 February 1968.

know enough about it. But I do know that people and their problems are of prime importance to us."[264]

That May, the school board for St. John of the Cross held an open meeting in the school gym that was very well attended and extremely contentious. The school decided not to join Operation Hospitality, but Rev. William J. Bennett, the founding pastor of the parish, overruled the board and enrolled the school in the program anyway.[265] St. John of the Cross was soon busing in five to six students from St. Thaddeus Catholic Church on the South Side of Chicago.[266] Zita Wheeler, who was a teacher at the time and who was the school's assistant principal when I interviewed her, recalled that a few families removed their children from the school, but that had been the only noticeable disruption; a police presence was provided for the arrival of the first few black families.[267]

His original prodding of the parish council aside, Falls's role and level of involvement throughout the discussion is unknown, but his interest in this issue is clearly in keeping with his thoughts regarding the need to focus on integration in education during and following the hospital integration lawsuit. Going into the fall 1972 school year, the school board of the Archdiocese of Chicago decided to end Operation Hospitality. Children already in the program could continue until they graduated, but no new children would be accepted.[268] From the point of view of adding some diversity to its grade school, St. John of the Cross considered Operation Hospitality a success, and to this day St. John of the Cross and St. Thaddeus have a strong relationship as "sharing parishes."[269]

In July 1968, the Parish Committee on Community Life published a parishioner survey on housing discrimination in the Sunday bulletin. When

264. Wolfe, quoted in JCBulletins, 25 February 1968.

265. Fr. William J. Bennett was the pastor of St. John of the Cross from 1960 until he retired in 1980. He had previously been an assistant pastor at St. John Fisher Catholic Church in Chicago. Koenig, *A History of the Parishes*, 1611–12.

266. Dowdle, interview by author; Wheeler, interview by author; O'Brien, interview by author.

267. JCBulletins 5 May 1968; Dowdle, interview by author; Wheeler, interview by author.

268. *Integrated Education*, "Chronicle of Race and Schools," 29.

269. Bill Bright, "Sharing Parishes." As "sharing parishes," St. John of the Cross provides financial support to St. Thaddeus in exchange for a sharing of the gifts of St. Thaddeus. In October 2011, the St. Thaddeus Choir provided the music for the 5:00 pm mass and stayed for a reception. Saint John of the Cross Catholic Church, "Sharing Parish St. Thaddeus Choir Visits."

asked if there was "strong discriminatory feeling in our community against non-whites," 110 answered "yes" while 19 said "no." When asked if they would sell their home to a non-white person, 47 answered "yes" while 80 said "no." When asked if a city ordinance was necessary in Western Springs to prevent discrimination in home sales, 48 answered "yes" while 80 answered "no."[270] With these responses, the parishioners clearly revealed that racial discrimination was a problem in their community and that they did not want to take any confrontational steps to remedy it. Falls's role in this initiative is again unknown, but a project based on collecting information, publishing it, and noting the discrepancy between an obvious problem and the will to change it echoes the type of activity that Falls was involved with his entire life.

By the spring of 1969, Falls was a regular parish council member, as well as a member of the education committee. He would serve on the parish council until 1971.[271] The council consisted entirely of men and Falls wished to remedy this situation. Each member was told that an alternate could stand in for him if he missed a meeting. Falls brought a woman who lived down the street from his home to serve as his alternate.[272] Also around this time, St. John of the Cross began allowing lay eucharistic ministers and Falls was one of the first appointed.[273] (Initially, there were a noticeable number of parishioners who refused to receive from Falls, but this blatant act of racial prejudice soon stopped.)[274] One of his tasks as a eucharistic minister was to find a boy to hold a tray in front of each person as they received communion so that none of the host would fall on the ground. Falls purposely brought a girl to hold the tray for him. This was not allowed by the Catholic Church at the time, but the pastor allowed him to do this without interference.[275] In each of these actions, Falls's desire was to begin breaking down the gender barrier

---

270. JCBulletins, 7 July 1968.

271. Ibid., 20 April 1969; 10 September 1972.

272. Falls, interview by Troester. There are various instances of Arthur's interest in women's rights issues throughout his life. In 29 March 1952, he was the only male speaker at an event sponsored by the B'nai B'rith Women's Council entitled: "Women's Role in Human Relations." Chicago Council Against Racial and Religious Discrimination, "Human Relations Calendar," *Against Discrimination: The Monthly Newsletter of the Chicago Council Against Racial and Religious Discrimination*, March 1952, in *Against Discrimination Newsletters*, Chicago Historical Society, call number: HN80 C4 A35.

273. John Kravcik, interview by author.

274. Joan Kravcik, interview by author.

275. Falls, interview by Troester. Falls does not give a date for this, but he does indicate that it was before the practice was permitted.

that existed in his parish. Falls never wrote or spoke on the issue of women priests, however, so his exact thoughts on that matter cannot be known.

Arthur and Lillian at a social gathering. Date unknown.
Courtesy of Vilma Childs.

Falls became so associated with his role as a eucharistic minister at the 5 p.m. mass on Sundays that there was even a notice of his "retirement" from it in August 1989, after fifteen years of service. Part of the reason for officially thanking him was because it was notoriously difficult to find eucharistic ministers for that mass.[276] Although the date of Falls's retirement from surgical practice is unknown, it was also around 1989 that Falls decided to close his private practice, which he had maintained since first becoming a doctor.[277] Both of these events occurred shortly after Lillian's death on Easter Sunday 1988.[278] Although Arthur and Lillian had had a tumultuous beginning in Western Springs, they had eventually made friends and grown to like it there.[279] Arthur died on 9 January 2000 at the age of ninety-eight. He spent his last few years living quietly in a small home near his niece

---

276. JCBulletins, 13 August 1989. At some point after Vatican II, Falls was also asked to serve as a deacon, but declined. Falls, interview by Troester.

277. Scott, interview by author.

278. Falls, interview by Troester.

279. This view was confirmed by Arthur's granddaughter and niece. Sykes, interview by author; Scott, interview by author.

Vilma in Kalamazoo, Michigan.[280] He and Lillian were both interred in the Queen of All Saints Mausoleum at Queen of Heaven Catholic Cemetery in Hillside, Illinois.

CONCLUSION

Falls dedicated his life to the achievement of racial justice in a number of different spheres. His method in each instance depended on the circumstances and what he felt was the most practical yet Christian manner to achieve racial justice. None of the archbishops of Chicago were ever willing to work with Falls on racial justice, but it is clear that Falls would always have been willing to work with them. After the early 1940s, Falls no longer worked with Catholic groups in the field of race relations, other than with his parish community. Although he would always remain a dedicated Catholic, he had concluded that these groups did not present the best avenue for achieving results in racial justice.

Arthur's parents and wife played critical roles in influencing his dedication and method in the realm of racial justice. His parents instilled in him the Christian notion of the common brotherhood and sisterhood of humanity. His father had displayed the virtue of standing firm on one's principles despite little support. His mother, who came from a long line of Catholics, was involved with the Chicago Urban League and encouraged Arthur's involvement. Because Lillian was an astute student of the social sciences, Arthur became an avid reader of texts in that field. In addition, she was a lifelong partner in the quest for racial justice, and put her own physical safety at risk when they moved to Western Springs. The three people that Arthur most respected in his life were themselves shining examples of how to live out the gospel of Jesus Christ.

Falls asserted that racial harmony could be achieved only by blacks and whites working together. For this reason, despite the problems that subsequently arose with the FCC, Falls always believed that Turner had made a mistake in resisting the organization's change of name and focus. We have also seen how Falls was able to organize with white members of the Catholic Worker movement in a way that had lifelong consequences for them, with some of these members going on to prominent positions in the city of Chicago and the Catholic press.

280. Unsworth, "Lonely Prophet Falls in Chicago," 18; Sykes, interview by author.

3 The Thought and Writings of Dr. Arthur G. Falls

DR. ARTHUR G. FALLS tailored his thought and writings to specific circumstances—just as he did with his actions. Nevertheless, certain theological principles and notions of how substantial change occurred in society were foundational to his thought and writings. These principles and notions had become established after he acquired a theological praxis from the Chicago Urban League and the Federated Colored Catholics that was strongly grounded in Catholic theology and the necessity of struggle to achieve positive results.[1] Arthur's writings were more practical than theoretical in orientation, with the theology implicit rather than in the foreground when his audience was not Christian. These ideas were revealed in his memoir and in numerous journal and magazine articles, as well as through interviews and remembrances from friends and family. The ideas in this chapter span from the late 1920s to the late 1990s, though his most prolific writing period began in the early 1930s and ended in the early 1960s. This section will begin with one of Falls's foundational Christian doctrines—the mystical body of Christ—followed by his ideas concerning sin, discipleship, interracialism, the social sciences, white privilege, the role of blacks and whites in racial justice, and the necessity of struggle to create authentic opportunities.

THE MYTHICAL BODY OF CHRIST

Falls's fight against racism rested on a firm theological foundation. There were a number of Catholic doctrines that he was particularly fond of

---

1. Although Falls did not utilize the term "praxis," he would be familiar with the concept. On one occasion, Falls defined belief as "practices as well as verbal utterances." Falls, "Chicago Fights Race Prejudice."

invoking in order to unmask the incompatibility of racism with Christianity, but none was more important to him than the mystical body of Christ. The doctrine of the mystical body of Christ came into vogue in liturgical and social justice circles in America as Falls began his involvement in racial justice. Patrick W. Carey observes that there was a "flowering of lay activity" in the United States and worldwide. This flourishing of lay activity in the United States was closely aligned with the liturgical movement, "which saw the Eucharistic celebration as the center of a deep Catholic spirituality and the church itself as the Mystical Body of Christ . . . These laity were self-consciously aware of their membership in the Mystical Body of Christ and therefore of their responsibility for justice and peace in public life."[2]

In essence, the doctrine of the mystical body of Christ was an insight into the sacramental and personal bond of the Catholic with Jesus Christ that empowered one to take responsibility for this relationship through active work for charity and justice in the Church and in the world.[3] Perhaps the most famous expositor of the mystical body of Christ in the United States was Virgil Michel, with whom Falls was friends. Michel understood the mystical body of Christ to be the spiritual bedrock for communal living. Following this doctrine to its logical conclusion, Christians united in Christ are also "intimately united to each other in Christ."[4] Being a part of the mystical body of Christ includes a responsibility for each member to "share in maintaining the supernatural life of the entire mystical body; each one has the duty, as far as circumstances allow, to come to the help of his fellow members, and thus to maintain the common life of the entire body."[5] Dorothy Day and the Catholic Worker movement were also influenced by the liturgical renewal movement started by Michel. In 1935, when Falls would have been an avid reader of the *New York Catholic Worker*, Day wrote: "The Mystical Body of Christ is a union—a unit—and action within the Body is common action. In the Liturgy we have the means to teach Catholics, thrown apart by Individualism into snobbery, apathy, prejudice, blind unreason, that they ARE members of one body and that 'an injury to one is an injury to all.'"[6]

2. Carey, "Lay Leadership," 238–39.

3. Ibid., 239. For more information about the how the mystical body of Christ was utilized during this period, see Kelleher, "Liturgical and Social Transformation," 58–70.

4. Michel, *Christian Social Reconstruction*, 7.

5. Ibid., 7.

6. Dorothy Day, "Liturgy and Sociology," 4.

Although LaFarge did not put the same social justice emphasis on it, he too referred to "His Mystical Body" in reference to the universal nature of the Church, which includes people of all races and nations.[7] Friendship House in Chicago likewise utilized this doctrine to address racial injustice. Shortly after it opened in 1942, it sponsored an interracial discussion on the mystical body in relation to racial justice.[8] Without a doubt, the notion of the mystical body of Christ was well known and discussed in many Catholic quarters as a foundation or argument for social and racial justice.

During his involvement in the Catholic Worker, Falls was a regular contributor to the *Chicago Catholic Worker* newspaper. Of special note is an article he wrote for its March 1941 issue, concerning segregation in Chicago. In expressing why Catholics in particular should be concerned about race relations, he stated, "Catholics are adherents of a faith which proclaims the doctrine of the Mystical Body of Christ, which Body still remains mythical, not mystical to too many of its members." He went on to testify that "the overwhelming majority of our Chicago Catholics have been either active leaders or passive followers in these discriminatory practices."[9] In this particular article, "discriminatory practices" referred to restrictive housing covenants, which denied blacks the opportunity to live in certain neighborhoods. In the opinion of Falls, "Catholic doctrines meant nothing to the promoters of restrictive covenants."[10] Restrictive covenants, which resulted in the overcrowding of African Americans in slum conditions, often led to the outbreak of deadly fires. Falls compared the black restrictive ghettos of Chicago to the Jewish ghettos of Adolf Hitler, which Americans supposedly abhorred. Hitler's Germany may have been crueler to Jews than Americans were to blacks, but the "average American" and the "average Catholic" shared a similar ideology regarding the people contained in their respective

7. LaFarge, *Interracial Justice*, 173.

8. Avella, *This Confident Church*, 297.

9. Falls, "Restrictive Covenants," 1941, 2. Falls borrowed the expression "the mythical body of Christ" from fellow Chicago Catholic Worker John Bowers, who would state that Catholics believe in "the mythical body of Christ," not "the mystical body of Christ." Falls, a letter quoted in packet for Summer School of Social Action, 1937–1938, Reynold Hillenbrand Papers, University of Notre Dame Archives, Notre Dame, IN, Box CMRH 5/19, Folder, Summer School of Social Action, 1937–1938. The original date or to whom the letter was sent is unknown. Hereafter referred to as "Summer School of Social Action." Thank you to Karen Johnson for sharing this document with me.

10. AGF, Box 2, Folder 2, disc 25-side 1, p. 3. Falls wrote this in 1962, twenty-one years after he wrote the above article. For more information the history of restrictive covenants in Chicago, see Plotkin, "Hemmed In," 39–69.

ghettos.[11] Like LaFarge, Falls believed that if the Catholic Church would firmly address racial justice, it could be "the most powerful factor in the development of a new social order in which opportunity for all individuals will be more equalized."[12] Being fully aware that Catholics made up over one-third of the population in Chicago and that prominent Catholics were often behind prejudicial practices within unions, hospitals, and other businesses, Falls was convinced that the elimination of racism in the Catholic Church would have played a significant role in ameliorating racism in the city of Chicago.[13]

For Falls, the collaboration of whites and blacks was not only an issue of justice, but also of common sense. In April 1937, he wrote an article for the *New York Catholic Worker* about housing covenants and segregation. He described the dilapidated buildings in black ghettos and the higher rents that led to overcrowding, prostitution, and other desperate acts in order to survive. He believed that if changes were not made in the near future to correct this horrific situation, there would be riots started by African Americans who had nothing else to lose—like the Harlem riot of 1935.[14] There would be race riots in America during the coming decade, but like previous riots, they were almost solely white-on-black violence. Black-on-white violence in the form of a riot would not occur in Chicago until the 1960s. Regardless, Falls contended that Chicago's 1.25 million Catholics could choose the outcome of their future by either opting to work for justice in the form of equal housing opportunities for all or opting to maintain the injustice by continuing their apathetic acceptance of a prejudicial social order.[15] In the meantime, Falls would keep readers of the *New York Catholic Worker* updated on the dreadful conditions in Chicago's slums as well as activities seeking to remedy the situation.[16]

Falls noticed that white Christians were regrettably rarely up to the task of confronting racism. According to Falls, "too often . . . when he [a black person] walks in Christianity *dies* out." Essentially, "the Christian

11. Falls, "Restrictive Covenants," p. 2.

12. Falls to St. Columban's Seminary in St. Colbumbans, NE, carbon copy to New York Catholic Worker, 13 July 1934, DDCW, Series W-2.2, Box 1, Folder 11.

13. Falls, "Honesty in Race-Relations," 159; Falls, "Chicago Letter," June 1935, 8.

14. Falls, "Danger of Riots in Chicago Slums," April 1937, 1, 4.

15. Falls, "Danger of Riots in Chicago Slums, 1, 4."

16. See, for example, Falls, "The Communist Says," April 1934, 1, 8; "Chicago Letter," June 1935, 8; "Chicago Fights Race Prejudice," September 1935, 2, 6; letter the editor, April 1937, 1, 4.

Church, as now constructed, has failed [African Americans]."[17] Falls would often hear the complaint that when he openly confronted racism in the Catholic Church, he was "fighting the Church" or "fighting the clergy." This was a completely false assessment in his eyes. The one who openly confronts racism in the Catholic Church "is not combating any of the laws or teachings of the Church, but is combating the sinful abuse of the position which the clergyman occupies. It is the priest or sister who causes this discrimination who is guilty of 'fighting the Church.'" Falls believed that the clergy were "direct descendants of the apostles . . . *but only insofar as they give us the word of God.*"[18] For Falls, it was important to focus on the prejudice exhibited by the clergy and the teachers of Catholic children. As long as teachers and role models of Catholic children were racist and even, in some instances, denying the sacraments to black Catholics, one could not realistically expect these children to "have a Christian concept of race-relations when they grow older."[19] This is an earlier view of Falls, which presents racism in the Catholic Church on a more individual level. Later on, he became aware that the problem was "institutionalized discrimination, not simply the human weakness of an individual member of the clergy or of the sisterhood."[20]

Those who preferred to ignore the racism found in the Catholic Church were "emulating the example of the ostrich who, it is said, hides his head in the sand when in danger." Such a solution is unworkable and will never eradicate racism within the Church. It will be "only by an intelligent and forceful repudiation of the abuses of Catholics . . . [that] the Catholic Church be accepted as the firm rock of justice and love."[21]

The use of the doctrine of the mystical body of Christ was not a passing fancy for Falls: he again used the image of the mystical body of Christ while writing his memoir in 1962, stating that "the practical application of this theology of the doctrine of the mystical body of Christ either had to be demonstrated or else the whole structure seemed shaky to me."[22] This

17. Falls, "Race and Its Opportunity," 1934, 10. Emphasis in the original.
18. Falls, "Honesty in Race-Relations," (1933) 158–59. Emphasis in the original.
19. Falls, "The Chicago Letter," October 1936, 4.
20. AGF, Box 1, Folder 2, p. 55.
21. Falls, "Honesty in Race-Relations," 159.
22. AGF, Box 1, Folder 5, pp. 158–59 (2). I have placed parenthesis around the number 2 because this is the second time in the memoir that Falls uses this number. Unfortunately, there is a section of the memoir where he repeats page numbers 145–210. These pages neither fit into his primary numbering system for the first 600 pages nor list disc

quote was in response to the Catholic Church's claim of being the "one true church."[23] For Falls, the "one true church" was a precarious claim if it was not authentically inclusive of all races. Falls took pride in the doctrines of the Catholic Church, but experienced considerable tension with its lack of practice concerning these doctrines.[24]

Falls did not question Church doctrine and assumed that all the Church's teachings were more than adequate.[25] He never understood "how so much intolerance did develop among people whose fundamental principles would seem to rule this out."[26] Falls stated that he never left the Catholic Church because it "has given me the foundation, which has enabled me to fight [racism]." He brought this "solid foundation" to other parts of his work with others, even though "I may not have announced it as Catholic doctrine—I announce it as basic principles of human relations—but it is Catholic doctrine."[27]

RACISM AS SIN

Within Catholic and Christian frameworks, racism is most often classified as sin. Falls also referred to racism as sin and defined sin as the act of "deny[ing] any individual those things which we claim to be the right of all human beings."[28] At first sight, this may seem to be a strange definition of sin. For St. Thomas Aquinas, the great thirteenth-century Catholic theologian, sin was understood as disorder.[29] Sin was disorder because God created the universe with a natural order. Falls's definition of sin placed an emphasis on the disordered distribution of the gifts of God. To give a specific example, in addressing the lack of quality medical care available to African Americans, Falls stated that it was "my philosophy that every hu-

---

numbers on top. Sorry for the confusion.

23. Ibid., p. 158 (2).

24. Falls was not the only Catholic of this time to refer to the heretical nature of racism. Merrill also stated that racism was a heresy. Unlike Falls, the discussion was more theoretical and not grounded in a concrete situation of racial prejudice. Merrill, "The Theology of Racism," 56–57.

25. Falls, "Colored Churches," 27.

26. AGF, Box 1, Folder 2, p. 43.

27. Falls, interview with Sicius.

28. Falls, "Industrial and Social Problems," (1931) 679.

29. Aquinas, *Summa Theologica*, I-II, question. 72, article. 1

man being has an inherent right to equal access to all medical facilities; that when he is unable to secure that access it is the duty of society, as expressed through government, to aid him in this endeavor."[30]

Falls also assigned sin to Catholics not following the Church's teachings. In this regard, Falls argued that the Church must "clean house" to effectively confront racism in broader society.[31] Falls argued that the origin of the sin of racism was fear: "Probe a little, and you'll find *fear*."[32] In 1931, he asserted this fear was grounded in "the two bugaboos of race-relations": social equality and marriage. Regarding social equality, there is a fear that justice for blacks will result in having African Americans coming into the homes of whites as close friends. Falls stated that this would not be the case. The social equality desired by blacks was the "opportunity" to participate in all the activities of the parish, not to enter the homes of unwelcoming white people. In reference to intermarriage, he reiterated to the white person that no marriage occurs without the consent of both parties. Nevertheless, blacks "must be allowed that freedom of choice which the Catholic Church teaches is essential to the marriage contract."[33]

For Falls, disregarding the teachings of Christ and the Church was sinful and, as a result, led to disorder and injustice in society. These sinful acts were rooted in fear of an unwanted closer association with African Americans. Admittedly, his analysis of racism as sin was not very in-depth. Nonetheless, Falls saw an integral web of interconnections between sin, doctrine, and discipleship. Therefore, he believed that heretical doctrine was expressed in disordered behavior and vice versa. And in the case of both sin and heresy, the call to be followers of Jesus in Christian discipleship was capitulated to the "existing local situation."

DISCIPLESHIP

Falls also appropriated other theological concepts in his writings, including discipleship. He grounded his notion of discipleship on the person and life of Christ. Falls employed the death of Jesus Christ to address more than the expiation of sins. In examining one of the historical reasons for the death

---

30. Falls, quoted in "Says Medical Bias is City's Worst Problem," *Chicago Daily Defender*, 1960, 3.

31. Falls, "Industrial and Social Problems," 679.

32. Ibid., 680. See also, Falls, "Colored Churches," 27.

33. Falls, "Industrial and Social Problems," 680–81.

of Christ, Falls concluded: "He taught the will of His Father in opposition to the 'existing local situation.'"³⁴ By the "existing local situation," Falls was referring to the cultural evils that appeared to be a given in certain societies, with little hope for change in the near future. The "existing local situation" was a phrase he had acquired from contemporary Catholics, it being the reason they gave for the Catholic Church not faithfully living out its teaching on racism.³⁵ For Falls, "Our Lord on earth clearly has demonstrated that there can be no such thing as 'modified' truth or justice; that there can be no compromise if one wishes to remain on this road toward the goal of human brotherhood."³⁶ Falls noted that it was not only Jesus who defied local custom; the apostles, the thousands of Christians fed to the lions, and the twenty-two Ugandan martyrs in the 1880s had all been willing to sacrifice their lives to uphold the "teachings of the Church, no matter what the 'existing local situation.'"³⁷ Near the end of his life, Falls spoke again about those who had in his opinion capitulated to the "existing local situation" instead of pursuing racial justice: "This is an unchristian thought . . . but when I die I want to go to Heaven and sit next to St. Peter at the Last Judgment and listen to all those explanations about why the time was never ripe."³⁸

In 1931, Falls published an address he had delivered at the national convention of the Federated Colored Catholics the previous September. In the text, Falls affirmed a common Catholic prejudice of the time: he held that Catholics, unlike Protestants, "*practice* all the teachings of Christ and not those alone which happen to conform to our particular desires."³⁹ Therefore, when Catholics refuse to "give the Negro justice and fair-play in all our religious activities . . . there is no possible way that we can claim to be true disciples of Christ."⁴⁰ Unfortunately, "the lives of [Christians] serve, in many cases, as examples of the extent to which many religious groups have departed from the teachings of Christ."⁴¹ In this sense, the degree to

34. Falls, "Colored Churches," 27.

35. Ibid.

36. Falls, "Honesty in Race-Relations," 158.

37. Falls, "Colored Churches," 27. In Arthur's analysis here we can clearly see a liberative theological framework at work. His experience of injustice at the hands of Catholics who blamed the local situation permitted Falls to see a similar occurrence in the Gospels that he can bring to bear on the contemporary situation.

38. Falls, quoted in Unsworth, *Catholics on the Edge*, 138.

39. Falls, "Industrial and Social Problems," 678. Emphasis in original.

40. Ibid., 678, 681.

41. Falls, "Interracial Cooperation in Chicago," (August 1935) 123.

which a parish community or denomination is embroiled in racist practices can act as a measuring stick for how much needs to be corrected until that community can be properly called "church" once more. If the Church wants to prove the importance of its teachings for rest of the world, it first needs to illustrate and confirm their importance by trying to live them out.

During this time period, Catholics were expected to attend and support the parish within whose boundaries they were lived. Additionally, parishes were entrusted with the care of all the souls within their assigned boundaries.[42] Since each Catholic knew that he or she "is obliged to support the parish in which he [or she] lives and to receive administration of services from his [or her] parish," black Catholics should not be expected to travel across town to receive basic services from the "colored church."[43] Therefore, Catholics who denied the Church's teaching regarding the necessity to support and to be administered to by one's local parish were effectively admitting that they hold a double standard for African Americans.[44] Within secular affairs, justice is even more of a mandate, because "the wealth of America has been built upon the co-operation of all groups, and that the Negro has more than contributed his share."[45] It is safe to assume that Falls is referring to the contributions that African Americans have made to the United States for which they have not been properly compensated, whether during slavery or afterward, with the black person statistically earning less than a white person for the same job. The only religious group that Falls saw to be practicing authentic inclusion with African Americans was the Bahá'í.[46] In addition, Falls commented that "*the Communist Party* is interracial throughout and includes its stand for interracial justice in all its platforms and selection of candidates."[47] In short, communists were better followers of Christ in the area of race relations than Catholics. Falls contended that a return to early Christianity in which theory and practice were not separated would have to occur for racism to be eradicated from the Church: "It would appear that religious groups cannot be expected to provide leadership or even much cooperation until their members return

---

42. For more information about parish boundaries during the time of Falls, see McGreevy, *Parish Boundaries*, 13–25.

43. Falls, "Colored Churches," 27.

44. Ibid.

45. Falls, "Industrial and Social Problems," 679.

46. Falls, "Interracial Cooperation in Chicago," (August 1935) 124.

47. Ibid., 125. Emphasis in original.

to the attitude of the early Christians—the acceptance in practice as well as in theory of the fundamental doctrines of Christianity and the repudiation of their present attempt to maintain the status quo."[48]

Although Falls's use of scripture was not extensive, he did make use of it on occasion.[49] The following are five New Testament passages that Falls quoted to disclose scriptural warrants against racism. Even though only one of the quotes is attributed in scripture to Jesus, Falls ascribed all of them to Our Lord. From the Gospel of Matthew: "And the second is like to it: Thou shalt love thy neighbor as thyself. On these two commandments hangeth the whole law and the prophets."[50] He also quoted 1 John 3:15 "Everyone who hateth his brother is a murderer. And ye know that no murderer hath life everlasting abiding in himself." For those who would state that the Catholic Church should only deal with the spiritual realm, he cited James 1:22 and 26: "Be ye doers of the word, and not hearers only, deceiving yourself. If any man thinks himself religious, not bridling his tongue, but deceiving his heart, this man's religion is vain." The "true Catholic" or follower of Christ allowed his or her faith to affect the everyday actions of his or her life; it was not limited to attending Mass on Sundays. Falls likely saw himself as someone trying to heed Ephesians 6:14–15: "Stand, therefore, having your loins girt in truth, and having on the breast plate of justice, and your feet shod with the preparation of the gospel of peace."[51] Being a follower of Christ meant getting actively involved in the struggle to love one's neighbor by creating a more just society.

In Falls's mind, the constant refusal of white Catholics to accept African Americans as equal members of the body of Christ was a rejection of the call to discipleship and the life that Christ lived. A Catholic could not in good conscience regard himself or herself as a disciple of Christ while treating blacks inhumanely, particularly those who lived within their parish

---

48. Falls, "Interracial Cooperation in Chicago," 141.

49. Arthur's minimal use of scripture was not uncommon for the time. During the 1930s, if scripture was used to support a position, it was often an afterthought. The use of scripture in this way is referred to as proof-texting. For further discussion on this topic, see Gula, *Reason Informed by Faith*, 166.

50. Matthew 22:39–40. For this section, I am using the translation of the passages given by Falls, which is from the Douay-Rhiems Catholic Bible. Falls, "Honesty in Race-Relations," 158–59.

51. Falls, "Honesty in Race-Relations," 158–59. Lastly, he used 1 Corinthians 13:1: "If I speak with the tongues of men and of the Angels, and have not charity, I am become as sounding brass, or a tinkling cymbal."

boundaries. Catholics were regularly reminded that they had an obligation to the parish in whose boundary they resided, and the parish likewise had an obligation to care for all the souls within its boundaries. Falls's understanding of discipleship as the following of all the teachings of Christ may sound legalistic to the contemporary ear, but it offered him a simple and clear way to reveal the hypocrisy of many white Catholics.

BLACK MILITANCY

Falls was very cognizant of the need for African Americans to play a key role in obtaining justice for themselves, and he was often critical of blacks who did not take the initiative to better their own situation. He observed, to his disappointment, that blacks were not often well organized and were "too willing to accept an inferior position." This was largely the result of a lack of "stamina and self-determination [within the midst of] suffering."[52] In 1935, he lamented that because African Americans "as a whole have not entered [Parent-Teacher Associations] as widely as they might, the potential has not been realized."[53] During that same year, Falls blamed much of the segregation found within Catholic parish organizations on "the failure of colored members to utilize to the fullest extent the opportunity afforded" to integrate certain organizations.[54] He later stated, "The majority of Negroes are not sufficiently anxious to avail themselves of the opportunities afforded to other groups, to be willing to work unremittingly for the securing of these opportunities . . . Not only must they be informed of those advantages which they now freely can enjoy in Chicago, but they must also be taught constantly the opportunity of further progress."[55] In addition, Falls never understood why African Americans would often choose to segregate themselves. As a medical student at Northwestern, he usually ate lunch in the university's sole cafeteria. There were eight other black students in his medical class, but he never saw any of them during lunch, until "one day, through chance, I happened to pass a room underneath the stairs leading to the basement where the brooms and mops were kept."[56] He found most of the African American students eating there. Apparently, one of the students

52. Falls, "Race and Its Opportunity," 10.
53. Falls, "Interracial Cooperation in Chicago," (July 1935) 107.
54. Falls, "Interracial Cooperation in Chicago," (August 1935) 123.
55. Falls, "Interracial Cooperation in Chicago," (September 1935) 141.
56. AGF, Box 1, Folder 3, pp. 106, 111.

also worked as a janitor for the building and had a key to the room, but "how this group of colored students ever decided to eat their lunch there I never knew."[57] Falls also believed that the segregation at beaches in Chicago was largely "self-imposed by Negroes themselves for reasons which I was not able to understand except to 'lack of desire to fight.'"[58]

In his 1962 memoir, he wrote again regarding the self-segregation of many African Americans: "I have always felt, and still feel, that in the city of Chicago, at least, Negroes do not need to be as deprived as they are of certain basic opportunities. The solution obviously is a determined, militant and unending fight against every vestige of discrimination and segregation in the city of Chicago."[59] He then listed a number of arguments that he had heard from fellow African Americans over the years against taking advantage of opportunities for integration, such as "I don't want my feelings hurt," "I don't want to go where I'm not wanted," "I go for pleasure and not for battle," and "I don't want to be a pioneer." For Falls, the honest answer was a "lack of courage."[60] The situation that Falls saw developing in Europe in the early 1930s regarding anti-Semitism led to his belief that without constantly fighting, one could lose the opportunities that one already possesses.[61]

In his nineties, however, Falls proposed a reason he had not previously given for the lack of African American involvement in racial justice: "People who are discriminated against are loath to discuss it. It's very painful. So, it was very hard to get even colored Catholics to challenge the Church to abide by its own teachings."[62] It seems that by his nineties, Falls had learned to empathize, to a greater degree, with why some blacks would not work for racial justice.

Early on in his involvement with race relations, he did hear about an instance of organized black "militancy." As the Great Depression worsened, unemployment and segregation had increased in Chicago, as well as calls for employers to fire blacks and hire whites. In August 1930, two African American men had been lynched in Marion, Indiana, which Falls felt was

57. Ibid., p. 112.
58. AGF, Box 1, Folder 13, disc 19-side 2, p. 7.
59. Ibid., p. 11.
60. Ibid., p. 11.
61. Ibid., pp. 11–12.
62. Falls, quoted in Unsworth, *Catholics on the Edge*, 127.

much too close to Chicago.⁶³ Over thirty years later, Falls wrote about what happened next:

> One of the results of the situation was an increasing militancy on the part of Negroes in Chicago—a militancy which bore direct fruit on September 16th. The construction company which had been building street car tracks from South Parkway to Cottage Grove on 51st Street had persistently refused to hire colored workers. On this day about five hundred Negroes congregated in the area, took the tools away from the men, and told the foreman there would be no further work there until Negroes were hired on the job. As a result, twenty-five Negroes were employed the next day.⁶⁴

In this seemingly minor historical event, Falls saw a group of African Americans who had organized themselves and created a disturbance, at great personal risk. This group of African Americans could have been jailed, beaten, and/or killed. There had been no guarantee that their action would succeed, but it was guaranteed that none of them would be working on the track if they did nothing.

Falls was also very familiar with the tactics of Gandhi in India during the early 1930s. He envied Gandhi's ability "to obtain the support of thousands of people who willingly went to jail."⁶⁵ This type of action had led in March 1931 to the Gandhi-Irwin Pact, an agreement that included a cessation of civil disobedience on the part of Indians in exchange for the release of almost all political prisoners by the British and greater freedom for the Indian National Congress.⁶⁶ Although Falls knew the situation in the United States was "very different," he "could not help wondering when Negroes in the United States would be able to have real victories in their resistance to oppression."⁶⁷

In July 1931, he met with Rev. Arnold J. Garvy, S.J., who was then teaching at Loyola University in Chicago. He knew Garvy to be "sincerely" concerned over the injustice that African Americans faced in the Catholic Church. During their conversation, Falls proposed the necessity of "militant action" in addition to education. Garvy disagreed and alleged that

---

63. AGF, Box 1, Folder 9, pp. 465–67.

64. AGF, Box 1, Folder 9, pp. 465–67. Fall's story is confirmed by *Chicago Daily Tribune*, "Police Quell Trouble," 15.

65. AGF, Box 1, Folder 10, p. 479.

66. For more information on the Gandhi-Irwin Pact, see Winslow and Elwin, *Gandhi*.

67. AGF, Box 1, Folder 10, pp. 479–80.

ignorance was the sole factor in the prejudicial attitudes of white Catholics in Chicago. Garvy worried that a militant stance by black Catholics would lead to the anti-clericalism that had been problematic in Europe. Missing in Garvy's assessment was the reality that most non-Catholic African Americans already viewed the Catholic Church and its clergy as the enemy. In his memoir, Falls stated that Garvy, years later, "a sad and disillusioned man, finally admitted that his program was not going to be the program which would produce results."[68]

An overrated value in the Catholic community was patience. "Patience" was a word that caused in Falls the greatest impatience. When Falls and the Grievance Committee of the Chicago FCC met with Bishop Sheil in 1932, Bishop Sheil underscored the need for black Catholics in Chicago to be patient. Sheil told them that, in time, the problem of racism would work itself out. For Falls, the practice of patience by African Americans "had always proved to be fallacious in the absence of any direct action."[69] "Patience, perseverance, industry, and thrift" guaranteed nothing: "particularly in the South . . . the years of such patience and industry often were swept away within an hour by the lynch mob."[70]

On a practical note, Falls wrote an article for the *Chicago Defender* in 1931 in which he touted the need for African Americans to pay attention to their health. Falls knew that sickness and disease were more prominent in the black ghettos of Chicago than in the white areas of the city. He recommended that blacks focus on developing nutritious eating habits, getting proper amounts of sleep, undergoing regular medical examinations, and consulting a physician at the first sign of an illness. He argued that "Negroes can improve their health status and in so doing improve their economic status." In essence, if blacks addressed their health problems, they "cannot be held back in their march toward economic security."[71] In 1942, Falls published another article related to health in the *Chicago Defender*, in which he communicated to a black audience the facts about tuberculosis and when one might need to go to the sanitarium.[72] Because of work by Falls and others during the 1930s to eliminate racial discrimination at the Municipal Tuberculosis Sanitarium, by 1941 African Americans in Chicago no longer

68. Ibid., pp. 499, 504–05.
69. Ibid., p. 528.
70. Falls, "Race and Its Opportunity," 10.
71. Falls, "Health and Jobs," 1931, 15.
72. Falls, "Your Health is Wealth," 1942, 15.

had a higher rate of tuberculosis than whites.[73] In both articles, Falls did not focus at all on the agency of whites in improving the situation of blacks. Falls's purpose was to instill hope in impoverished African Americans about their ability to start improving their situation on their own without waiting for someone else.

Without a doubt, Falls perceived an active militant and confrontational role for African Americans in working toward their liberation. Although whites also have a role to play, which shall be covered in the next section, blacks should not wait for white cooperation or accept faulty white leadership. Regarding the militancy that Falls proposed, it could not be equated with violence, though he firmly believed in the right to self-defense in cases of imminent danger. "Militancy" referred to employing every moral means at one's disposal for achieving racial justice and refusing to compromise with any cultural evils of the day.

WHITE COOPERATION AND SOLIDARITY

Obviously, since Falls was an integrationist, he believed that whites had a role to play in working toward racial justice. Often, though, whites were a source of disappointment for Falls. In frustration, he regularly observed "the apathy or indifference or cowardice of white people" when confronted with prejudice from another white person.[74] One of his first experiences of this type was as a medical student at Northwestern University. When he was denied access to white female patients at the clinic by a newly arrived doctor, none of his professors or fellow students came to his defense—even those who were sympathetic.[75] Additionally, after Falls's class was admitted, more than twenty years elapsed before Northwestern's medical school accepted another African American student.[76] If whites at Northwestern had been willing to fight alongside Falls at this time, perhaps the denial of future black applicants would have been prevented. It was in response to situations like this that Falls related the story of an FCC meeting in which "we discussed whether or not there was such a thing as a decent white man."[77]

---

73. AGF, Box 2, Folder 3, disc 28-side 2, pp. 2, 7–8.
74. AGF, Box 1, Folder 3, pp. 142, 152–53.
75. Ibid., pp. 138–42.
76. Ibid., pp. 143, 151–52; Young, interview with author.
77. Falls, quoted in Unsworth, *Catholics on the Edge*, 126.

Falls experienced another instance of disappointment during the Educational Institute of the Catholic Youth Center in early October 1940. The conference was mostly for young people, but adults were allowed in attendance. On the evening of 5 October, the entirely African American choir of St. Elizabeth's High School performed at the conference and was ecstatically applauded by the audience. The next day, however, when one of the youth proposed a resolution for the desegregation of Catholic high schools, it fell on deaf ears. In fact, many of the youth were adamantly opposed to the motion, and the priests in attendance refused to offer any advice to the participants. In the end, no action was taken.[78] For Falls, this was another example of cowardice on the part of supposedly sympathetic white clerics and students in adequately addressing racial injustice. Falls would later write, "In spite of the clear cut statements of the Pope and of the Hierarchy of the Church and in spite of the enlightened discussions in such publications as the *Interracial Review*, most Catholics, both laity and clerical, absolutely failed to take a position for justice when the chips were down."[79]

In contrast to the whites whom Falls viewed as apathetic, there were whites who thought they knew what was best for African Americans, without any consultation. Falls complained that paternalistic whites with good intentions would advise that the solution for African Americans would be found in education, politics, or Christianity; these solutions were subterfuges for asking that whites be permitted to resolve racial injustice. Falls asserted that these solutions were ineffective and insulting "because in practically all cases, something was being done for the Negro, and not with him."[80] They represented some of the worst kind of arrogance.

Communists, on the other hand, were known to work "*with* Negroes, not for Negroes."[81] Falls believed that this difference in procedure and their proven policy of non-discrimination in all matters were the main reasons that Communism was popular among African Americans.[82] He believed that the movement had made inroads with blacks not because "they accept the ideology of the movement or the actions of the leaders in Russia, but

---

78. AGF, Box 2, Folder 1, disc 24-side 2, pp. 8–9.

79. Ibid., p. 9.

80. Falls, "Race and Its Opportunity," 10. Falls obviously made use of education, politics, and Christianity during his lifetime, but he was critical of how whites often expected him to make use of these avenues.

81. Falls, "Summer School of Social Action." Emphasis in original.

82. Ibid.

solely because they feel that Communism may offer the only chance to get an 'even break,' even if that 'break' is not all that might be desired."[83] Falls agreed with the assessment that if the regime of Communist Russia "were to be transplanted here, Negroes would be far better off than they are in this so-called Christian and democratic order." He believed that that should serve as a warning to white Christians, who could easily attract African Americans to their ideology if they would simply live out their doctrines.[84]

Another issue that often plagued white Catholics with good intentions was ignorance. In 1941, under the editorship of Rev. Edward B. Dailey, the official newspaper of the Chicago Archdiocese, the *New World*, began providing greater space to the issue of interracial cooperation. Regrettably, some of the articles that Dailey permitted to be published included such terms as "darkies" and "Negress." Falls wrote Dailey to inform him that these words were offensive to African Americans and should not be printed.[85]

From the above, it becomes apparent that Falls believed that whites could, and should, work with blacks in working toward racial justice. Nonetheless, when whites— even those with good intentions—tried to aid the cause of racial justice without taking the time to listen and work with African Americans, they were taking on a paternalistic attitude that betrayed an ignorance and an arrogance concerning how racial justice could be attained and the extent to which their own racist attitudes had compromised their best intentions.

INTERRACIALISM

In his memoir, Falls recounted a "tragic" event that occurred on 20 March 1934. W. E. B. Du Bois gave a talk in Chicago concerning his change in stance. Up to that point, Du Bois had supported focusing solely on integration, but he now said that African Americans needed also to focus on establishing a separate culture and society. Du Bois was willing to use any

83. Ibid.
84. Ibid.
85. AGF, Box 2, Folder 2, disc- 26-side 2, p. 1. Unfortunately, the past issues of the *Chicago New World* are not yet searchable, but from paging through 1941 copies of the paper, I did find the world Negress used. Agar, "'Granny,' Born in Slavery," 6. Also, as Falls stated, the paper had a number of articles highlighting interracial cooperation. Here are three examples: *Chicago New World*, "Meeting to Urge Better Relations," 7; *Chicago New World*, "Bill Overcomes Race Preference," 11; *Chicago New World*, "Interracial Group Urged by Bishop," 1.

means or situation necessary to address the desperate plight of blacks.[86] Falls remembered the dismay he had felt that night: "We could hardly believe our ears because Dr. Du Bois had served throughout as the outstanding example of militant Negro leadership. Now [he] . . . was advocating that Negroes accept discrimination and 'make the most of the situation.'"[87] Falls believed that this "defection" could be attributed to Du Bois's loss of hope in the field of race relations.[88] For Falls, however, there were available opportunities for fighting at one's disposal, so any compromise with segregation was unacceptable.

Falls believed that the only way to achieve the goal of racial justice—a truly interracial society—was through organized interracial groups. This section will show that his reasons for interracialism were not only theological, as indicated in the above discussion on the mystical body of Christ, but also very practical. And, although Falls was a strong proponent of interracialism, this did not result in Falls passively waiting for whites to take the lead in promoting racial justice. Falls viewed prejudice as "a two-edged sword" that was harmful for blacks and whites alike. While it "humiliates and insults Negroes, it also stultifies the conscience of whites and frustrates the normal workings of democracy and Christianity."[89] To adequately confront this problem, whites and blacks must band together as "fellow-Catholics" and "fellow-Americans." Working with blacks is a necessity for whites because "white Catholics can never be good Catholics as long as they keep Negroes from being good Catholics."[90] Racism was harmful to African American Catholics because it excluded blacks from fully participating in the life of the Catholic Church and its saving grace.

Although Falls hoped that African Americans would become more organized and practice greater self-determination, he rejected the idea that

---

86. AGF, Box 1, Folder 13, disc 19-side 1, p. 19. The *Chicago Defender*, which covered the event with shock, was so bold as to ask, "Is he a quitter?" Jones, "Why Fight Segregation?" A10. It should be noted that Du Bois still believed that racial justice could only be finally achieved with the attainment of an integrated society. In addition, to be fair to Du Bois, he had always practiced his "new" philosophy, he had just never written or spoke about how segregation could be used for the advantage of African Americans in achieving racial justice in particular situations. For more information on this topic, see Lewis, *W. E. B. Du Bois*, 335–45.

87. AGF, Box 1, Folder 13, disc 19-side 1, p. 19.

88. Ibid., p. 20.

89. Falls, "Industrial and Social Problems," 681.

90. Ibid.

racial justice could be accomplished by blacks alone, for reasons that extended beyond the theological realm. American society was too complex, and the fate of African Americans "is so interwoven with the lives of other groups that there can be no separate development." As such, Falls insisted that blacks must work with whites to attain racial justice, which in itself would aid with the "elimination of much of the prejudice and discrimination which now exist."[91] In addition, he argued that blacks should view themselves more in terms of being citizens than as blacks. He wrote this to emphasize that African Americans should feel willing and able to participate in those activities that can improve not only their situation, but the situation of all in society. Additionally, if one is willing to step out of the black ghetto, the chances to participate in interracial cooperation and to create a more just society are "far greater than most people realize."[92]

Falls also believed that interracialism was larger than blacks working with whites. He thought it would be helpful if there were joint collaborations between "the Jew, the Negro, the foreign-born laborer—[because] all these have an insight which members of the dominant group seem to miss."[93]

In 1931, Falls wrote an article in the *Chronicle* regarding the success of communism among African Americans. Falls was obviously envious of communists when it came to the level of integration they practiced. He cited an unknown newspaper account that stated that 80 percent of evictions in Chicago were directed at blacks. Not only were communists in Chicago aiding black party members in illegally moving their belongings back into their apartments within a day, when white communists referred to a black communist as "Comrade," they "seem[ed] to mean it."[94] The Catholic Church would be wise to follow suit in treating the black person as an equal. Falls asserted that "active support" for the FCC and the National Urban League would not only prevent the spread of communism among African Americans, but lead to effective change in society regarding racism.[95]

91. Falls, "Race and Its Opportunity," 10.
92. Ibid.
93. Falls, "Summer School of Social Action."
94. Falls, "The Spread of Communism," (1931) 577–78.
95. Ibid., 578. See also, Falls, "Industrial and Social Problems," 681. Falls belief that African Americans would become communists if other avenues were not made available was not idle speculation. He had seen a number of blacks with whom he was working for racial justice become communists, including Claude Lightfoot, the politician and author, and John Gray, former president of the International Negro Youth Movement. AGF, Box 1, Folder 13, disc 19-side 1 p. 21.

In an April 1934 article for the Catholic Worker, Falls relayed his experience of a concert and dance hosted by the local Communist party. Falls attended the event with a friend as a part of his duties as chair of the Interracial Commission of the Chicago Urban League. The concert featured a variety of acts, including an African American woman presenting her drawing of the most recent lynching in Maryland, and white and black children performing a play called *They Lynch Little Children in Alabama*.[96] After the entertainment, there was a dance in which many black and white individuals danced together. Someone whom Falls knew stated, "In this organization there is no discrimination; if anyone comes in who isn't willing to subscribe to this stand, he is put out at once."[97]

This was all in contrast to the presence of three segregated Catholic institutions in the same neighborhood where the dance was held. Although the neighborhood was mostly African American, there was a Catholic maternity hospital for whites only, a Catholic homeless shelter that housed only white boys, and a parish whose priest temporarily succeeded in blocking the occupancy of a social agency that served mostly blacks near his white congregation. With this juxtaposition in mind, Falls asked his readers to consider which situation a black non-Catholic would respond to more positively: "to the 'beautiful liturgy' and sound theology of the [Catholic] Church, or to the practical demonstration of human brotherhood demonstrated by the [communists]?"[98]

Despite Falls's admiration of communist integration, he would never become a communist. In addition to the obvious difference of opinion on the efficacy of religion, there had been other bad experiences with communists. In early 1934, Falls was involved with the religious committee of the American League Against War and Fascism. The league had a strong contingent of communists. Though he was "impressed with the sincerity and the devotion of the Communists in pursuing their aims," he "was utterly disgusted at the lack of principles which seemed to motivate some Communists and the lack of . . . regard for any basic democratic procedures."[99] He found their contempt for anyone who did not agree with their avenue for change to be disconcerting.[100]

96. Falls, "The Communist Says," 1.
97. Ibid., 8.
98. Ibid.
99. AGF, Box 1, Folder 13, disc 19-side 1 p. 13.
100. Ibid.

Healing the Racial Divide

THE SOCIAL SCIENCES

In 1937, Falls reviewed John LaFarge's recently published book, *Interracial Justice*, writing that the book fulfilled a need for clearly laying out the problems faced by all African Americans. In addition, the book revealed the absolute incompatibility of racism with Catholic doctrine. Falls noted that missing from the book was a "discussion of methods of approach which have been found effective in various situations." Falls hoped that this would be the focus of a future work by LaFarge.[101] Falls believed that in its current state, LaFarge's book lacked a perspective informed by the social sciences for adequately addressing racism.

Not being an academic, Falls's use of the social sciences was not extensive, but he did view them as imperative to the pursuit of racial justice. In one article, Falls asserted that "the study of race-relations is the study of human relations and belongs properly in the field of Sociology."[102] In other words, without a basic understanding of human societal behavior, one could not address racism. He realized that social scientists could provide insights into the current situation of racism as well as more effective ways to address it. Although Falls's writings on the social sciences are all from the 1930s, they obviously informed his activities for the rest of his life.

In 1932, Falls wrote an article for the *Chronicle*, in which he corrected a priest who had published his "misconceptions" about African Americans in a previous issue.[103] Falls chastised Fr. Mark Moeslein for his broad generalizations about black and white culture—particularly Moeslein's derisive perspective of "Negro culture"—by citing relevant data from the social sciences about how people of different races who possessed the same social status were more similar to one another than people within racial groups as a whole.[104] Falls quoted Moeslein's worst assertion: "Should colored people

---

101. Falls, review of *Interracial Justice*, (1937) 246.

102. Falls, "Honesty in Race-Relations," 158–60.

103. Falls, "Some Misconceptions on 'Negro Culture,'" (1932) 70–71. Falls is responding to Moeslein, "That He Might Present Himself a Glorious Church," 54–55.

104. Falls, "Some Misconceptions on 'Negro Culture,'" 70. For his argument, Falls utilizes Frazier, *The Negro Family in Chicago*. This book makes use of interviews, census data, and other available statistics to analyze the family unit among African Americans in Chicago. Frazier concludes that slavery and poverty have been detrimental to familial stability while a good paying job is the most essential element for familial stability among blacks in Chicago. In particular, see Frazier, *The Negro Family in Chicago*, 246–250. Falls was probably also influenced in this area by his wife, Lillian who received her Masters Degree in Social Service Administration from the University of Chicago. Her thesis

cling to their culture, as it is, only miracles of grace can bring about what the Federated Colored Catholics urge so earnestly."[105] Moeslein was a kindred spirit of LaFarge, who likewise believed only in the ontological equality of the races, perceiving European culture to be superior. Falls questioned the desirability of assimilating all of society into European culture and offered the Negro spirituals as a universally appreciated aspect of African American culture.[106] Moeslein had also questioned the usefulness of legislative responses to racism, which Falls argued was naïve. Falls's reading of history made it clear to him that injustices were not easily rectified with moral suasion and that very "constructive pieces of legislation" had come about "as the result of a long and bitter fight."[107] Conversely, Moeslein advised black Catholics to be patient because justice would arrive. Falls rejected this notion: "The large body of colored people finally are beginning to understand that nothing is going 'to come to them.' What they will accomplish will be the result of intelligent, co-operative efforts of colored and white friends."[108] Falls finished this particular article by counseling black and white Catholics to "obtain facts and not emotional reactions or opinions" with regard to racism.[109]

In reaction to Falls's article, a priest wrote a letter to the editor of a well-read journal of the time called *The Sign*, in which he criticized Falls's perspective and asserted that Moeslein's views were correct. He concluded the letter by claiming that blacks could best aid their cause by placing their

---

studied the potential of black children in particular social and cultural settings and found that social class was the main determining factor in academics, not race. See Proctor, "A Case Study of Thirty Superior Colored Children."

105. Falls, "Some Misconceptions on 'Negro Culture,'" 70.

106. Ibid., 70–71. In his memoir, Falls recounted that he never heard a Negro Spiritual until medical college when he had interaction with African Americans who had come from the South. AGF, Box 1, Folder 3, p. 67.

107. Moeslein, "That He Might Present Himself as a Glorious Church," 54–55; Falls, "Some Misconceptions on 'Negro Culture,'" 71. For his understanding of history, Falls cites Adams, *The Epic of America*. This history book, which was published during the Great Depression, was a bestseller and is known for coining the term, "American Dream." Adams strongly believed in the ideals of America, where every person would have an opportunity for a fulfilling life, but that this would not be accomplished by the masses trusting the government and large corporations. The accomplishment of the American Dream is "a long and arduous road to travel," because "no ruling class has ever willingly abdicated." Adams, *The Epic of America*, 414–16.

108. Falls, "Some Misconceptions on 'Negro Culture,'" 71; Moeslein, "That He Might Present Himself as a Glorious Church," 54–55.

109. Falls, "Some Misconceptions on 'Negro Culture,'" 71.

faith in the Catholic Church.¹¹⁰ In response, Falls gave five concrete examples of how the Catholic Church in Chicago was not a friend to African Americans and in fact promoted segregation. One example was the recent opening of a Catholic maternity hospital in a mostly black neighborhood; the hospital advertised itself as a facility "for mothers of Catholic families of the white race."¹¹¹ Practices such as these necessitated the existence of the Federated Colored Catholics. The solution in overcoming racial injustices was "close cooperation between white and colored Catholics." In order to achieve cooperation, "perhaps a little moral suasion is needed—and then perhaps there is needed a long fight using every honest means of getting justice. Whatever is needed, that the Federation proposes to do!"¹¹²

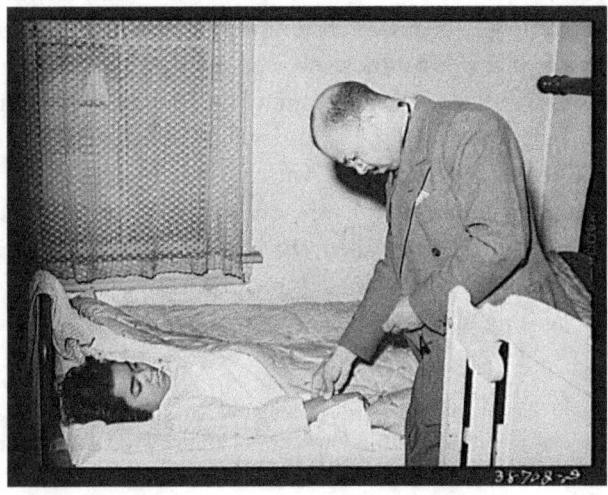

Dr. Falls visiting a family on relief during the Great Depression. Chicago Illinois: 1941. Courtesy of the Library of Congress, LC-USF34- 038702-D

Falls was also aware of what later writers and social scientists would refer to as "white privilege." Racism does not simply harm blacks, it also benefits whites: "It is well to remember that prejudice pays—pays in hard,

110. Ahern, letter to the editor, 611.

111. One of the ads for the hospital can be found in Lewis Memorial Maternity Hospital, "Lewis Memorial Maternity Hospital," 6.

112. Falls, letter to the editor, (June 1932) 675. Arthur's view on the need for militant struggle would not change. In his 1962 memoir, he wrote: "I have always regarded the fight for human relations as warfare—warfare which broke out in battle after battle on the very same subject." AGF, Box 1, Folder 13, disc 19-side 2, p. 6.

cold cash, for someone, whether it be the 'Aryan' doctor who drives out his Jewish competitor from a paying position, or the Chicago realtor who derives exorbitant rent from slum property because the occupants can't move."[113] Additionally, in situations where African Americans were able to achieve a greater "educational and cultural" status, they faced discrimination from whites worried about their own status.[114] Falls further stated that racial animosity and hostility in the United States were based on "the greed and selfishness and paganism of millions of human beings, including, sadly enough, many of us Catholics."[115] Within the same article, Falls implied that racist Catholics were heretics as well as classifying them as pagans. His emphasis on millions of people indicates that Falls was fully aware that the racism was harmful because it had permeated the minds and souls of countless individuals. Racism was not only part of the legal fabric of society, it was also part of the cultural fabric, and ordinary white individuals regularly profited from it.

In 1934, fascism was a stark reality in Spain and Italy, and the situations in Germany and Russia had much in common with fascism, in Falls's opinion. He wrote of the "spread of Fascism in the United States," observing that fascism had always been a part of the African American experience and that a common denominator in fascist regimes was "the terrorization of minority groups" to conceal the underlying problems of a country.[116] Falls noted that in Germany and the United States, fascism had resulted in racially and religiously motivated discrimination and violence against Jews, blacks, and Catholics. Therefore, white Catholics should be concerned about the growing trend toward fascism in the United States. Falls even mentioned a handful of fascist groups in the Chicago area and concluded by arguing that "one of the most effective bulwarks against the establishment of Fascism in this country is the unity of white and colored

---

113. Falls, "Restrictive Covenants Create Negro Ghettos," 2. In spring 1931, Falls gave an address to the group entitled, "Is the Rising Unrest Among the Darker Races Threatening White Supremacy?" Unfortunately, no copy of this talk was preserved. Chicago Urban League, "The Chicago Urban League: Season 1930–1931," CUL, Box 1, Folder 27.

114. Falls, "Race and Its Opportunity," 10.

115. Falls, "Restrictive Covenants," 3. Obviously, if Falls was writing today he probably would not refer to racists as pagans. He used this term in a derogatory sense that is similar to how theologians like Cone, Massingale, and Copeland employ the term idolatry. All are attempting to make clear that Christians that willingly participate in racism are very far from the teachings of Christ.

116. Falls, "The Graver Menace," (1934) 102.

people, understanding that their problems are common."[117] The Catholic Church could play a critical role in fighting fascism by seriously investing energy in the interracial organizations already in existence.[118] Through his work with the Morgan Park–Beverly Hills Interracial Group (mentioned in the previous chapter), Falls tried to implement this interracial vision with the incorporation of social science instruction on race relations to both whites and blacks.[119]

In another article by Falls, written shortly afterward, he noted the need for the social sciences to analyze human situations because it took "a great deal more than a spirit of sympathy or good-will . . . for a person to be able to cope with prejudice and discrimination in American life."[120] With the aid of the social sciences, which even in the 1930s were available in a wide body of literature, "one is able to pierce through the labyrinth of misconceptions, falsehoods, and sophistries which exist in [race relations]."[121]

THE NECESSITY OF SOCIAL STRUGGLE

Despite its limited success, Falls believed there was a role for moral suasion, which was appealing to the consciences of whites and those in power about the need for charity and justice for African Americans in society and the Church.[122] As stated above, Falls asserted that moral suasion needed to be coupled with a dedication to a long and bitter struggle.[123] The tools that Falls employed to fight racism evolved based on changing circumstances and available options, but the commitment to fight and, at times, to put one's life on the line—as he and Lillian did in moving to Western Springs—are essential ingredients for racial justice.

Even though Falls applied political pressure to the mayor in Chicago and worked to have legislation passed on the city and state levels, Falls

---

117. Ibid., 102–03. Believing that racism has affected all people of color, Falls joined a local committee of the World Committee to Aid the Victims of German Fascism in early 1934 to help raise funds for European Jews to travel to the United States. AGF, Box 1, Folder 13, disc 19-side 2, p. 3.

118. Falls, "The Graver Menace," 103.

119. AGF, Box 1, Folder 10, pp. 541–44.

120. Falls, "Honesty in Race Relations," 158.

121. Ibid.

122. Falls, "Industrial and Social Problems," 679.

123. Falls, "Some Misconceptions on 'Negro Culture,'" 71.

never supported a political candidate or party. Although he did identify as a Republican during the 1930s and 1940s, he did not find voting helpful. In his experience, political parties that were aware that they were a better choice for African Americans expected the black vote and, consequently, took no action to improve their situation.[124] A better avenue was "organized opposition," deemed by Falls as the only way to achieve justice for African Americans on a large scale. He focused his energy not only on society, but also on the Catholic Church.[125] Again, he considered his actions most effective when they were performed within the context of a group that had specific goals and a plan of action. Group action was preferable for those who were not wealthy, because their power was in numbers. Falls noted that the wealthy could act alone with the use of money to sway decisions in the mind of a person or institution practicing prejudice: in 1928, when H. L. Swift, a donor to the University of Chicago, sent one of his African American employees to the new Billings Memorial Hospital located on its campus, she was refused admittance until Swift threatened to discontinue any further contributions to the university, Falls noted, "She was admitted."[126]

Another example of organized opposition was buying power, which Falls considered a helpful tool in achieving racial justice.[127] Stores that existed in predominantly black neighborhoods could not exist without African American customers, so Falls urged those customers not to patronize a store unless it employed a decent number of black workers.[128] Along these lines, Falls believed that worker and consumer cooperatives could play an integral role in creating more just remuneration for African Americans and others who found themselves in a more vulnerable position in society. In December 1935, he documented the existence of the Farmers' Cooperative Milk Company in the wake of a recent milk strike. Because the middleman, in this instance a distributor, took such a large cut of the profit, many of the smaller farmers were not receiving adequate wages. The small dairy farmers were not only paid an adequate wage by the milk cooperative, but they could sell their milk for less than the large distributors because they were not concerned about their profit margin.[129] Falls believed cooperatives

124. Falls, "Race and Its Opportunity," 10.
125. Johnston, "Colored Churches," 26.
126. AGF, Box 1, Folder 7, disc 12-side 1 p. 8.
127. Falls, "Race and Its Opportunity," 10.
128. Falls, "The Chicago Letter," December 1935, 8.
129. Falls, "The Chicago Letter," December 1935, p. 8.

needed to be utilized by blacks and others to oppose the rich and large corporations that were hoarding profits and decent paying jobs. The cooperative movement was also positive because it valued cooperation instead of exploitation. It was inherently democratic and accepting of all races and creeds, and its "very construction . . . gives colored members, as well as all others, equal power in determining policies, including employment, a power which is most limited in the present chaotic system."[130] His promotion of cooperatives coincides with his belief in the universal destination of goods: "The earth and everything on it was created by God—and for the use of mankind, all mankind, not just Americans."[131] If God's creation is to be shared by all, then there needs to be an endorsement of economic models that work toward such a goal.

In addition to moral suasion and struggle, another essential element in the long battle toward racial justice is hope. Without the hope that change can and will occur, groups will fold after a short period of time. For Falls, hope was closely related to belief. For example, even though the Catholic Church often rejected Falls, he believed that "Catholic" meant "universal" and he was determined to have the Catholic Church live up to its ideals: "The Catholic Church never really welcomed me, but if you believe in something, you have to stick with it."[132]

THE CIVIL RIGHTS AND BLACK POWER MOVEMENTS OF THE 1960s

Unfortunately, there is not much information regarding Falls's opinion of the civil rights or black power movements during the late 1950s and 1960s. During this period, he was involved with the CED, the lawsuit against the Chicago-area hospitals, and his church, as well as regularly speaking on racial justice matters.[133] In 1968, however, Falls did give an interview to the

---

130. Ibid. Falls never explicitly attacked capitalism as a system, but many of his ventures are concerned with working toward an economic reality that is more democratic.

131. Falls, "Restrictive Covenants," 2.

132. Falls quoted in Unsworth, *Catholics on the Edge*, 130.

133. For documentation of his talks, see "Dr. Falls to Speak at Housing Meeting," Unknown newspaper clipping, 7 November 1964, WSHS, Folder: Dr. Arthur G. Falls; *Alton Evening Telegraph*, "Says Doctors Fail to Face Racial Problem," 18; *Chicago Daily Defender*, "League Head to Talk," 17; Despres, "Alderman Reports Integrating Medical Services," 4; *Chicago Daily Defender*, "Calendar of Community Events," 13. According to this notice, Falls would be presenting a review of *Black Rage* by William H. Grier, M.D. and Price M. Cobbs, M.D.

Chicago Tribune about the civil rights and black power movements, characterizing them as "a great deal of vocalization and very little cerebration."[134] Based on his personal engagement with college graduates in these movements, he maintained that they lacked any cogent plan for addressing racism. He believed that if they were more organized, they might be able to accomplish some magnificent feats. He pointed out that groups like the Urban League, the NAACP, and the Council for Biomedical Careers were not receiving much news coverage in 1968, but that they were better suited to the pursuit of equality in society because of their clear goals and organization. Though Falls was extremely familiar with African American history, he stated, "I realize it's not as dramatic a cry to shout, 'We want competent teachers' instead of 'We want black teachers and black history courses,' . . . but that's what's needed."[135] Falls continued: "I'd rather have them think science than think black . . . We've already heard all the things the 'white man' has done—they haven't left any out—now the thing to think about is what do we do now."[136] This thought coincides with the argument Falls had made over thirty years earlier, when he said that blacks should view themselves more as citizens than as blacks.[137] For Falls, the common humanity shared by every person of every race was more important than racial differences. Additionally, this corresponds with Falls's opinion in early 1969 that although the issue of racial injustice was complex, "I feel that the main reason for the few students [in medical schools] lies within ourselves."[138] In response to this opinion, which a *Chicago Defender* writer referred to as Falls's "unpopular stance," Doris E. Saunders wrote, "Dr. Falls is probably one of our heroes who won't be appreciated until the night of his wake, but then, prophets are usually unappreciated in their own home town."[139]

134. Falls, quoted in Schueler, "W. Springs Doctor."

135. Ibid. In addition to the familiarity he would have gained about African American history during his time with the De Saible Club, he also gave one of the welcoming addresses at the Annual Meeting and the Celebration of the Twentieth Anniversary of the Association for the Study of Negro Life and History in Chicago, which focused on African American achievements in music and art, the immediate antebellum period, and West African culture. *The Journal of Negro History*, "Proceedings of the Annual Meeting," 373–78. It should be noted that he had the same critique of the National Catholic Interracial Federation being disorganized without a "definite program" in the late 1930s. AGF, Box 1, Folder 14, disc 22-side 1, p. 8.

136. Falls, quoted in "W. Springs Doctor."

137. Falls, "Race and Its Opportunity," 10.

138. Falls, quoted in Doris E. Saunders, "Confetti," 12.

139. Doris E. Saunders, "Confetti," 12.

Healing the Racial Divide

A niece on Lillian's side of the family remembers her father and Arthur arguing about affirmative action, with Arthur arguing against the use of affirmative action. As she recalled, Arthur viewed it as special treatment, as opposed to being given a fair chance.[140] Arthur's granddaughter recalls that he just wanted everyone to have an opportunity. He was supportive of affirmative action only in cases where an opportunity was currently being denied to African Americans. His experience in the early 1920s had left him opposed to such ideas: at Northwestern, about one third of his class had flunked out of the medical school as part of its quota system. Out of the nine African American students in that class, he was the only one to return for his second year. Falls believed that medicine should be a field open to anyone who worked hard and was qualified.[141]

One issue that Falls did not address is that of schools with limited resources and how they might be in a position to accept only a set number of students. Since whites, as a whole, are likely to have better financial and educational backgrounds from which to succeed, how are opportunities to be afforded to blacks when opportunities are limited? If Falls did have a response to this concern, it has not been preserved.

It would likely be illuminating if Falls had written or said more about the civil rights and black power movements. Based on his use of concrete goals, we can assume that he was supportive of the push to pass the Civil Rights Act of 1964. Nonetheless, by 1968, he believed that the goals of the civil rights movement lacked an adequate focus. With regard to the importance that Falls placed on concrete goals, his actions speak for themselves. During the late sixties, his focus had shifted to addressing school segregation in Chicago and creating career opportunities for those interested in medicine, as was covered in the last chapter.

---

140. Scott, interview with author.

141. Sykes, interview with author. Dr. Sykes, while working on her thesis about the lives of her grandparents, interviewed Arthur and Lillian in depth. Her knowledge regarding so many parts of Arthur's life before she was born makes her a credible source for including this secondhand information. In his memoir, Falls vividly recounted that on the second day of school all the students were brought to the auditorium and told that one third would not make it to sophomore year—a threat with which the school followed through. AGF, Box 1, Folder 3, pp. 105–6, 137–38.

CONCLUSION

Even though Falls was not a theologian, there is a depth to his thought and writings on Catholic racial justice that is, unlike those of his contemporary John LaFarge, informed by personal experiences of racism. Along with his own involvement in working against racism, Falls gave rich and practical meaning to the doctrine of the mystical body of Christ, the concept of sin, and the notion of Christian discipleship. These Christian ideas, combined with an analysis of the contemporary situation through the social sciences, became foundational for promoting effective strategies for the attainment of racial justice.

The relationship present in Falls's understanding of Christian doctrine, his use of the social sciences, his own experiences with racism, and his experiments in racial justice was not linear. Each area was a source of mutual enrichment for the other. His notion of Christian discipleship was influenced by his reading of the scriptures in light of his contemporary situation in Catholic Chicago. His vision of an integrated society was in turn informed by his reading of the life of Christ as one dedicated to the healing of all humanity despite the "existing local situation."

Unfortunately, one area of his life that we know very little about was his prayer life. As stated in the previous chapter, we know that he participated in Compline in the late 1930s during his time with the Catholic Worker and that he regularly attended mass his entire life. In addition, it is known that he read the works of Virgil Michel and the popular Catholic magazines and newspapers of his day. Nevertheless, there is no account of his preferred methods of prayer or what his prayer life entailed outside of an organized setting. But, even though we lack this knowledge, Falls's informed and thoughtful application of the doctrines of the Catholic Church to his contemporary situation indicates a rich spiritual life that is presently hidden from us.

4 A New Understanding of Catholic Racial Justice—Inspired by Falls

FALLS LEFT BEHIND MORE than four full decades of actions and writings dedicated to improving race relations in the United States. As the two previous chapters attest, Falls did not haphazardly address issues of racial injustice. He utilized his Catholic faith tradition while constantly experimenting with different methods, which he subsequently adjusted, based on the results. He also employed his knowledge of history and the social sciences to make the best decisions possible. Using a definition of Catholic racial justice inspired by Falls as its foundation, this chapter will bring certain insights and methods from the previous two chapters into conversation with contemporary views and methods of confronting racism to explore a more adequate Catholic theological racial justice framework.

More specifically, after proposing a definition of Catholic racial justice that is inspired by the life and writings of Falls, this chapter will probe certain facets of the definition to confirm its validity and ascertain its implications. I will then address contemporary manifestations of racism as noted by the social sciences to more greatly ensure that racism will be efficaciously addressed in the twenty-first century. Next, there will be an examination of the concept of sin and its limits in addressing racism. This will be followed by an investigation into the legitimacy of classifying racism as a heresy by evaluating racism in light of traditional Christian heresies. Next, the manner in which the Church has traditionally responded to heresy will be summarized. Additionally, there will be an examination of the tension experienced by Falls and other African Americans in their attempts to live faithfully in a racist church. Lastly, the chapter will cover the need for active struggle and the necessity of hope.

A NEW DEFINITION OF RACIAL JUSTICE

One obvious question that has not been addressed is: What is Catholic racial justice? This section will offer a new definition of Catholic racial justice that the remainder of the chapter will scrutinize. Any definition of racial justice will be dependent upon our understanding of racial injustice. In short, racial justice is about trying to accurately assess and address the problem of racial injustice in order to apply the most appropriate and efficient solution. For Cone, racial injustice is grounded in the slavery of African Americans and can be rectified only through liberation. Falls placed the emphasis of racial injustice on a lack of opportunities for blacks in American culture. Therefore, his definition of racial justice stressed creating opportunities so that African Americans could truly be integrated into society and Church.[1] For both Cone and Falls, the problem and the solution are both deeply influenced by their Christian faith. Between the two of them, racial injustice is clothed in the language of sin, idolatry, and heresy, while racial justice is clothed in notions such as discipleship, militancy, and liberation. A working definition of Catholic racial justice that is informed by the life and writings of Falls could be as follows: *an organized struggle for the realization of the mystical body of Christ in the context of racial injustice in our society and within our Church.*

Implicit in this definition—and based on an authentic understanding of the mystical body of Christ—is a struggle for racial justice that joins together black and white agency as well as further work in the retrieval of African American and black Catholic narratives. Although Falls's life and writings have been a substantial source for improving our understanding of Catholic racial justice, there are countless other African Americans and black Catholics whose voices should be added to his so as to continuously improve our conception of Catholic racial justice. As noted in chapter 1, Massingale's examination of Malcolm X and Copeland's retrieval of Henriette Delille are two examples of new and potent insights brought into the realm of Catholic racial justice that were previously absent in Catholic theology. Additionally, the insights provided by our study of Falls in chapters 2 and 3 demonstrated the significance that the life and writings of even one black Catholic can have in penetrating more deeply into the harm of racism from a theological perspective as well as offering concrete responses.

---

1. LaFarge also stressed an "equality of opportunity" for all groups or individuals, regardless of race, but misunderstood the nature of racism and the degree to which racism had permeated American Catholic culture. LaFarge, *Race Question and the Negro*, 84.

Therefore, it is fair and necessary to state the following conclusion: from this point forward, no theory of Catholic racial justice can be considered adequate, acceptable, or effective unless it incorporates the voices of black Catholics and other African Americans, and this position needs to be relentlessly defended.

In this definition of Catholic racial justice, the "mystical body of Christ" has additional faith connotations. A faithful response to racial injustice from a Christian perspective must be grounded in a liberative and inclusive vision of Christianity as well as a struggle that is based in hope. Falls's reading of history from the social sciences and the background he received in African American history from the De Saible Club also aided him in being conscious that hope could be, to a certain degree, established by previous victories in racial justice. In addition, the Christian education that Falls received from his parents, the Federated Colored Catholics, and the Catholic Worker put in place a firm foundation for his work toward the greater inclusion of African Americans in the Catholic Church and society.

Furthermore, the doctrine of the mystical body of Christ insinuates that the problem is not always the "Church against the world" situation—it is more than that. It will involve struggling against injustice within the Catholic fold—even with priests and nuns. In the fight for racial justice, we must not forget that the Church itself has been infected with racism and that future work for racial justice will require a battle on two fronts: Church and society. The Church, as it is composed of members of a culture, is not immune to the biases of a culture. Falls experienced the sinful and racist nature of his own Church in not being able to attend his parish's grade school, not being able to work in his Church's hospitals, and having fellow Catholics and Christians trying to segregate his living quarters to a Chicago ghetto.

During his life, Falls was always involved in organizations because he knew that more could be accomplished through a group than on his own. This is one way of interpreting the word "organized." Falls understood that power among the oppressed could be best wielded with greater numbers. None of the groups with which he was involved, with the possible exception of the Catholic Church, was more important than the goals to be achieved. Therefore, Falls often left groups or joined additional groups to best address a new situation or gain a new insight into a situation. The other interpretation that follows from "organized" is the planned nature of actions. Falls did not find it helpful or useful to lash out blindly at our racist culture. Actions against this culture required an accurate diagnosis and surgical precision in applying a remedy.

Lastly, the work for racial justice will not be accomplished solely through moral suasion. Although theory, reason, and argument are necessary for change, they are only one component. Since the injustice of racism is so ingrained in the hearts and minds of Americans, change will only occur with "struggle." Although Cone would say that the form of the struggle should take "any means necessary," Falls would qualify that statement by saying we should make use of any moral means at our disposal. "Moral means" would include letter writing, boycotts, meetings, co-operatives, lawsuits, protests, civil disobedience, educational programs, and political pressure, but would exclude violence. Even though Falls accepted violence as a means of self-defense, he did not advocate it as an instrument for achieving justice. Additionally, this organized struggle should be informed by the social sciences. The social sciences furnished Falls with a more accurate assessment of and solution for the evil of racism.

RACIAL JUSTICE IN THE SOCIAL SCIENCES

Through his wife, Lillian, Arthur was immersed in the social sciences of his day. He utilized certain insights from her field and valued its existence. The same could be said, to varying degrees, for all the theologians covered in the second half of chapter 1. For example, Cone asserts that the social sciences are an indispensable tool for practically analyzing racism and considering different methods of confrontation.[2] Exactly how one is to work for racial liberation is not always explicitly stated in Cone's work, because "black religion is not a social theory that can be a substitute for scientific analysis of societal oppression."[3] Two weaknesses that Cone believes were especially present in early black theology were the lack of social and economic analyses. It should be noted that it was during this time period that Falls gave his negative assessment of the black power movement. For Cone, an omission of these tools occasions an unrealistic dependence on moral suasion to respond to racism. The solution to poverty and racism

---

2. Cone, *Speaking the Truth*, 123. The use of the social sciences by those agents listed in the first half of chapter one is more limited. Official U.S. bishops' documents from 1968's *The National Race Crisis* onward began employing the social sciences, but in very limited capacity.

3. Cone, *Speaking the Truth*, 32, 46.

is more complicated than making persuasive arguments to the white and privileged.[4] Study of the origins and causes of racism, poverty, and oppression is required to put forth realistic solutions.[5]

Therefore, it is appropriate to consider the latest findings in the social sciences about current manifestations of racism and how to best address them if we are to take Falls seriously. This section will review the work of social scientists Matthew Desmond and Mustafa Emirbayer, whose work on racism and racial justice is current and comprehensive.[6] Although the audience of their book is primarily white college students, their framework can be expanded to include the non-college-educated and people of color.

There is a popular notion that racism no longer exists in the United States.[7] Although laws are in place to prevent discrimination in residential, educational, and economic areas of American life, racism still exists as a cultural phenomenon that has severe consequences. To illuminate how racism endures in the twenty-first century, consider these recent statistics. (Statistics are helpful because of their ability to view racism on a large scale where its systematic effects are most clearly visible.) For example, between 1995 and 2004, the FBI has recorded over forty thousand race-based hate crimes in the United States. In 2004, there were over 3,800 race-based hate crimes, with 67 percent of those perpetrated against African Americans. In 2005, 25 percent of African Americans were living in poverty, compared to 8 percent of whites. Additionally, since 1940, the unemployment rate for blacks has remained at a level around twice that of whites. In 2006, the unemployment rate for blacks was 9.2 percent, compared with 4 percent of whites.[8] This disparity also remained consistent during the Great Recession. In January 2012, the unemployment rate for blacks was 13.6 percent, compared with 7.4 percent for whites.[9] Despite these obvious inequalities, half of whites believe that there is relative economic equality between whites and blacks.[10] Desmond and Emirbayer contend: "Like a recessive tumor, twenty-first-century racism has disguised itself, calling itself by

---

4. Cone, *For My People*, 88–96.
5. Cone, *Speaking the Truth*, 123.
6. Desmond and Emirbayer, *Racial Domination, Racial Progress*.
7. Numerous examples are given in the following texts: Bonilla-Silva, *Racism Without Racists*; Brown et al., *White-Washing Race*; Feagin, Vera, and Batur, *White Racism*.
8. Desmond and Emirbayer, *Racial Domination, Racial Progress*, 2.
9. Luhby, "Big Drop in Unemployment Rate."
10. Desmond and Emirbayer, *Racial Domination, Racial Progress*, 2.

other names and cloaking itself behind seemingly 'race neutral' laws, policies, and language. But it is still with us, influencing our relationships, our institutions, and our world. And it will not simply fade out of existence if we turn a blind eye toward it. A tumor will destroy a body regardless of whether its bearer recognizes it or not."[11]

The racial inequalities of the present are the result of a long-existing culture of racism, which has been compounded by the inheritance of "social conditions, historical contexts, and state policies" most dreadfully realized in the institutions of slavery and Jim Crow.[12] This inheritance has resulted in a present-day situation in which the median net wealth of white families is twenty times that of African American households. In 2005, the disparity was eleven to one, but the current economic crisis has been more injurious to the already precarious situation of many black families.[13]

Desmond and Emirbayer delineate five fallacies about racism that prevent our society from adequately addressing it. First, there is the individualistic fallacy, through which racism is usually thought of solely on the interpersonal level as an intentional act between two people, even though "intentionality is in no way a prerequisite for racism. Racism is often habitual, unintentional, commonplace, polite, implicit, and well-meaning."[14] This fallacy also fails to account for the many systematic and structural forms of racism. Second, there is a legalistic fallacy that assumes that eliminating laws that sanction racism will purge racism. For instance, school systems all across the country are still severely segregated almost sixty years after *Brown v. Board of Education*, which was supposed to eliminate segregation in schools by making it illegal to compel segregation. Third, there is the tokenistic fallacy, which wrongly assumes that if a few African Americans are successful, then economic and political power are now equally available to all races. For example, the election of Barack Obama to the U.S. presidency and the ascension of Oprah Winfrey to her position as one of the richest people on the planet are not fair indicators that economic and political opportunities are legitimately available to people of all races.[15]

11. Ibid., 4.

12. Ibid., 5, 12.

13. Kochhar, Fry, and Taylor, "Wealth Gaps Rise." According to this report, the median net wealth of a white family in 2009 was $113,149 compared to $5,677 for an African American family.

14. Desmond and Emirbayer, *Racial Domination, Racial Progress*, 27.

15. Ibid., 27–28. As Desmond and Emirbayer point out, the first black congressman, Joseph Rainey, was elected in 1870, but his election did not mark the end of racism.

Fourth, there is the ahistorical fallacy, which implies that past instances of racism are of no consequence today. On the contrary, past instances of limited opportunities and lower net wealth have resulted in African Americans needing to put forth greater exertion in order to attain a standard of living equal to that of the average white family. Fifth, there is the fixed fallacy, which presumes that racism does not change forms. Under this notion, if the previous forms of racism are addressed, through improvements such as allowing black Catholics to enroll in predominantly white Catholic schools, then it can be concluded that racism as a whole has been eliminated. Moreover, the most horrific manifestations of racism should not be considered the norm for dealing with the problem, because "to define racism only through extreme groups and their extreme acts is akin to defining weather only through hurricanes."[16]

In addition to the five fallacies, Desmond and Emirbayer proffer two further notions that are important preliminary points for any honest discussion of racism. First, since white is the "*dominant* category," which defines what is normal in American society, it should not be seen as simply another race among others. Whiteness provides "many cultural, political, economic, and social advantages and privileges for white people and withholds such advantages and privileges from nonwhite people."[17] "White privilege" is the term used to refer to this set of advantages for whites or those who appear to be white. Second, like Massingale, who notes the way that the Christian narrative—authentically told—can replace the dominant racist narrative, Desmond and Emirbayer propose a cultural narrative based an alternative reading of the American narrative. Their reading emphasizes personal and civic responsibility and the ability of a dedicated minority to change the current situation.[18] An alternative reading of the American narrative is a common foundation for many social scientists who address racial domination.[19]

16. Ibid., 27, 30.

17. Ibid., 38. Emphasis in the original.

18. Ibid., 40, 501–5, 518–19, 541. One important reason they probably use a version of the American narrative is because it is considered acceptable to teach in the social sciences departments of public universities.

19. For example, Jeffrey C. Alexander posits that through stories such as the creation of the Bill of Rights, the Constitution, as well as those of George Washington and America's involvement in World War II, there is a "cultural structure at the heart of democratic life" that promotes solidarity, liberty, and a politics of responsibility. Alexander, *Civil Sphere*, ix, 60–62. In contrast, Charles Taylor grounds his thought in "citizen dignity"

Desmond and Emirbayer advocate addressing four overlapping areas to effectively transform current domination structures: "(1) ourselves, (2) our inner circle, (3) our institutions, and (4) our nation."[20] Change of self for whites means a dedication to listening, learning, and being aware of our almost unconscious racist attitudes. For African Americans, it means acknowledging and resisting culturally influenced feelings of "self-hate" that are created by the normalization of European standards. Addressing our inner circle includes challenging the prejudicial attitudes of family and friends, as well as being cognizant of the best ways to have a meaningful conversation. Confronting our institutions requires individual and multiracial coalitions to influence and transform the institutions of which we are a part. This type of change will require personal sacrifice and could easily lead to a loss of promotion, job, or bodily safety. Since federal and local political policies contribute to racial domination and influence the flow of money and power, a reform of political structures is imperative, as are changes in policy. Substantial change on this last level occurs principally "through methods of public protest, including strikes, sustained boycotts, public demonstrations, civil disobedience, racial uprising, and full-scale revolutions."[21] Coalitions are indispensable because the dominated require numbers to exert their influence. Lastly, a long commitment will be required, along with a willingness to break particular laws in order to expose certain kinds of domination.[22] In agreement with Desmond and Emirbayer, Frances Fox Piven contends that extensive change happens in the political sphere only when people "rise up in anger and hope, defy the rules that ordinarily govern their lives, and by doing so, disrupt the workings of the institutions in which they are enmeshed."[23] On a large scale, such actions will force politicians to give attention to injustices that are often ignored because of corruption within government and the influence of the wealthy and big business on electoral politics and government policies.[24]

In combating racism on all its various levels, one needs to believe that winning is possible. To add to this hope, Desmond and Emirbayer allege

---

because he feels it is the only concept for mutual recognition that everyone shares in a democracy. Taylor, "The Politics of Recognition," 27.

20. Desmond and Emirbayer, *Racial Domination, Racial Progress*, 523.
21. Ibid., 34, 523–36.
22. Ibid., 537–41.
23. Piven, *Challenging Authority*, 1.
24. Ibid., 1–18.

that social change is rarely the result of a large-scale involvement, but rather the dedication of anywhere from 20 percent to less than 1 percent of the entire population.[25] Jeffrey C. Alexander, with a slightly different opinion, asserts that significant achievements in racial justice require the mobilization of the oppressed with an apparatus in place to communicate their injustice in a manner that permits a large number of the dominant group to empathize. Regarding racism in the United States, this will not occur until "a new social movement" appears that is able to unite "the increasingly fragmented black community" and effectively communicate its struggle to the average white American.[26]

Although Falls's use of the social sciences was more limited because of what was available at the time, his life illustrates how he employed them to prove the intellectual and cultural equality of African Americans with whites as well as to demonstrate that militant, determined struggle was a prerequisite for substantial societal change. Falls accomplished change in many areas of Chicago life by collaborating with a small group of dedicated people who believed that change was possible. Without necessarily being aware of it, Falls was a model and forerunner in all four of the areas that Desmond and Emirbayer propose for implementing change. First, he worked on constantly developing his own understanding of racism. He learned about American history and his racial heritage in order to better understand the evil of racism. He also conversed with his family, or inner circle, regarding the best way to address racism. Additionally, he labored to change the Catholic and medical institutions with which he was involved. Finally, he attempted to change government policy by having laws enacted on the city and state level, pressuring the mayor to appoint an African American to the school board, and suing in federal court to ensure that government funds given to white hospitals would be available for African American physicians and patients.

The social sciences are no less important today than they were for Falls in his organized struggle against racism. To a certain extent, they have been utilized by the theologians in the second half of chapter 1, but greater use could aid these theologians and others in proposing practical paths for confronting racial injustice through theological praxis. Concerning most ecclesial documents on racism, the need for employing the social sciences is even more pronounced. As Cone alleges, without the social sciences, Catholic

---

25. Desmond and Emirbayer, *Racial Domination, Racial Progress*, 541.
26. Alexander, *Civil Sphere*, 390.

racial justice is usually reduced to moral suasion.[27] With the use of the social sciences, moral suasion can be transformed into organized struggle.

THE INADEQUACY OF RACISM AS SIN

Although Falls referred to racism as sin, it was clearly also more than that in his eyes. Racism attacked the integrity of the mystical body of Christ, the Church. This section will briefly review modern notions of sin to determine to what extent it is adequate to call racism sinful. It is outside the context of this work to present an exhaustive overview of sin; therefore, I will paint some broad strokes and touch on certain dimensions of sin that will be helpful for this project. A sinful action can be examined objectively and subjectively. The objective aspect of the sin refers to the wrongness of an action independent of whether one is aware of or intends the evil that one is performing. The subjective aspect of sin refers to what degree a sinful act should attribute guilt to the person performing the action.[28] Our examination of sin will focus on the objective aspect of sin. This will allow for an easier comparison with heresy below. For, as we will see, being a heretic is not dependent on whether one is aware of his or her heretical beliefs or behaviors. Therefore, in order to narrow our comparison, this section will not address the subjective qualities.

Karl Rahner, the great German theologian of the twentieth century, defined "guilt," which was closely allied with sin, as "closing oneself to [the] offer of God's absolute communication."[29] For Rahner, this rejection of God could occur in either an explicit or unreflective manner. The American moral theologian Daniel C. Maguire defines "guilty behavior"—a term that he prefers to "sin"—as a "*conscious and free behavior (active or passive) which does real unnecessary harm to persons and/or their environment.*"[30] Maguire's definition,

---

27. It should be noted that Massingale has made this same claim. He states that in ignoring social analysis, "American Catholic teaching on race often presumes that it is addressing a rational audience of well-intentioned people, and thus assumes that racism can be overcome principally by education, dialogue, and moral persuasion." Massingale, *Racial Justice*, 75.

28. *New Catholic Encyclopedia Supplement 2010*, 2nd ed., s.v. "Sin (Theology of)."

29. Rahner, *Foundations of Christian Faith*, 93. Emphasis in the original.

30. Maguire, *The Moral Choice*, 392. Emphasis in the original. The reference to sin as guilt in the work Rahner and Maguire is to emphasize the subjective nature of sin. Therefore, it should be noted that Rahner's definition also stresses the free and conscious decision of the subject.

in contrast to Rahner, emphasizes the harmful effect that sin has on creation. Both theologians are pointing to different aspects of the same reality, and combining their complementary definitions of sin could be helpful: sin is a rejection of God that causes material harm in the created world. Obviously, racism can be classified as sinful under these terms because of the manifest harm it causes to human society and individual people, which is a rejection of Jesus and his command to love one another.

Cone's understanding of sin mirrors that of Rahner and Maguire, but also stresses the communal nature of sin.[31] As Massingale observes, Cone's communal analysis of sin is grounded in his utilization of Exodus.[32] In this context, Cone defines "sin" as "a religious concept that defines the human condition as separated from the essence of the community . . . To be in sin, then, is to deny the values that make the community what it is. It is living according to one's private interests and not according to the goals of the community. It is believing that one can live independently of the source that is responsible for the community's existence."[33]

In other words, sin is intimately associated with right living in community—particularly one's religious community. Since God's relationship with Israel is centered on the liberating event of the exodus, in which the Hebrews were set free from slavery, any action against liberation, whether personal or communal, would be a sinful act against God and the community.[34] Cone's communal understanding of sin could be applied to interpret the dominant culture in the United States as a sinful culture of white privilege.

Although racism is clearly sinful in that it is a rejection of God and does harm to humanity, it is more. As Nilson so eloquently explains, racism harms the very integrity of the Church in a way that is not equaled by sinful acts such as adultery, eating steak on Good Friday, or cheating on one's taxes. As discussed in chapter 1, he sees racism as a heresy that betrays a lack of authenticity among Catholic theologians. Since the notion of sin does not adequately address all the implications of racism, the next section will explore the possibility of recognizing racism as heresy, and whether heresy can be understood not only as a belief, but also as a practice.

31. For more on Cone's understanding of communal and personal sin, see Cone, *Black Theology and Black Power*, 63–64; *Black Theology of Liberation*, 110–12; *Spirituals and the Blues*, 82. As recognized by Massingale, Cone's notion of personal sin is grounded in his understanding of Genesis. Massingale, "Social Dimensions of Sin," 81–84.

32. Massingale, "Social Dimensions of Sin," 85–91.

33. Cone, *Black Theology of Liberation*, 110.

34. Ibid., 111–12.

RACISM AS HERESY

A Traditional Understanding of Heresy

If we are going to seriously consider racism as a heretical practice against the mythical body of Christ, a brief account of heresy in the Christian tradition needs to be explored. After this section, we can then revisit Falls's notion of heresy along with those of other modern theologians in light of this examination. "Heresy," from the Greek *hairesis*, is a fluid term in the Christian tradition. In the New Testament, the term referred primarily to a sect, such as the Pharisees or Sadducees, though 2 Peter 2:1 used the term to indicate "lying teachers." Later, during the patristic era, "heresy" was often synonymous and interchangeable with "schism," since heretics were viewed as individuals separating themselves from the Catholic Church.[35]

Alister McGrath defines "heresy" as "a doctrine that ultimately destroys, destabilizes, or distorts a mystery rather than preserving it."[36] He makes the important distinction that heresy has its origin in belief and is not a total rejection of the faith, although he considers it destructive like a virus. For example, Marcion (85–160) and Valentinus (100–160) were early heretics who thought they were defending orthodoxy. Both of them, disappointed that their ideas did not take hold within the Roman Christian community, founded their own communities.[37] In these two early examples, we see that heresy became a Church-dividing issue. In the Middle Ages, heresy was seen not only as threatening the integrity of the faith, but displaying disdain for the teaching authority of the Catholic Church. It often dealt with disputes surrounding papal authority rather than theological ideas.[38]

Since the seventeenth century, heresy has more often been used as a doctrinal censure or condemnation of a teaching that was viewed as contravening an essential aspect of the faith.[39] In the 1917 edition of the Code of Canon Law, heretics were defined as baptized persons who still retain a Christian identity but reject a vital aspect of the Christian faith.[40] At Vatican

---

35. *New Catholic Encyclopedia*, 2nd ed., s.v. "Heresy"; McGrath, *Heresy*, 103.

36. McGrath, *Heresy*, 31.

37. Ibid., 33–34, 62, 103, 171, 201.

38. *New Catholic Encyclopedia*, 2nd ed., s.v. "Heresy"; McGrath, *Heresy*, 103. Three examples of "heresies" based more on a contention with papal authority are the Hussites, Waldensians, and Lollards.

39. *New Catholic Encyclopedia*, 2nd ed., s.v. "Heresy."

40. *New Catholic Encyclopedia*, 2nd ed., supplement 2009, s.v. "Heresy (Canon Law)."

II and since, the term "heretic" has been avoided when referring to other Christian denominations in favor of the term "separated brethren."[41] Also since Vatican II, the Congregation for the Doctrine of the Faith (CDF), which is the Vatican congregation charged with protecting the integrity of the faith, has placed more emphasis on teaching the faith than punishing those holding heretical teachings.[42]

Throughout the Christian tradition, the definition and understanding of heresy has undergone constant evolution and revision. Nonetheless, there are certain common elements. Heretics view themselves as defending a cultural tradition that they believe to be essential to the faith. In addition, heresy has been seen primarily as related to either the acceptance or rejection of certain doctrines rather than actions. By stating that many white Catholics in Chicago were implicitly assenting to the mythical body of Christ, Falls was placing a strong emphasis on practical mediation or the relationship between faith and practice. But can an implicit assent to a religious error visible in one's actions be heretical? The next section will compare racism with traditional heresies in order to further probe this possibility.

A Comparison of Traditional Heresies and Racism

Although traditional heresies have been normally associated with erroneous doctrines, there are a number of similarities between heresy and racism. Since there is a relationship between thought and action, it is logical that there should also be a relationship between traditional doctrinal heresies and practices. This section will compare some of the traditional heresies with racism in order to detect whether one can legitimately claim that these heresies have substantial commonality with racism. Approaching racism as heresy is not without problems. Mark Edwards, in his recent work on heresies within the early Church, reveals that many viewpoints that were

---

Canon 1325, paragraph 2. This same paragraph states that one who completely rejects the Christian faith is an apostate. I used the following copy of the 1917 code of canon law: *Canon Law*, eds., Bouscaren and Ellis. The 1983 Code of Canon Law changes the wording slightly from the 1917 version, but the sentiment is the same. Code of Canon Law, c. 751, in *Code of Canon Law*.

41. *New Catholic Encyclopedia*, 2nd ed., supplement 2009, s.v. "Heresy (Canon Law)." Second Vatican Council, Decree on Ecumenism, 1, 3–4, 7–11, 20, 24.

42. *New Catholic Encyclopedia*, 2nd ed., supplement 2010, s.v. "History of Heresy: IV: After Vatican II." Nevertheless, there have been notable censures of theologians by the CDF since Vatican II.

A New Understanding of Catholic Racial Justice—Inspired by Falls

initially condemned as heretical were later incorporated into the orthodox teachings of the Catholic Church.[43] Nevertheless, there are certain heresies from the early history of the Church that are still deemed heretical that will allow for a comparison.

In the second century, Marcion rejected both the Old Testament and Jesus's Jewish roots. For him, the Old Testament was too morally questionable to be associated with the person and message of Jesus Christ. Jesus was sent by the God of love, while the Jewish god was an inferior, hateful, vengeful deity. McGrath asserts that it is not an accident that Marcionism reappears during outbursts of anti-Semitism: "It is a heresy about the dignity and historical significance of the Jewish people."[44] Similarly, racism denies the dignity and historical significance of African Americans.

Another heresy of the early Church was docetism, which taught that Jesus only appeared to be human and that he did not die on the cross. In effect, the notion of God being joined to a human nature was too horrific to contemplate.[45] Both docetism and racism are based on cultural notions that a group finds too difficult to consider. Docetists could not assent to any sort of joining of the divine with the human. In like manner, many racists can not assent to a church community that permits the interaction of whites and blacks within the same worship space or neighborhood, much less a scenario where blacks and whites are a community of genuine equals.

Similar to the traditional heresies, racism in the twenty-first century is perpetuated by individuals who are capitulating religious truth to cultural notions about race that are incompatible with the Christian faith. Racists believe that they are protecting the purity of the Church and will to separate themselves from contact with blacks by withdrawing their children from "contaminated" schools or fleeing from areas in which African Americans reside. Racism rejects any form of Christianity that affirms the value of African American history or culture. Unlike traditional heretics, racists do not explicitly disavow any specific Catholic doctrine, but as Falls asserts, their concrete practice betrays implicit heretical beliefs. Nonetheless, certain heretics, such as the Marcionists, had beliefs that were indubitably lived out in a practice of exclusion. Although not officially viewed as heretics at the time, the circumcision party that Paul rejected certainly had beliefs that proceeded to particular practices.

43. Edwards, *Catholicity and Heresy*. This is not the case with racism.
44. McGrath, *Heresy*, 131.
45. Ibid., 111–16.

Nevertheless, can an authentic understanding of heresy place more emphasis on praxis and still be heresy? As previously mentioned, many writers refer to racism as idolatry. Originally, in the Old Testament, idolatry had a strict definition based on either a rejection of the Jewish God and the worship of other deities or the worship of other deities in addition to the Jewish God. Beginning in the New Testament, idolatry was also used in a metaphorical sense to refer to Christians who placed disproportionate importance on wealth and other material objects.[46] For those writers, a Christian's sinful actions could be used to detect an unproclaimed idolatry. It is in this metaphorical sense that modern theologians refer to racism as idolatry. This precedent for a development in meaning could legitimize a similar advance regarding heresy, especially since certain heresies have had a close relationship to practice.

A controversial matter that is raised when racism is classified as a heresy is the logical conclusion that many in positions of Church authority are heretics. Although Falls did not specifically apply the heresy of the mythical body of Christ to bishops, he made the same accusations of white superiority toward certain bishops that he alleged against white lay Catholics. That numerous bishops could be heretics has a historical precedent in the Arian heresy of the fourth century.[47] The more problematic issue concerns the fact that a number of popes in the past have supported slavery based on racial determination.[48] Even though this is a delicate matter that deserves consideration, it is outside the scope of this work to further assess this issue. In any case, if we assume for the time being that racism can rightly be called heretical in the twenty-first century, it is appropriate to consider how recent writers have viewed racism as heresy.

Addressing Racism as Heresy in the Twenty-First Century

The previous two chapters examined Falls's battling with those who lived by a heretical, or inauthentic, notion of the mystical body of Christ—the

---

46. *New Catholic Encyclopedia*, 2nd ed., s.v. "Idolatry (in the Bible)." Two examples of idolatry in this context are in Ephesians 5:5 and Colossians 3:5.

47. Newman, *The Arians of the Fourth Century*, 251, 275–79.

48. Nicholas V, *Dum diversas*. Pope Innocent VIII accepted one hundred dark-skinned slaves as a gift from King Ferdinand of Aragon in 1488 and gave some of them to his favored cardinals. Stark, *For the Glory of God*, 330. From 1600 to 1800, the papal navy was composed of 2,000 slaves who were almost totally Muslim, which may indicate they were almost all black. Noonan, *A Church that Can and Cannot Change*, 102.

so-called mythical body of Christ. To reiterate, Falls never unequivocally stated that the mythical body of Christ was a heresy. Nevertheless, it is clear from his writings that racism, which is an outright rejection of the mystical body of Christ, is more than mere sin. For Falls, it was the primary Church-dividing issue in Catholic Chicago during the twentieth century. This section will briefly examine racism as heresy in the work of Cone, Nilson, and Copeland. Their insights on this topic will augment the previous section and provide a firmer theological basis for classifying racism as a heresy.

Cone defines heresy as "any activity or teaching that contradicts the liberating truth of Christ."[49] Traditional definitions of heresy focus on the denial of a doctrinal truth that is essential for the Christian faith. Cone's approach to heresy is broader in the sense that it includes actions, and narrower in the sense that it is concerned with one divine truth: "the liberating truth of Christ." Cone admits that theology and ethics are not the same; nevertheless, they are "closely interrelated."[50] The ethical dimension in his definition of heresy is also found in his classification of Christ. He defines Christ by his work for freedom and liberation instead of using metaphysical classifications.[51] In addition, he believes that heresy prompts one to mistake "untruth" for "truth" and to readily allow a separation of theory and praxis.[52] In other words, one cannot only believe that Christ came to liberate the oppressed; one must also struggle to make Christ's mission present today. For Cone, heresy is not simply an issue for historians, but a real and present danger. Heresy needs to be addressed again in our time, "*not* for the purpose

---

49. Cone, *God of the Oppressed*, 33. Although it is possible to perform an analysis of Cone's thought on racism as heresy, the main thrust of his work more properly displays that racism is an idol that must be destroyed. Cone, "Preface to the 1986 Edition," in *Black Theology of Liberation*, xvii. It should be noted that Cone, Copeland, and Massingale prefer to classify racism as idolatry. Cone, *Black Theology of Liberation*, 61; Copeland, "Racism and the Vocation of the Christian Theologian," 17; Copeland, *Enfleshing Freedom*, 109–10; Massingale, "Response," 130–35. Although it is outside the scope of this book to compare the merits of viewing racism as heresy versus idolatry, a few words concerning the difference between heresy and idolatry would be helpful. Generally speaking, heresy is concerned more with church unity, the hope of reconciling the heretic back into the Church, and involves a truth of the faith that is overemphasized to the detriment of the faith as a whole. Idolatry is concerned with the identity of the church (or a lack of church) because another object has replaced the centrality of God. With idolatry, conversion is necessary in order to return to the church. Undoubtedly, the notions of heresy and idolatry do have overlapping qualities.

50. Cone, *God of the Oppressed*, 34.

51. Ibid., 82.

52. Cone, *Speaking the Truth*, 10.

of witch-hunting, but for the sake of the Church's life."[53] The church's life is at stake because when the church lapses into heresy, the church ceases to be church. According to Cone, the church—the Christian community—has three tasks in order to justify the appellation of "Christian": (1) to preach liberation, (2) to share in the struggle for liberation, and (3) to be a visible manifestation of the Gospel.[54] When the three tasks are not all present, church is not present and the gathered community is in a heretical state. In essence, heresy is not merely notional, as the Code of Canon Law contends, but ethical—it involves praxis.

Based on his apprenticeship with Cone and other black theologians, Nilson also recognizes the heretical nature of racism. He posits that racism is not simply a behavior that is discordant with the fundamental doctrines of Christianity, which would make it solely an ethical problem, but also a "theological problem."[55] He quotes a white German theologian who powerfully describes the heretical nature of racism: "The theological justification of racist structures must be condemned as heresy. This is not a matter of 'heresy' in a figurative, ethical, sense. Heresies are a challenge to the essential being of the church, not simply the truth of a particular belief. Racism is a heresy in that basic sense of the word: under the appearance of credal legitimacy it undermines the unity of the church."[56]

Although Copeland does not refer to racism as a heresy, the christological implications that she relates to racism have strong heretical overtones. For instance, Copeland calls believers to follow Christ, and to be the body of Christ: "If my sister or brother is not at the table, we are not the flesh of Christ."[57] In other words, to be the body of Christ, we must emulate Jesus's radical inclusivity with those whom society despises. Copeland makes the christological implications of racism quite clear: we are not Christ's flesh if we oppress others. Moreover, Copeland employs the doctrine of the mystical body of Christ to emphasize her christology: "a praxis of solidarity for human liberation . . . make[s] the mystical body of Christ publicly visible in our situation."[58]

---

53. Cone, *God of the Oppressed*, 34. Emphasis in the original.
54. Cone, *Black Theology of Liberation*, 138–39.
55. Nilson, *Hearing past the Pain*, 56–57, 68.
56. Nilson, *Hearing past the Pain*, 69, quoted in Raiser, *Ecumenism in Transition*, 10.
57. Copeland, *Enfleshing Freedom*, 82.
58. Ibid., 105.

Based on the evidence collected here, it is fair to conclude that heresy is a better way to classify racism than sin because it directly attacks the integrity of the Church. Viewing racism as heresy implies that the Christian's faith is compromised when one assents to racist practices. Whereas a Christian lives a life of orthopraxis (i.e., correct belief lived through practice), a heretic lives a life of heteropraxis (i.e., compromised belief lived correspondingly through incorrect practice). If we assert that racism is heretical, the next logical area to explore is how heresy has been addressed. By knowing how heresy has been addressed in the past, decisions about how to best approach racism from a theological perspective in the present can be formulated.

Traditional Responses to Heresy

This section will give a brief overview of responses to heresy in the Christian tradition. This section is not meant to serve as an exhaustive examination of the topic, but to provide an opportunity to incorporate the larger tradition into modern confrontations with the evil of racism. In order to bypass complications in current scholarship regarding the worth of certain heresies, the focus will be on responses to heresies that the broad consensus of Christian scholars still find troubling and about which there is less debate regarding the possibility or usefulness of their incorporation into orthodox theology.

As noted above, Valentinus and Marcion began their own churches after their views were rejected by Roman Christians. During most of the second century, there was neither a firm authoritative apparatus nor a power structure in place to take any concrete actions against heretics.[59] Therefore, most actions against heretics took the form of writing, with the best known author being St. Irenaeus of Lyons. Irenaeus hoped to bring heretics back to "the Truth" by persuasion—or at least by compelling them to change their current reasoning once it had been proven deficient and false.[60]

Extraordinary changes in the manner in which heresy was addressed occurred after the emperors Constantine and Licinius issued the Edict of Milan in 313, which granted religious freedom and the return of confiscated property to Christians. In response to the Arian heresy that was dividing the Church, Constantine called the Council of Nicaea in May 325 to unify

59. McGrath, *Heresy*, 132–33.
60. Irenaeus, *Against the Heresies*, Book 2, Chapter 11, Section 2, 37–38.

Christians to create a more stable political environment. In the end, the council condemned Arianism, and Constantine exiled those in authority or positions of influence who refused to accept the results of Nicaea. Despite the condemnation, canons were also passed that clearly stated that those who rejected heresy would be welcomed back.[61]

After Constantine's edict, religious coercion became a factor in addressing heresy. St. Augustine (354–430) was the first theologian to write frankly about the issue and to endorse coercion as a way to stop heresy and bring people back to the Catholic Church.[62] This issue came to the forefront for Augustine regarding the Donatists in North Africa, who believed that the church should not readmit Christians who denied their faith during the Diocletian persecution from 303 to 311. Initially, Augustine was against the use of force and promoted the idea that all people—both Donatists and Catholics—should be exposed to the arguments of both sides so that each person could make an informed decision for the truth. Later, particularly after Augustine had witnessed the ability of force to induce the acceptance of the Catholic viewpoint on Donatists, he took a favorable stance toward coercion for religious purposes under specific circumstances and conditions. Augustine compared such conduct to that of a physician who is forced to treat a recalcitrant patient. With this in mind, he instructed that such actions should be carried out with a loving restraint that is careful not to give way to malice or greed.[63]

St. Jerome (347–420) had strong words against heretics. He believed that they needed to be cut out of the community as soon as they were noticed. Comparing them to cancer and dangerous hot embers, he stated:

> The cancer gradually festers in the body and, according to the familiar proverb, one sheep's disease pollutes the entire flock. Therefore, the ember must be extinguished as soon as it appears so that the house does not burn down. Yeast must be kept far from the batch [of flour] so that it does not spoil. Putrid flesh must be

---

61. McGrath, *Heresy*, 136–49, 203. The condemnation can be found in the creed agreed upon by the council and a letter that was composed by the council for the Church of Alexandria. Council of Nicaea, "The Nicene Creed," 3; Council of Nicaea, "The Synodal Letter," 53. Canons eight and nineteen describe conditions for accepting back heretics, with the ordained normally being able to retain their position. Council of Nicaea, "The Canons of the 318," 19–20, 40.

62. Swift, *The Early Fathers on War*, 110.

63. Mattox, *Saint Augustine*, 66–69; Augustine, Letter 93, chapters 1–5, 12, pp. 382–401.

amputated so that the body does not rot. And the diseased animal must be sequestered from the sheepfolds so that the flocks do not die. Arius was one ember in Alexandria, but because he was not extinguished at once, his flame destroyed the entire city.[64]

Although Jerome was prone to hyperbole, his point was clear: heresy is harmful, unacceptable, and cannot be allowed to flourish within the Church under any circumstance.

St. Thomas Aquinas (1225–1274) lived during the Cathar heresy, which was a religious movement with a dualistic theology that was strongly entrenched in southern France. To a large extent, Aquinas's order, the Dominicans, was founded with the purpose of preaching among the Cathars. Since Aquinas's *Summa Theologiae* was written as a theology handbook for his order, many of whom would be preaching among the Cathars, his comments on heresy were not hypothetical.[65] After heretics had rejected a number of pleas to return to the Church, they were to be excommunicated and handed over to the secular authorities for death. For Thomas, "if heretics be altogether uprooted by death, this is not contrary to our Lord's command."[66] Heretics that repented were always to be welcomed back into the Church the first time. The penitent could also be accepted back into the Church a second time if need be, but at that point should also be handed over to the secular authorities for death. This was to be done for the good of the weaker members of the faithful community who might be further scandalized and possibly lose their own salvation if the heretic fell back into error a third or fourth time.[67]

Especially in light of *Dignitatis humanae*, the Second Vatican Council's document on religious freedom, coercion in religious matters is no longer considered acceptable. The document regards the innate dignity of the human person as of greater importance than religious unity. Therefore, statements against the use of coercion in religious matters are reiterated numerous times. Regardless, the truths of the Church are still to be proclaimed in earnest, to the point of shedding one's own blood, but never the blood of another.[68]

---

64. Jerome, *Commentary on Galatians*, 5.9, pp. 210–11.

65. Torrell, *Saint Thomas Aquinas*, 144–145.

66. *STh*, II-II, Q. 11, art. 3, reply; answer 3, pp. 89–91. The above quote is from the reply of the second article.

67. *STh*, II-II, Q. 11, art. 4, reply, p. 93

68. Second Vatican Council, *Dignitatis humanae*, 1–4, 9–12, 14.

This notion echoes Falls's belief from the 1930s that racial justice should be worked toward "using every honest means of getting justice."[69] His stance included responses such as moral suasion and militant struggle, depending on the circumstances. In his 1962 memoir, he wrote, "I have always regarded the fight for human relations as warfare—warfare which broke out in battle after battle on the very same subject."[70] Falls was obviously using "warfare" in a symbolic sense. Although racist heretics should never face violence for their actions, this overview demonstrates that the matter is serious enough that it needs to be addressed in a manner more confrontational than moral suasion. An assault on racism is required that will attend to its personal, social, cultural, and structural aspects. Since heresy is something that not only affects society, but greatly harms the Church, the next section will appraise how one lives in a faith community contaminated by heresy.

The Tension of Living in a Heretical Church

Cone has always been suspicious of white churches, like the Catholic Church, and does not have any intention of joining such a church. Even so, he views the separation of white and black churches as a "scandal" that cannot be rectified until they both decide to "achieve their Christian identity only through an unqualified solidarity with the victims of oppression, seeing their struggles of liberation as God's eschatological sign to make us all one."[71] He has also been "critical of black churches for their imitation of the white ones from which they are separated."[72] He sees this similarity in the stress many black churches place on doctrinal confessions instead of liberation. In fact, "many have adopted the same attitude toward the poor as have the white churches . . . [and] are more concerned about buying and building new church structures than they are about feeding, clothing, and housing the poor."[73] It is worth mentioning that while Cone does not advocate a segregated society, he is very suspicious of integrated churches

---

69. Falls, letter to the editor (June 1932) 675.
70. AGF, Box 1, Folder 13, disc 19-side 2, p. 6.
71. Cone, *Speaking the Truth*, 81–82.
72. Ibid., 81
73. Ibid., 122.

A New Understanding of Catholic Racial Justice—Inspired by Falls

based on the past and current failures of these churches to promote racial justice. For Cone, integrated churches are white churches.[74]

Massingale has a heartfelt and poignant section within his book about being in a racist Church that is entitled, "A Concluding Black Catholic Reflection: 'Sometimes I Feel Like a Motherless Child.'"[75] He writes about the reality of white privilege in the Catholic Church, where there is a pervasive "racist" perspective that "European aesthetics, music, theology, and persons—and only these—are standard, normative, universal, and truly 'Catholic.'"[76] Though this section ends only with questions regarding the issue of being a black Catholic in a white church, he later remarks that he has often been "weary to the depths of my soul and overwhelmed by the challenges of keeping my sanity in a white culture and its institutions. I have experienced such despair as a true 'dark night' of sense, will, and spirit in which all I have to cling to is the naked faith that being a theologian in the Catholic Church is what God has called me to do."[77] Massingale believes that the voices of black Catholic theologians allow for the possibility in the American Catholic Church of a theology that is "truly 'catholic'" and "provides an alternative model and/or needed corrective" for the Catholic Church.[78]

Falls clearly struggled with being in a racist Church. On the one hand, he could not imagine voluntarily joining the Catholic Church because of its deeply ingrained racist practices from the level of lay person to bishop. On the other hand, as I discussed in chapter 3, Falls never left the Catholic Church because it had given him the foundation to fight racism.[79] The mystical body of Christ that was exemplified in the notion of a unified Church and society prevented Falls from ever considering the creation of a segregated society separate from whites.

---

74. Cone, *For My People*, 34, 46–52; *Black Theology and Black Power*, 71–82; *Speaking the Truth*, 54–60, 143–47.

75. Massingale, *Racial Justice*, 78–82.

76. Ibid.

77. Ibid., 82, 167.

78. Ibid., 172–73.

79. AGF, Box 1, Folder 10, pp. 506–07; Falls, interview with Sicius. The first part of the sentence is reference to the following quote of Falls that was given in the second chapter: "It is very fortunate that I was born into the Roman Catholic Church because under no stretch of [the] imagination could I conceive that I ever voluntarily would have joined it because of the discrimination and segregation which existed." AGF, Box 1, Folder 10, pp. 506–7.

Falls, like the black Catholic theologians covered, does not question the fundamental doctrines of the Church. These doctrines became a life-giving font for Falls that provided the basic tools and inspiration to confront racism. Nonetheless, his writings are saturated with the pain and agony caused by the apathy of so many fellow Catholics toward the prophetic demands of these same doctrines and the witness of Jesus Christ. Falls was not willing to sacrifice genuine Christian practices for the "beautiful liturgy" and sound doctrine. He wanted both and he focused his energy on sound theological praxis.[80]

Falls and current black Catholic theologians are also strongly in favor of inclusion. Falls found his reasons for inclusion in doctrines such as the mystical body of Christ. Any church that did not strive to include all peoples was not worthy of the name "church." While agreeing with Falls, Massingale incorporated black Protestant sources, including the images of the welcome table and the beloved community, into his vision of an interracial theology, permitting a development of the Catholic viewpoint to one that is more than European.[81] This type of multicultural expansion allows Catholic theology to become truly universal and "catholic."

Copeland's work likewise underscores the importance of an interracial setting for Catholic theology. Her argument for integration is informed by the Catholic concept of "Eucharistic solidarity." There is a strong connection between the body of Jesus Christ and the faithful bodies of his disciples—both black and white. There is also an ardent connection in "Eucharistic solidarity" to the eucharistic meal, for the "Eucharistic banquet re-orders us, re-members us, restores us, and makes us one."[82] If Catholics refuse to accede to the inclusive reality and power of the eucharist, they are rejecting a core mystery of the Catholic faith.

To a large extent, the tension present from living in a racist church is irreconcilable. Even though Catholic doctrine provides invaluable tools for opposing racism, the vocation to push one's church to live out the Gospel is filled with frustration and constant rejection. For the Catholic struggling with this tension, the only undertaking that can bridge this contradiction is active struggle. With this task in mind, we move on to the next section, which explores the necessity for organized struggle and praxis in our work toward Catholic racial justice.

80. Falls, "The Communist Says," p. 8.
81. Massingale, *Racial Justice*, 122–25, 132–43.
82. Copeland, *Enfleshing Freedom*, 126–28.

THE NECESSITY FOR ORGANIZED ACTIVE STRUGGLE AND PRAXIS

In his life and writings, Falls illustrated a clear belief that meaningful change did not occur without active struggle. Of course, Falls did not randomly lash out in anger against the injustices he experienced and witnessed. He joined or gathered with a group of people, formed a plan that he thought had a possibility for success, and then executed that plan. Just as Desmond and Emirbayer have observed, racial justice requires collective action and multiracial coalitions. Falls's conviction was in contrast with that of John LaFarge, who was not against recourse to courts, judges, legislators, and working with non-Catholic groups per se, but placed the primary emphasis on moral suasion and educating whites. Essentially, any work toward structural change through coalitions was secondary and seemingly superfluous.[83]

Falls had mixed results in his work for racial justice. Sometimes, as with the building of his home in Western Springs, he was successful. Other times, such as with his effort to build an integrated neighborhood in Deerfield, he failed. Whether he succeeded or failed, he took what he had learned and adjusted his methods to more effectively address future problems.

Although Falls would have been unfamiliar with the term "theological praxis," it is not anachronistic to say that Falls implicitly used this method.[84] Falls's praxis may be partially due to his being a medical doctor, a profession in which theory and action are in constant dialogue. In a number of articles, he wrote about innovative treatments he had tested on patients, for which he analyzed the results and then offered advice for future treatments.[85] For Falls, there could be no separation between doctrine and action. If one believed in the reality of Christ and the teachings of Christ and his Church, one was also responsible for living out these doctrines in a life of Christian discipleship that almost always required personal sacrifice. In Falls's work, there was a fluid relationship between doctrine and practice, with each informing and enriching the other. Although the doctrine of the mystical body of Christ, which was popularized by Michel, was regularly used to promote lay participation in the cause of social justice, Falls applied the doctrine to his own context of fighting housing covenants in Catholic

---

83. LaFarge, *Catholic Viewpoint on Race Relations*, 72, 141.

84. As Cone points out, all theology is contextual and, therefore, responds to contemporary concerns and circumstances. Cone, *God of the Oppressed*, 36–41.

85. Falls, "Protein (Milk) Therapy," (1928) 117–21; "Management of Pulmonary Tuberculosis," (1955) 399–402; "Ammonium Chloride and Novasurol," (927) 65–67, 72–73.

Chicago. Such an application deepened the meaning and application of the doctrine within an interracial context in which white Catholics benefited from the oppression of their fellow Christians.

Furthermore, struggle is the constant companion of one truly dedicated to racial justice. Cone asserts that God is best known through "a participation of the whole person in the liberation struggle."[86] As I discussed in chapter 1, this perspective leads Cone to state that the black experience must be the starting point for black Christians.[87]

For Copeland, the experiences of Delille point to the actuality that the "Christian witness demands an engagement with bodies, not their denial; a struggle with history, not surrender to it."[88] Her separation from the cultural practice of plaçage was an action against predetermined cultural expectations. Instead of reasoning with her culture to repent, she dedicated herself to the education of free and enslaved African Americans, which offered an embarrassing witness to how white Christians should have been living.

Massingale states that for the black scholar, "'speaking the truth' is an activity engaged in, on behalf of, and in solidarity with a community-in-struggle."[89] Massingale's remark is not surprising since he sees "struggle" to be the one word that defines the African American experience in the United States.[90] If "struggle" characterizes the experience of blacks trying to simply survive, it undoubtedly describes the experience of any person laboring for authentic opportunities for African Americans.

FALLS AS A SIGN OF HOPE

Just as hope is an integral aspect of the Christian faith, it is also constitutive of the Catholic racial justice project. Falls was aware, in no uncertain terms, that one could not accomplish anything if one did not try. In an interview that Falls gave near the end of his life, he stated that he would often remind people in the various groups he participated in that "if you are right, you don't always lose." He said this to combat the common fear of the problem being unworkable and the solution not worth trying.[91] Despite writing very

---

86. Cone, *Black Theology of Liberation*, 98.
87. Cone, "Preface to the 1997 Edition," *God of the Oppressed*, xi–xii.
88. Copeland, *The Subversive Power of Love*, 57.
89. Massingale, *Racial Justice*, 155.
90. Ibid., 20.
91. Falls, interview by Troester.

little on the notion of hope, Falls implicitly exuded hope. One could not dedicate one's entire life to a cause that one felt was hopeless. Falls joined all his campaigns under the assumption that there was a possibility of success.

Hope also plays an important role in the work of the theologians I have covered. It is a prevalent theme in the work of Cone: "Victory over evil is certain because God has taken up the cause of the oppressed."[92] Scripturally, Cone grounds hope in the exodus event and the resurrection of Christ. Because Jesus has been raised, African Americans do not need to fear death in their struggle for liberation—Christ has conquered death.[93]

Massingale dedicates a considerable amount of space to hope in his book on racial justice. For him, hope is a prerequisite for any journey that intends justice in an oppressive situation. Because the aim of hope runs counter to the dominant cultural order, it is even "subversive."[94] Often, in the African American experience, hope is implicitly present in the cries and songs of lament—similar to those found in the psalms of the Old Testament that cry out in pain regarding Israel's situation, but are firm in the hope that God will correct the wrong.[95]

Hope also played a key role for Henriette Delille, who in 1836 wrote the following prayer in the opening pages of a prayer book that she used at mass: "I believe in God. I hope in God. I love. I wish to live and die for God."[96] Copeland, in conflating this prayer with the life of Delille, proclaims that Delille lived a new way of being within the bounds of tepid Catholicism "with eschatological and situated hope."[97]

The relevance of hope cannot be overemphasized. In addition to it being an integral aspect of the Christian faith, the social sciences confirm its necessity in inspiring people to work for change. Hope must continue to be a part of any racial justice framework. Positive change can and does happen on this side of heaven. In the lives of Delille and Falls, we see that much was accomplished to bring dignity to the lives of African Americans, but that much is still unfinished. The reality of justice unrealized in race

---

92. Cone, *God of the Oppressed*, 91.

93. Ibid., 91, 120–21, 127–49.

94. Massingale, *Racial Justice*, 145–47. Emphasis in the original.

95. Ibid., 105–10, 147–49.

96. In the original French, she wrote, "*Je Crois en Dieu. J'espère en Dieu. J'aime. Je v[eux] vivre et mourir pour Dieu.*" Delille, quoted in Copeland, *The Subversive Power of Love*, 27–28.

97. Copeland, *The Subversive Power of Love*, 66.

relations should not be cause for despair. The victories of the past witness to new and unforeseen possibilities. In other words, there have been many achievements in the past despite dire circumstances.

CONCLUSION

This book began with the hope of making the following three contributions: (1) to draw attention to the necessity of African American sources and focusing on black agency in Catholic racial justice, (2) to expose a new generation of Catholics to the life of Arthur Grand Pré Falls, and (3) to deepen our current understanding of Catholic racial justice. The life and writings of Falls are important components of the Catholic tradition that affirm much of the work being done by those few Catholic ethicists who are addressing racial injustice. Specifically, I used the life of Falls in order to verify the necessity of black agency and the use of African American sources for Catholic racial justice. I then postulated a definition of Catholic racial justice inspired by Falls: *an organized struggle for the realization of the mystical body of Christ in the context of racial injustice in our society and within our Church*. This chapter has scrutinized and explored certain aspects of this definition—especially the implication of racism as a heresy. Allowing that more work should be done to confirm this proposition, my tentative assessment is that racism can be rightly called heretical.

The second and third chapters of this book gave ample space to the life and writings of Falls. The insights reached in this chapter vindicate the need for a historical emphasis in the realm of moral theology and corroborate the urgency for more historical research in the area of Catholic racial justice. Even though a doctrinal emphasis in ethics, as we see in Falls, can be an indication of an overly legalistic solution, his theological praxis embodied how doctrines such as the mystical body of Christ can provide dynamic guideposts for Christian discipleship.

Whether this book will succeed in introducing Falls to a new generation of Catholics remains to be seen. Chapters 2 and 3 encompass countless hours of research on the life and writings of Falls. But in order for this final goal to be successful, more work on Falls by this author and others will be required to ensure that his legacy can be communicated to the average Catholic in the pew. Falls's simple yet provocative style of writing means that his work does not need to be translated from academic lingo to plain English. Apart from his writing for medical journals, the work of Falls was

A New Understanding of Catholic Racial Justice—Inspired by Falls

not scholarly, but it still reached a depth of importance that most scholars can only hope to attain one day.

To further demonstrate the practicality of Falls's thought, I have written one more chapter, which extrapolates a vision for a virtuous life inspired by Falls.

5 Virtues for the Oppressed

IN 2007, CHRISTOPHER VOGT, an associate professor of theology at St. John's University in Queens, New York, published an article in *Theological Studies* that proposed three virtues whose promotion he believed would encourage the notion of the common good in the United States: solidarity, compassion, and hospitality. This chapter hopes to serve as a sequel or companion piece, to that article. Vogt proposed three virtues to be practiced by all Catholics to aid in the creation of a society more amenable to the notion of the common good, but I will argue that his virtues are most appropriate for those in positions of power and privilege.[1] Although Vogt's virtues are helpful and in fact desperately needed for those with privilege, I will recommend three additional virtues for those living on the margins: justice, militancy, and hope.

This chapter will begin with a brief summary of Vogt's work on virtue. It will then examine work by Lisa Tessman and Bernard Lonergan. Tessman has composed a layered framework that analyzes virtue from the context of one's life—particularly as to whether one is leading a life that is prohibitively burdened. Her framework will be useful for analyzing the necessary difference between the virtues proposed by Vogt and the additional virtues that will be offered. Lonergan's insight into the bias often held by members of a dominant group will reveal that an oppressed group is already aware of the problems that plague the marginalized and they are in less need of the virtues suggested by Vogt.

I will then propose three virtues that are especially suited for the oppressed in working toward the common good. It should be noted that, with certain qualifications, these virtues can be practiced by privileged persons

---

1. Vogt, "Commitment to the Common Good," 416–17.

who have already internalized Vogt's virtues. This section will be guided and influenced by the life of Dr. Arthur G. Falls. Finally, after addressing each virtue individually, I will present a contemporary case study to provide a concrete example of these virtues in action.

VOGT, TESSMAN, AND LONERGAN

This section will not be a comprehensive summary of previous work done on virtue; instead, it will summarize the above-mentioned article written by Vogt and other works that are pertinent to this project. Vogt's article asserts that American society is more defined by contract than covenant. In other words, Americans view their relations with one another more from the standpoint of personal benefit than familial obligation. Therefore, Vogt asserts that Catholic social teaching, which is normally communicated in the form of doctrine, values, and/or principles, is too foreign and abstract to be appropriated into the hearts and minds of Catholics in the United States.[2] Vogt argues that the encouragement of certain virtues would be more efficacious toward instilling openness to the common good, given its covenantal view of society.[3] As Vogt eloquently states, "virtue ethics is concerned not merely with the shape of the *telos* itself, but equally with the question of how a person's dispositions, practices, and ways of living must be formed in order to lead to that goal."[4]

Before Vogt explicates the three virtues that he believes have special relevance for creating an atmosphere conducive to the common good, he utilizes Jean Porter's definition of virtue: "a stable quality of the intellect, will, or passions through which an individual can do what morality demands in a particular instance, and do it the right way, i.e., with an appropriate motivation."[5] Vogt finds this definition useful because of its holistic nature; essentially, the best virtuous schemes will work within an interrelated framework, transforming the intellect, will (action), and

2. Ibid., 396–98.

3. Vogt, citing contentious debate regarding the notion of the common good, never explicitly defines the term beyond its covenantal aspects (Vogt, "Commitment to the Common Good," 394–97). For our purposes here, it may be a helpful to include *Guadium et spes*' defintition of the common good: "the sum of those conditions of social life which allow social groups and their individual members relatively thorough and ready access to their own fulfillment" (*Guadium et spes* no. 26).

4. Vogt, "Commitment to the Common Good," 394, 399–400.

5. Ibid., 401; Porter, "Virtue," 1316.

passions (emotion). In this context, he proposes the virtues of solidarity, compassion, and hospitality; solidarity is related to intellect, compassion is related to passions, and hospitality is related to will.[6]

Vogt understands solidarity as a way to comprehend the world and the intimate connections between privilege and oppression. This understanding should aid the person in rearranging not only one's priorities, but also the priorities of societal institutions. Compassion moves the oppressor to empathize and feel the pain of the marginalized in society. Without this virtue, the oppressor will often rationalize oppressive manifestations found in personal behavior and social structures. Hospitality is an action grounded in a preferential option for the poor that provides the space and opportunity for compassion to occur.[7]

Although not expressly noted in the article, Vogt's examples and case study reveal that these virtues are for the privileged. One example relates the case of a retired couple who come to care for a widowed woman with two children who lived next door. It is apparent that the couple is economically stable (or privileged) while the widowed woman is in financial distress (or socially marginalized). The case study undertakes the problems faced by undocumented migrant workers in Long Island, New York. The actions recommended, such as the "receiving community" building a "hiring hall" for the migrant workers, focus completely on what the privileged can do for the marginalized.[8] In both situations, it is difficult, if not impossible, to conceive of how the marginalized person or group would offer hospitality to the privileged. By the very nature of the situations, the marginalized are practically forced to accept hospitality. It is unlikely that the privileged could be forced to accept hospitality from the marginalized. In this respect, the practicing of these virtues is a one-way street. In addition, the purpose of hospitality is to awaken compassion for the poor. In most cases, the poor do not have to practice hospitality to be moved to compassion for the plight of impoverished people. The poor are quite cognizant of their troubling situation. As noted above, even though Falls was not opposed to hospitality, he saw it as a misuse of resources. He preferred to focus his energy on promoting justice.

---

6. Vogt, "Commitment to the Common Good," 400–401. In this section, Vogt maintains that justice guides all three of the virtues that he advances.

7. Ibid., 402–10.

8. Ibid., 402, 413–16.

To be clear, I do not want to be perceived as condemning Vogt's article. It is a fine piece of scholarship that ascertains virtues genuinely needed among the privileged. These virtues have operated in an effectual manner for many modern American Christians, such as those whom one sees in the Catholic Worker movement. On the other hand, the article does not address the need for corresponding virtues that could be equally helpful from the context of the marginalized for promoting the common good. Even Vogt urges a word of caution regarding how his virtues, especially hospitality, could be exploited by the privileged to control the oppressed and create a situation of dependence.[9]

Mention of Lisa Tessman's *Burdened Virtues: Virtue Ethics for Liberatory Struggles* is appropriate at this juncture because of its work in realizing the potency of different virtues for disparate socioeconomic contexts. Tessman, an associate professor of philosophy and women's studies at Binghamton University in New York, focuses on virtues that often materialize in society because of troubling circumstances. Although she proposes a liberative revision of the Aristotelian virtue framework, her framework still promotes a vision of society based on human flourishing, or an eudaimonistic viewpoint. Aristotle, in his work on virtue, assumed a life that was not oppressed. With such large portions of the world population living in poverty and distress, Tessman finds such a vision of the virtues to be deficient. Therefore, she suggests four different sets of virtues that are each based on various socioeconomic circumstances. The first set of virtues, which largely resembles those suggested by Aristotle, includes generosity, compassion, friendliness, trustworthiness, honesty, creativity, and temperance. Once again, this first set of virtues is conducive to a person who does not lack material needs, is virtually unburdened by any serious problems, and does not live in a world to which injustice would call him or her to act. The second set of virtues she offers is based on a situation in which privileged people come into contact with suffering. These virtues more closely resemble those put forth by Vogt and are grounded in "sensitivity and attention to others' suffering."[10] Her third set of virtues is helpful for the oppressed in eventually working toward the improvement of their circumstances. These virtues include anger at injustice, a lack of compassion for oppressors, courage, and loyalty toward companions and the cause. These traits, taken as a whole, are obviously context specific and in some

---

9. Ibid., 413.
10. Tessman, *Burdened Virtues*, 161–64.

instances would not be considered virtues. There is also the danger that this set of virtues could be cultivated and abused to justify "morally horrifying actions."[11] Additionally, she presents a fourth set of virtues, which have the express purpose of aiding one in surviving grim circumstances. Examples of this set of virtues would be lying in order to procure food for one's family or practicing "psychological denial" in order to bear the brunt of terrible occasions of mistreatment that one cannot escape.[12] This last set of virtues is far removed from the flourishing and bliss present for practitioners of the first set of virtues. Tessman's more realistic and nuanced view of the virtues establishes the background for the work this chapter proposes. After addressing the concept of group bias in the work of Bernard Lonergan, I will focus on the third set of virtues proposed by Tessman, which are practiced by those on the margins for the attainment of justice. The virtues that will be proposed below will differ in emphasis from Tessman's virtues because of their explicit Catholic inspiration and Christian framework.

Bernard Lonergan, the Canadian Jesuit priest and philosopher-theologian, proposes a structure for understanding three different types of bias: individual bias, group bias, and general bias. He defined "bias" as an unwanted insight that is always to be avoided. There is also a measure of personal responsibility for the three biases listed. In brief, an individual bias is a purposeful lack of insight based in egoism; group bias is egoism on a group level that places the well-being of one's own group over and above that of another; general bias is indicative of an oversight in which all groups in a society are blind to reality regarding a certain problem.[13]

According to Lonergan, group bias represents "an interference with the development of practical common sense" on a group level. The group suffering from a bias is able to exercise common sense only to the extent that it does not contradict its own egotistical ends. It is typical for a privileged group in society to erect mechanisms that preserve its status to the detriment of a marginalized group. While this inequality creates an inherent contradiction in society that will in time become apparent to the dominant group, it is quite apparent to the marginalized group from the beginning. The marginalized group will usually be at the epicenter of the bias-correcting process and they will often counter the bias with "militant action." In response, the dominant group may work to correct the problem,

---

11. Ibid., 164–65.
12. Ibid., 166.
13. Lonergan, *Insight*, 214, 244–67.

react vehemently against any loss of privilege, or attempt to make it appear that a reversal has occurred.[14]

In the words of Lonergan, group bias, of its own accord, "awakens the resentment, the opposition, the hostility of other groups, and thereby creates a force for its own demise."[15] In contrast, the dominant group "provides a market for doctrines and theories that will justify its way of proceeding and attribute the misfortunes of others to their indolence and stupidity, their lack of energy and good will. Society divides into the haves and the have-nots, and the dominant group has its own ideology justifying itself and is very surprised when the other group works out an opposite ideology to bring about the revolutionary situation."[16]

One can be certain that one is no longer suffering from group bias when there is an agreement across diverse groups that the inequality has been solved.[17] Lonergan asserts that the elimination of bias in the dominant group demands conversion, which has the ability to break down bias. Conversion occurs through encounter: "meeting persons, appreciating the values they represent, criticizing their defects, and allowing one's living to be challenged at its very roots by their words and by their deeds."[18]

There are a number of implications that can be drawn from Lonergan's insights for overcoming group bias as it pertains to societal evils such as racism. Perhaps the most important for our purpose is that insights for overcoming white supremacy are to be found in the oppressed group. Lonergan's philosophy clearly teaches that the understanding of the common good that Vogt's virtues are supposed to elicit will generally not be any secret to the oppressed group. In other words, although whites in the United States largely suffer from the group bias that racism is no longer a problem, African Americans do not suffer from this illusion. In addition, if whites want to be cognizant of their racial bias, they need to test their opinions against the viewpoints of minority groups. In order for whites to overcome racial bias, they are in need of conversion, which Lonergan argued occurs via encounter. In essence, whites can work toward overcoming racial bias only through interaction and serious conversation with African Americans.

14. Ibid., 247–52.
15. Lonergan, *Macroeconomic Dynamics*, 94.
16. Lonergan, *Early Works*, 507–8.
17. Lonergan, *Insight*, 574.
18. Lonergan, *Method in Theology*, 246–47. For an excellent summary of Lonergan's notion of conversion, see Loynes, "Response to Drs. Nilson, Massingale, and Copeland."

This reasoning is not meant to imply or ensure that an oppressed group grasps how to adequately address group bias; the obtaining of that type of knowledge will be covered below. What a marginalized community can undoubtedly provide is whether the problem of group bias is improving or worsening. Too often in the history of Catholic racial justice in America, paternalistic white priests, still suffering from racial bias, performed actions that perpetuated racial injustice and accentuated the reality of white supremacy.

VIRTUES FOR THE OPPRESSED

In the previous section, the work of Tessman was helpful in delineating virtues into different contexts. Her work on virtues, while taking a liberative perspective, is not religious or theological in nature. Lonergan proposed a Catholic framework that demands the aid of oppressed groups in addressing group bias. As Lonergan was only parsing out a general structure for his philosophy and metaphysics, he did not explain in detail or use concrete examples of how group bias was reversed and how this reversal plays out in the relationship between the dominant and oppressed groups. Although Vogt's virtues can play a key role in the privileged person's recognition of their participation in group bias, insights are necessary from the oppressed to prevent the dominant group from falling into paternalism. The virtues being set forth in this chapter will help clarify the proper relationship between oppressors and oppressed in working toward the common good.

The virtues in this section are inspired by the life and writings of Falls. Since his work for racial justice was grounded in his Catholic faith, he can serve as an example of a virtuous life from a marginalized vantage point that is distinctly grounded in the dogmas and doctrines of the Catholic Church. Three virtues that were lived and advocated by Falls during his struggles against racial injustice were justice, militancy, and hope. As with Vogt's virtues, these are also meant to be holistic in nature with distinct correlations to intellect, will (action), and passions (emotion), though there will be some gray areas in two of the virtues. In this case, justice will be associated with both intellect and will, militancy with both passion and will, and hope with passions. The following three sections will explore each of the proposed virtues in depth while using Falls as a touchstone.

Justice

For St. Thomas Aquinas, justice is one of the cardinal virtues, and he places it within the realm of the will (action).[19] According to Aquinas, justice is directed toward one's relation with others and connotes a kind of equality.[20] As Porter notes, there is an intrinsic relationship between justice and the common good.[21] The argument could be made that instead of beginning with justice, I should start with prudence, which has traditionally been associated with intellect.[22] For my purposes here, when I refer to the virtue of justice, it more properly is the work of prudence in its formulation of creating and implementing a world more defined by equality.

For Falls, the doctrine of the mystical body of Christ played a pivotal role in his theological understanding of equality and opportunity. Within the theological framework of Falls, meditation on the doctrine of the mystical body of Christ should lead one to the conclusion that it was composed of the privileged *and* the marginalized. Essentially, excluding the marginalized from justice brought one into the realm of heresy.

Additionally, Falls believed that compromise in the area of justice was unacceptable and he offered the life of Jesus as justification for this stance: "Our Lord on earth clearly has demonstrated that there can be no such thing as 'modified' truth or justice; that there can be no compromise if one wishes to remain on this road toward the goal of human brotherhood."[23] As I mentioned in chapter 3, in the section on discipleship, Falls wrote about the apostles, the Christians fed to the lions, and the Ugandan martyrs as additional examples of this unwillingness to compromise.[24] Falls wanted Catholics to model their commitment to justice on Jesus and the saints.

The next logical question to be raised is: how does one discern what is an appropriate and meaningful justice-related framework within a society that appears to be increasing in complexity every day? The role of the social sciences becomes indispensable for this task. Although Falls appreciated the theological work on racial justice done by Fr. John LaFarge, Falls commented that the work lacked a "discussion of methods of approach

---

19. Aquinas, *Summa Theologiae* (hereafter *ST*) 1–2, q. 60, a. 2–3.
20. *ST* 2–2, q. 57, a.1.
21. Porter, *The Recovery of Virtue*, 125.
22. *ST* 1–2, q. 47, a. 1.
23. Falls, "Honesty in Race-Relations," 158.
24. Falls, "Colored Churches," 27.

which have been found effective in various situations."[25] Falls's reading of the social science literature of his day led him to adopt certain avenues of "organized opposition," focusing his energy both on the injustices present in society and within the Catholic Church.[26] He pointed to the success of this method in the battles waged by such groups as the Chicago Urban League, the International Labor Defense, the Federated Colored Women's Clubs, and the League of Struggle for Negro Rights: "To the extent that this mass force can be guided along well thought out lines, adapting the action to the needs of particular situations, will the effectiveness of this technic [sic] be best demonstrated."[27] This statement, which adds the necessity of force in employing a just plan, acts as a logical departure point for my next proposed virtue: militancy.

Militancy

Militancy has not traditionally been considered a virtue in Christian ethics, though it has been given a positive reception by black liberation theologians such as James Cone and George C. L. Cummings. Cone equates militancy with the "passion and anger" surrounding the cause of black liberation, and he takes pride in the militant African Americans throughout history who played a role in liberation.[28] Cummings writes that "God's freedom . . . is manifested in the persistent will of the oppressed to fight and kick against injustice and hopelessness."[29] For our purposes, "militancy" denotes action as well as a particular force and passion behind that action. The achievement of justice by the oppressed requires a tone that is stronger than moral suasion and usually under the guise of organized opposition.

From a Catholic perspective, William C. Mattison III refers to fortitude as containing a "militant" aspect, but he also reminds the reader that true fortitude is practiced only "when it is just." When fortitude leads one to "attack," the opponent should be "lovingly confronted with their harmful acts."[30] Although Aquinas classified fortitude as a passion, the writings of

25. Falls, review of *Interracial Justice*, 246.
26. Falls, "Colored Churches," 26.
27. Falls, "Interracial Cooperation in Chicago," (September 1935) 141.
28. Cone, *God of the Oppressed* ix; *Cross and the Lynching Tree*, 66, 71–72, 126–27, 138–40.
29. Cummings, "The Slave Narratives," 65–66.
30. Mattison, *Introducing Moral Theology*, 185, 188, 191.

Cone and Cummings on militancy span both the will and the passions.[31] This will also be the case as we analyze Falls's understanding of militancy.

As I discussed in chapter 3, Falls did not believe that moral suasion alone could solve the problem of white supremacy; as I mentioned in chapter 4, he characterized the struggle against racism as "warfare."[32] He never forgot about the blacks who, in 1930, confiscated tools from a group of white workers, forcing a company that had not employed African American workers to hire twenty-five the next day.[33] This minor historical event taught Falls that a small but organized group of people could significantly better their lives within a short period of time. Such an action is not without risk: the provocation could have escalated into riots and/or resulted in serious bodily harm to the blacks involved.

To be clear, militancy for Falls could not be equated with violence. He believed that results could be achieved with honest means that were confrontational without being violent. Having a militant stance is not without sacrifice. Militant action, even when informed by a proper understanding of justice, does not always succeed within a short period of time. It should be remembered that Gandhi's work for Indian independence from Great Britain took over forty years. Hence, there is always the danger that the marginalized will fall into complacency with their situation if it is not quickly resolved. Such a state of affairs can give the sense that the injustice is inevitable and hopeless. Therefore, the above two virtues, without the virtue of hope, are doomed to despair in the face of repeated failures.

Hope

In the thought of Aquinas, hope is considered a type of passion (emotion), but one that has its ultimate longing in God.[34] Hope is a virtue that is oriented toward the attainment of God. It is viewed as something that is difficult but not impossible to attain with the aid of God.[35] Although Falls's notion of hope had a supernatural aspect, the stress in this section will be less on the desire for the attainment of God and more on the belief that God's will for a just world can be achieved to a significant degree on earth.

31. *ST* 1–2, q. 60, a. 2–3.
32. AGF, Box 1, Folder 13, disc 19-side 2, p. 6.
33. AGF, Box 1, Folder 9, pp. 465–67.
34. *ST* 1–2, q. 40, a. 1.
35. *ST* 2–2, q. 17, a. 1.

As with Aquinas's yearned-for God, this more just world is difficult to attain, but not impossible.

Falls believed that without hope, groups would fold after a short period of time. As detailed above (under "Falls as a Sign of Hope"), Falls often reminded other activists that "if you are right, you don't always lose." Hope of success was necessary to prevent one from despairing and accepting an injustice.[36]

Although Falls wrote little on hope, his entire life implicitly exuded hope. Invigorated by previous successes and educated by past failures, he unceasingly battled against racism with the hope of winning the present battle. And if the present battle was lost, he knew that another attempt, that incorporated lessons learned, could very well be successful.

As was covered above, hope is also a prevalent theme with modern theologians who address racism, such as James Cone and Bryan Massingale. For Cone, hope is not wasted because the cause of liberation is God's cause, which guarantees success.[37] For Massingale, the "subversive" vision inspired by hope is crucial for racial justice because it allows a space for dreaming of new possibilities that cannot be imagined by those in despair.

ACTION NOW: A CASE STUDY

Action Now, a grassroots community organization, has been waging a campaign against the compounded problems of housing foreclosures and vacant buildings in the city of Chicago.[38] Analyzing the work of Action Now as a case study will better illustrate the above virtues.

Vacant buildings in Chicago, often caused by foreclosures, have been a perennial problem, which the Great Recession exacerbated. In addition to blighting a neighborhood, vacant homes reduce property values, invite vandalism, and create an atmosphere more welcoming to violence and crime. Action Now includes community organizers who often come from privileged backgrounds, but the organization is careful to be driven by the desires of the marginalized and oppressed, which safeguards the group against misguided and paternalistic ventures. Action Now accomplishes

---

36. Falls, interview by Troester.

37. Cone, *God of the Oppressed*, 91.

38. Action Now, "About Us." Although this case study will focus on Action Now's campaign against neglected properties, they also work on a variety of other issues, including the minimum wage, education, and violence.

this by hosting listening sessions that are incorporated into its plan for justice, having regular monthly meetings, going door-to-door, and involving the marginalized in "the planning, implementation and evaluation of issue campaigns."[39] The collaboration that exists in this group between the privileged and marginalized illustrates a way in which privileged members of society can espouse justice, militancy, and hope. The fact that the marginalized drive the group's agenda ensures that their vision for equality and opportunity is not compromised and rationalized by those from privileged backgrounds. As an organized group, Action Now is already employing an important insight of the social sciences that is present in the virtue of justice. In addition, regarding its vision, Action Now clearly states that "*everyone*" should have access to basic necessities and should be permitted a voice in decision making on all levels of society.[40] Essentially, its plan is not one of revenge, but of authentic opportunity for all people. Its plan to address vacant houses in Chicago has focused on two fronts: (1) putting mechanisms in place to prevent as many foreclosures as possible, and (2) holding financial institutions responsible for vacant buildings.

The plan that Action Now formulated includes not only moral suasion, but militant actions to place pressure on financial institutions to create a more just situation. From a legal standpoint, Action Now successfully pressured the city in June 2011 to pass an ordinance regarding the proper securing of vacant buildings and the proper upkeep of lawns and sidewalks.[41] Before the passage of this law, banks would purposely stop foreclosure proceedings once a family vacated a property so that the bank would not be responsible for the maintenance of the property. The passage of the city ordinance closed this loophole. Now banks are responsible for any property that is vacated because of the start of a foreclosure proceeding.[42] In December 2011, Action Now also successfully pressured Cook County, in which Chicago is located, to pass a similar ordinance where violators could be fined up to $1,000 per day for not securing or properly maintaining a property.[43]

In between the passage of these two bills, the situation with many of the vacant houses in Chicago was not improving, so five women who live in

39. Action Now, "Welcome to Action Now!"
40. Action Now, "About Us." Emphasis in the original.
41. CBS Chicago, "Ordinance Holds Banks Responsible."
42. Action Now, "Victory!"
43. Donovan, "New County Fines of Up to $1,000 a Day."

one of the blighted neighborhoods, ranging in age from fifty-five to eighty, spent a morning collecting garbage and broken furniture from the lawns of vacant properties. They then dumped it all in the lobby of the bank that owned the buildings—Bank of America. This action garnered media attention not only in Chicago, but nationally.[44] It was a militant way for residents to empower themselves while also embarrassing the banks into following the law.

During this same time period, Action Now also proposed and helped enact a mediation program with the purpose of aiding homeowners in exploring all of their options in the face of foreclosure. The mechanism that is the hub for this new program is the Circuit Court of Cook County.[45] These legal and symbolic actions permit the marginalized to take ownership of their situation and take concrete steps toward achieving justice.

Neither justice nor militant action can be sustained over a long period of time without hope. There are two sections on the website for Action Now that perform an excellent job of instilling hope. There is a section dedicated to documenting the previous victories of Action Now[46] and there is a section that documents each instance in which Action Now was covered by a local or national news agency.[47] Both of these sources encourage pride in one's hard work and express the hope that future tasks dedicated to justice in a militant fashion will achieve positive results.

CONCLUSION

For too long, Catholic ethicists have viewed moral suasion and depending on the kindness of those with privilege as the only legitimate means for the marginalized to address injustice. This chapter has attempted to lay the groundwork for the legitimate and active participation of the oppressed in their own liberation. As I discussed in chapter 3's section on interracialism, Falls believed that blacks and whites needed to work together for justice, because the fate of African Americans is interwoven with that of all other citizens. The example of Action Now demonstrates that such ventures can be interracial in nature, and that they can be a combined effort between the

---

44. CBS Chicago, "Women Dump Garbage"; Roy Strom, "Chicago Police Arrest 21 Protestors."

45. Action Now, "Housing/Foreclosure"; Circuit Court of Cook County, "About."

46. Action Now, "Neighborhood Victories."

47. Action Now, "In the News."

oppressed and the privileged. Nonetheless, progress for a more just society should not be dependent on the actions of those in positions of authority, influence, and privilege. Incorporating the insights from Lonergan detailed above, those in positions of privilege need to be extremely careful in implementing the virtues of justice, militancy, and hope. The privileged must listen intently to the voices of the marginalized in order to avoid paternalism.

Vogt's article made the argument that Catholics should be formed in the virtues of solidarity, compassion, and hospitality, but I would emphasize that the need for those virtues rests among Catholics in positions of power and privilege, especially when they pay attention to the marginalized.[48] Even so, oppressed people should not have to wait for those with privilege to right wrongs and reorganize unjust situations and institutions; therefore, the virtues proposed in Vogt's article should be advocated along with the additional set of virtues I offered here, as part of a dual approach to create a society more genuinely open to the notion of the common good. Although enlightened people of privilege can also habituate the virtues of justice, militancy, and hope, they must practice these virtues in close collaboration with the marginalized and/or via insights from the oppressed.

A final note for this chapter: although I have not extrapolated explicit connections to how the proposed virtues for the oppressed can be applied to oppressions other than race, I believe that these virtues can also aid other causes, such as feminism. Although Arthur was never involved in a large-scale feminist campaign, Lillian's feminist tendencies definitely had an impact on his thinking regarding women. In addition, although the feminist scholar Tessman assigns different sets of virtues to different socioeconomic contexts, she does not designate one set of virtues for combating racism and another set of virtues for combating sexism. Therefore, I hope that this work on virtue will be helpful for numerous other groups that suffer as a result of group bias from a dominant culture.

---

48. Vogt, "Commitment to the Common Good," 416–17.

Afterword

BILL BRIGHT, A WHITE resident of Western Springs since 1973, got to know Falls better at St. John of the Cross Catholic Church in the late 1980s. Near the end of Falls's time in Western Springs, they led a weekend retreat together called "Christ Renews His Parish," which is a national retreat program with the aim of bringing parishioners into closer relationship with Christ. Bright remembered a presentation when Falls "thought that we couldn't hear him because we were all leaning forward." When he apologized for his weak voice, Bright interrupted him and said, "Dr. Falls, it's not that we can't hear you. It's just that we want to hear every single syllable of what you're saying."[1] Falls still has something important to tell us that should keep us at the edge of our seats.

1. Bright, interview by author.

Bibliography

NOTE OF EXPLANATION AND ORGANIZATION

As THIS WORK IN Christian ethics relied heavily on archival material, the bibliography will be arranged in such a way as to highlight the archival material to make it easier for others to find primary sources for the life of Falls. I have begun by listing the archives that contain primary sources for Falls with a brief description of each archival collection and its contents. The following section presents citations in chronological order of every primary source for Falls that I discovered in the listed archives. The subsequent section lists published primary sources for Falls from journals, magazines, and newspapers.

The next section presents a list of archives that were used for secondary source material for the life of Falls. There is a brief description of each archive and the type of secondary material that was utilized from each of those collections. Next, a list of published materials that were used as secondary sources for Arthur's life is provided. This is followed by list of interviews that I performed for this work. Except for my interview with Cyprian Davis and Bryan Massingale, which were concerned with ecclesial documents published in the United States, the remainder of the interviews were performed to fill in details regarding the life of Falls. The section after this focuses on published works that were used to inform historical background regarding the time in which Falls lived and worked.

The remainder of the bibliography does not have Falls as the focus. It begins with ecclesial documents that were cited because of their focus on racial justice. This is followed by theological works that were cited because of their racial justice focus. Next, the contemporary sources that

Bibliography

were employed in examining the social sciences are listed. This is followed by sources that were specifically used for the sections in chapter four that addressed the notions of sin and heresy in the Christian tradition. Lastly, items that did not fit into any other category, including many of the works cited in the last chapter, are listed under Other Works.

ARCHIVES USED AS PRIMARY SOURCES FOR FALLS

Archdiocese of Chicago's Joseph Cardinal Bernardin Archives and Records Center, Chicago.

This is the archives for the Archdiocese of Chicago. Pertaining to this book, the archive includes correspondence between Falls and Cardinal Stritch, the record of Falls's baptism, material from the Catholic Interracial Council and other Archdiocesan initiatives concerning race. It also contains an interview with Edward Marciniak that was part of the PhD work of a Chicago priest.

Chicago Historical Society. Chicago Federation of Labor Collection, Chicago. 56.5 linear feet.

This collection includes minutes, correspondence, and files from the Chicago Federation of Labor from 1890 to 1983. There is one folder called "Negro and Civil Rights Items" that contains a letter from Falls to the Chicago Federation of Labor. It is from 12 August 1935 and identifies Falls as the secretary for the Joint Conference for the Defense of Ethiopia. This letter is not mentioned in the book, but is cited below.

National Archives Building, Chicago.

This National Archives in Chicago is one of the regional repositories for federal court cases. Pertaining to this book, it is notable for containing the suit that Falls and a number of other African American doctors made against seventy-five percent of all the hospital corporations in the Chicago area: Robert G. Morris, Jr., M.D., et al. v. Chicago Hospital Council, et al., 61 C232, U.S. District Court, 1819-1999, Civil Case Files, *1938-1985*, Record Group 21; National Archives Building, Chicago. There are a few sheets where Falls provides his own background and relates specific experiences of racism with Chicago hospitals. About 3,000 pages.

Raynor Memorial Libraries. Special Collections and University Archives. Marquette University, Milwaukee, WI. Dorothy Day-Catholic Worker Collection. Over 200 cubic feet.

This collection focuses not only on the founders of the Catholic Worker movement, Dorothy Day and Peter Maurin, but includes writings, letters, pictures, newsletters, newspapers, and logbooks from Catholic Worker communities across the world. Pertaining to Falls, it has a number of letters written by Falls to persons at the New York Catholic Worker, a few letters that were written to Falls, and all of Arthur's published writings in the *New York Catholic Worker* and *Chicago Catholic Worker* newspapers.

Raynor Memorial Libraries. Special Collections and University Archives. Marquette University, Milwaukee, WI. Arthur G. Falls, Reminiscence. About 800 pages.

This collection's contents are the limited to most of the unpublished memoir manuscript that was donated to the archives by Falls's niece, Vilma Childs. About 620 pages. There is also a copy of one missing section of the manuscript that is there with the permission of the Schomburg Center for Research in Black Culture at the New York Public Library. About 180 pages.

Richard J. Daley Center. Archives Room 1113. Clerk of the Circuit Court of Cook County, Chicago.

The Daley Center contains the court file for Western Springs Park District v. Arthur Falls, et al., 52C 14741, 1 December 1952. This includes the record of all the court dates, motions, and a petition by signed by many of the residents to have Arthur's home condemned for a new park.

Bibliography

Richard J. Daley Library. Special Collections and University Archives. University of Illinois at Chicago, Chicago, IL. Chicago Urban League Records, 1916-2000. 664 linear feet.

This collection includes minutes, reports, and correspondence from the Chicago Urban League. Falls was intimately involved with the Chicago Urban League from 1929 until 1936. During the 1940s and 1950s, he was again involved with League, but in a more peripheral manner. Unfortunately, records of the League during Arthur's first involvement are sparse. He is mainly mentioned in certain reports. Additionally, the records contain almost no record of the De Saible Club. The collection also includes the records of groups with which the League worked closely like the Council Against Discrimination of Greater Chicago. There are three primary sources for Falls in this collection: a letter he sent to the Chicago Urban League from South America and two other letters that he sent as part of different groups of which the Chicago Urban League kept copies.

Schomburg Center for Research in Black Culture. New York Public Library, New York, NY. August Meier Papers. 74 linear feet.

The August Meier Papers includes the personal correspondence, academic work, conference papers, speeches, and research of August Meier (d. 2003), who was an expert in African American history. Included in this collection are about 300 pages from Arthur's memoir. About 180 of these pages were not a part of the collection at Marquette University. With the permission of the Schomburg Center, copies of these pages have been included with the memoir at Marquette.

Western Springs Department of Community Development, Western Springs, IL. One folder of microfiche.

This site has a folder that contains microfiche copies of letters and permits pertaining to Arthur's 4812 Fair Elms Avenue address in Western Springs. Included in this are letters that Falls wrote the department over the years as well as soil sample tests that were sent to the department by the company that Falls had hired to perform the tests.

Bibliography

PRIMARY SOURCES FOR FALLS IN ARCHIVES

Falls, Arthur. Interview by Rosalie Reigle Troester, 10 January 1988. Transcript. Dorothy Day-Catholic Worker Collection, Marquette University, Milwaukee, WI, Series W-9, Box 4, Folder 12.

———. Chicago Catholic Worker 50th Anniversary Celebration, 5 December 1986. Cassette, Dorothy Day-Catholic Worker Collection, Marquette University, WI, Series W-9.1, Box C-27.

———. Falls Letter with Lillian Falls to Paul C. Nicholson, Village Manager, 2 November 1977. Western Springs Department of Community Development, Western Springs, IL, Folder: 4812 Fair Elms Avenue.

———. Interview by Francis Sicius, 16 June 1976. Cassette, Dorothy Day-Catholic Worker Collection, Marquette University, WI, Series W-9.1, Box C-3.

———. Falls Letter with Mark Lepper, M.D. to Friends of Medical Committee for Human Rights, 1965. Chicago Urban League Records, University of Illinois at Chicago, Series III, Box 14, Folder 177.

———. Reminiscence, 1962. Manuscript. Arthur G. Falls Papers. Raynor Library Catholic Social Action Collections, Marquette University, Milwaukee, WI. A little over 800 pages.

———. Unpublished Autobiography,1962. Manuscript. Schomburg Center for Research in Black Culture, New York Public Library, New York, NY. About 300 pages.

———. Samuel Cardinal Stritch, 4 May 1956.Chancery Correspondence, General Correspondence, Executive Records, Archives of the Archdiocese of Chicago, Chicago, Box 43891.04, Folder 7.

———. Falls letter et al. to Cardinal Samuel A. Stritch, 3 April 1956. Chancery Correspondence, General Correspondence, Executive Records, Archives of the Archdiocese of Chicago, Chicago, Box 43891.04, Folder 7.

———. Falls Letter to John H. Kennaugh, Assistant Village Manager, 26 July 1955. Western Springs Department of Community Development, Western Springs, IL, Folder: 4812 Fair Elms Avenue.

———. Falls Letter to George E. Smith, Village Manager, 24 June 1955. Western Springs Department of Community Development, Western Springs, IL, Folder: 4812 Fair Elms Avenue.

———. Falls, with Vernon DeYoung, A. M. Mercer, Alfred B. Stein, and Quentin Young (Committee to End Discrimination in Chicago Medical Institutions) to the President of the United States, January 1954. Chicago Urban League Records, Richard J. Daley Library, University of Illinois at Chicago, Series I, Box 263, Folder 2640.

———. Falls Letter to Samuel Cardinal Stritch, 18 June 1951. Chancery Correspondence, General Correspondence, Executive Records, Archives of the Archdiocese of Chicago, Chicago, Box 43878.02, Folder 10.

———. Falls Letter to Samuel Cardinal Stritch, 12 December 1949. Chancery Correspondence, General Correspondence, Executive Records, Archives of the Archdiocese of Chicago, Chicago, Box 43873.07, Folder 2.

———. Falls Letter to Mr. Sidney Williams, 6 October 1947. Chicago Urban League Records, Richard J. Daley Library, University of Illinois at Chicago, Series I, Box 50, Folder 556.

Bibliography

———. Falls Letter to Samuel Cardinal Stritch, 6 December 1946. Chancery Correspondence, General Correspondence, Executive Records, Archives of the Archdiocese of Chicago, Chicago, Box 43863.02, Folder 3.

———. Falls Letter to Archbishop Samuel A. Stritch, 26 December 1941. Chancery Correspondence, General Correspondence, Executive Records, Archives of the Archdiocese of Chicago, Chicago, Box 43849.04, Folder 5.

———. Falls Letter to Most Rev. Samuel A. Stritch, 9 August 1940. Chancery Correspondence, General Correspondence, Executive Records, Archives of the Archdiocese of Chicago, Chicago, Chicago, Box 43848.01, Folder 14.

———. A letter written by Falls was quoted in packet for Summer School of Social Action,1937-1938. Reynold Hillenbrand Papers, University of Notre Dame Archives, Notre Dame, IN, Box CMRH 5/19, Folder, Summer School of Social Action, 1937-1938. The original date or to whom the letter was sent is unknown.

———. Falls Letter to Edward K. Priest, 5 May 1936. Dorothy Day-Catholic Worker Collection, Marquette University, Milwaukee, WI, Series W-2.2, Box 1, Folder 11.

———. Falls Letter to Edward K. Priest, 14 March 1936. Dorothy Day-Catholic Worker Collection, Marquette University, Milwaukee, WI, Series W-2.2, Box 1, Folder 11.

———. Falls Letter to Executive Committee, Chicago Federation of Labor, 12 August 1935. Chicago Federation of Labor Collection, Chicago Historical Society, Chicago, Box 25, Folder: Negro and Civil Rights Items.

———. Falls Letter to Bishop J. F. Noll, 28 November 1934. Carbon copy to New York Catholic Worker. Dorothy Day-Catholic Worker Collection, Marquette University, Milwaukee, WI, Series W-2.1, Box 3, Folder 1.

———. Falls Letter to Bishop J.F. Noll, 16 November 1934. Carbon copy to New York Catholic Worker. Dorothy Day-Catholic Worker Collection, Marquette University, Milwaukee, WI, Series W-2.1, Box 3, Folder 1.

———. Falls Letter to St. Columban's Seminary in St. Colbumbans, NE, 13 July 1934. Carbon copy to New York Catholic Worker. Dorothy Day-Catholic Worker Collection, Marquette University, Milwaukee, WI, Series W-2.2, Box 1, Folder 11.

———. Falls Letter to Dorothy Day, 16 June 1934. Dorothy Day-Catholic Worker Collection, Marquette University, Milwaukee, WI, Series W-2.2, Box 1, Folder 11.

———. Falls Letter to Dorothy Day, 3 November 1933. Dorothy Day-Catholic Worker Collection, Marquette University, Milwaukee, WI, Series W-2.2, Box 1, Folder 11.

PRIMARY FALLS MATERIAL FROM JOURNALS, MAGAZINES, AND NEWSPAPERS

Falls, Arthur G. Letter to the Editor. *Daily Defender*, 10 June 1964, p. 15.

———. "The Search for Negro Medical Students." *Integrated Education* 1 (June 1963) 15-19.

———. In "Says Medical Bias is City's Worst Problem." *Chicago Daily Defender*, 5 December 1960, p. 3.

———. "Management of Pulmonary Tuberculosis." *Journal of the National Medical Association* 47 (November 1955) 399-402.

———. Letter to the Editor. *Western Springs Times*, 24 July 1953, p. 2.

———. "Your Health is Wealth." *Chicago Defender*, 18 April 1942, p. 15.

Bibliography

———. "Restrictive Covenants Create Negro Ghettos: Chicago No Example for Rest of World." *Chicago Catholic Worker*, March 1941, pp. 1-3.

———. Review of *Interracial Justice*, by John LaFarge. *Opportunity: Journal of Negro Life* 15 (August 1937) 246.

———. "Chicago Letter." *New York Catholic Worker*, May 1937, p 2.

———. Letter to the Editor. *New York Catholic Worker*, May 1937, p. 5.

———. "Chicago Letter." *New York Catholic Worker*, April 1937, p 7.

———. "Danger of Riots in Chicago Slums: Housing Conditions Make for Danger to Peace on South Side." *New York Catholic Worker*, April 1937, pp. 1, 4.

———. "Chicago Letter." *New York Catholic Worker*, March 1937, p. 2.

———. "Chicago Letter." *New York Catholic Worker*, February 1937, p. 2.

———. "Chicago Letter." *New York Catholic Worker*, January 1937, p. 6.

———. "Chicago Letter." *New York Catholic Worker*, November 1936, p. 7.

———. "The Chicago Letter." *New York Catholic Worker*, October 1936, p. 4.

———. "The Chicago Letter." *New York Catholic Worker*, September 1936, p 3.

———. "Chicago Letter." *New York Catholic Worker*, August 1936, p. 3.

———. "The Chicago Letter." *New York Catholic Worker*, June 1936, p. 3.

———. "The Chicago Letter." *New York Catholic Worker*, April 1936, p. 7.

———. "The Chicago Letter." *New York Catholic Worker*, December 1935, p 8.

———. "Chicago Fights Race Prejudice, 'Security' Wage." *New York Catholic Worker*, September 1935, pp. 2, 6.

———. "Interracial Cooperation in Chicago." *Interracial Review* 8 (September 1935) 141-42.

———. "Interracial Cooperation in Chicago." *Interracial Review* 8 (August 1935) 122-23.

———. "Rosary College Will Welcome Negro Students: Encouraging Catholic Interracial News Sent by Chicago Correspondent." *New York Catholic Worker*, July-August 1935, p. 3.

———. "Chicago Letter." *New York Catholic Worker*, June 1935, p. 8.

———. "Interracial Cooperation in Chicago." *Interracial Review* 8 (June 1935) 88-89.

———. "Interracial Cooperation in Chicago." *Interracial Review* 8 (May 1935) 74-75.

———. "The Graver Menace." *Interracial Review* 7, (August 1934) 102-03.

———. "The Communist Says: 'Welcome, Negro Brother!'" *New York Catholic Worker*, April 1934, pp. 1, 8.

———. "The Race and Its Opportunity." *Chicago Defender*, 10 February 1934, p. 10.

———. "Better Race Relations from a Catholic Viewpoint." *Interracial Review* 6 (October1933) 183-84.

———. Letter to the Editor. *America* (7 October 1933) 21.

———. "Honesty in Race Relations." *Interracial Review* 6 (September 1933) 158-60.

———. "Chicago Further Organizes." *Interracial Review* 6 (April 1933) 70.

———. "Chicago Catholics Flay Prejudice." *Chronicle: Official Organ of the Federated Colored Catholics of the United States* 9 (December 1932) 248-49.

———. Letter to the Editor. *Sign* 11 (June 1932) 674-75.

———. "Some Misconceptions on 'Negro Culture.'" *Chronicle: Official Organ of the Federated Colored Catholics of the United States* 9 (April 1932) 70-71.

———. "Colored Churches." *Chronicle: Official Organ of the Federated Colored Catholics of the United States* 9 (February 1932) 26-27.

———. "Our Lady of Solace Chapter." *Chronicle: Official Organ of the Federated Colored Catholics of the United States* 9 (February 1932) 40.

Bibliography

———. "Our Lady of Solace Chapter Formed." *Chronicle: Official Organ of the Federated Colored Catholics of the United States* 9 (January 1932) 15.

———. "Industrial and Social Problems." *Chronicle: Official Organ of the Federated Colored Catholics of the United States* 8 (December 1931) 678-81.

———. "The Spread of Communism Among Chicago's Negroes." *Chronicle: Official Organ of the Federated Colored Catholics of the United States* 8 (September 1931) 577-78.

———. "Health and Jobs." *Chicago Defender*, 2 May 1931, p. 15.

———. "As a Beginner Figures It Out." *Medical Economics* 6 (May 1929)16-18, 65, 67.

———. "Protein (Milk) Therapy of Pelvic Inflammations: Report of First Hundred Cases." *Journal of the National Medical Association* 20 (July-September 1928) 117-21.

———. "Ammonium Chloride and Novasurol: The Use of, as a Diuretic." *Journal of the National Medical Association* 19 (April-June 1927) 65-67, 72-73.

SECONDARY SOURCES FOR THE LIFE OF FALLS IN ARCHIVES

Amistad Research Center. Tulane University, New Orleans, LA. Henry Hugh Proctor and Adeline L. Davis Papers 1989 Addendum, 1919-1984. Unprocessed.

This collection includes a couple dozen letters that Arthur's wife, Lillian, wrote to her sisters. These letters are mostly from the last decade of Lillian's life and were helpful in adding a few minor details.

Amistad Research Center. Tulane University, New Orleans, LA. Julius Rosenwald Fund Records, 1920-1948. 3.75 linear feet.

This collection includes minutes, reports, and correspondence from members of the Julius Rosenwald Fund, which was an endowed foundation that donated monies to public schools, colleges, Jewish charities, as well as a number of persons and institutions concerned with the plight of African Americans. The one citation from this collection in this book is a letter to Falls from the president of the fund who was also chairman of the Mayor's Committee on Race Relations.

Archdiocese of Chicago's Joseph Cardinal Bernardin Archives and Records Center, Chicago.

This is the archives for the Archdiocese of Chicago. Pertaining to this work, the archive includes correspondence between Falls and Cardinal Stritch, the record of Arthur's baptism, material from the Catholic Interracial Council and other Archdiocesan initiatives concerning race. It also contains an interview with Edward Marciniak that was part of the PhD work of a Chicago priest.

Chicago Board of Education Archives. 125 S. Clark Street, 6th Floor, Chicago.

This archive includes minutes from the meetings of the Chicago Board of Education and old year books. The main source of information used for this book were the Proceedings of the Chicago Board of Education during the late 1960s when Falls was working with groups to provide opportunities for poor students to get into medical school. The archive also had a copy of a Englewood High School yearbook from 1918 that included Falls senior photo.

Chicago Historical Society, Chicago.

The Chicago Historical Society is located in the Chicago History Museum and has a substantial collection concerning anything important to the history of Chicago. Areas of the collection that are of importance for this work include files for Friendship House, a book concerning Chicago's 1960 Clergy Conference on Race, and the monthly newsletters of the Chicago Council Against Racial and Religious Discrimination.

Credit Union National Association Archives (CUNA). Located at the CUNA offices in Madison, WI. Access to records available upon request: 608-231-4104.

The CUNA archives do not contain the archives of individual credit unions, but of the national association. This includes minutes, financial statements, and their newsletter, Credit Union Bridge. This archive was utilized to

Bibliography

discover more about the People's Co-op Credit Union, with which Falls was involved. Information about this credit union was available in their newsletter. To the best of my knowledge, Falls is not specifically mentioned in their archives, but there is also no digital search engine with which this can be verified.

Madonna House Archive. Catherine de Hueck Doherty's Correspondence, Combermere, Canada.

This archive is located at Madonna House, which is a lay-training center that was founded in 1947 by Catherine Doherty. The archives for Catherine Doherty and Friendship House are held there. The lone letter cited from this archive was one that was written to Doherty and mentioned Falls. This letter was shared with me by Karen Johnson.

Moorland-Springarn Research Center, Washington, DC. Howard University. Thomas Wyatt Turner Papers. 9.5 linear feet.

This collection includes Dr. Turner's correspondence, newspaper clippings, writings, and documents relating to his involvement in the Federated Colored Catholics, Hampton Institute, and Howard University. The only reference to this collection was the following document: "Recommendations of the Federated Colored Catholics of Chicago. Changes in the Revised Constitution Submitted by the Committee on the Revision of the Constitution." This document was shared with me by Karen Johnson.

Raynor Memorial Libraries. Special Collections and University Archives. Marquette University, Milwaukee, WI. Dorothy Day-Catholic Worker Collection. Over 200 cubic feet.

This collection focuses not only on the founders of the Catholic Worker movement, Dorothy Day and Peter Maurin, but also includes writings, letters, pictures, newsletters, newspapers, and logbooks from Catholic Worker communities across the world. Pertaining to Falls, it has a number of letters written by Falls to persons at the New York Catholic Worker, a few letters that were written to Falls, and all of Falls's published writings in the *New York Catholic Worker* and *Chicago Catholic Worker* newspapers.

Richard J. Daley Center. Archives Room 1113. Clerk of the Circuit Court of Cook County, Chicago.

The Daley Center contains the court file for Western Springs Park District v. Arthur Falls, et al., 52C 14741, 1 December 1952. This includes the record of all the court dates, motions, and the petition by signed by many of the residents to have Arthur's home condemned for a new park.

Richard J. Daley Library. Special Collections and University Archives. University of Illinois at Chicago, Chicago, IL. Chicago Urban League Records, 1916-2000. 664 linear feet.

This collection includes minutes, reports, and correspondence from the Chicago Urban League. The collection includes the records of groups with which the League was involved like the Council Against Discrimination of Greater Chicago. Falls was intimately involved with the Chicago Urban League from 1929 until 1936. During the 1940s and 1950s, he was again involved with League, but in a more peripheral manner. Unfortunately, records of the League during Arthur's first involvement with the League are sparse. He is mainly mentioned in certain reports. Additionally, the collection contains almost no record of the De Saible Club.

National Archives Building, Chicago.

This National Archives in Chicago is one of the regional repositories for federal court cases. Pertaining to this work, it is notable for containing the suit that Falls and a number of other African American doctors made against seventy-five percent of all the hospital corporations in the Chicago area: Robert G. Morris, Jr., M.D., et al. v. Chicago Hospital Council, et al., 61 C232, U.S. District Court, 1819-1999, Civil Case Files, 1938-1985, Record Group 21; National Archives Building, Chicago. About 3,000 pages.

St. John of the Cross Catholic Church, Western Springs, IL.

The parish, of which Falls was a founding member in 1960 and served on its parish council, contains almost all of the bulletins for the parish dating back to its founding. They also have a commemorative booklet from the founding of the parish. Unfortunately, they have not archived minutes from the parish council or other parish groups.

Western Springs Department of Community Development, Western Springs, IL. One folder of microfiche.

This site has a folder that contains microfiche copies of letters and permits pertaining to Arthur's 4812 Fair Elms Avenue address in Western Springs. Included are letters that Falls wrote the department over the years as well as soil sample tests that were sent to the department by the company that Falls had hired to perform the tests.

Western Springs Historical Society, Western Springs, IL.

This site contains some basic information on Falls and a couple dozen newspaper clippings about Falls. Unfortunately, many of the newspaper clippings only have a publication date written on them and omit the name of the newspaper. It also contains a brief history of Arthur's purchase of property in Western Springs that was composed by the Deerfield Citizens for Human Rights. Falls integrated Western Springs after a long legal battle to prevent his home from being condemned in 1953. He lived there for over forty years.

Wisconsin Historical Society, Madison, WI. Congress on Racial Equality Collection. 43.5 cubic feet.

This collection includes minutes, reports, and correspondence. Despite the size of the collection, the majority of material in the collection is from the period 1959-1964, when the group received most of its national attention. Arthur's primary involvement was in the period 1941-1943, when the group first began. The material for this period is very sparse with only one document that cites Falls, which was also cited in this book.

PUBLISHED SECONDARY SOURCES ON THE LIFE OF FALLS

Ahern, C. J. Letter to the Editor. *Sign* 11 (May 1932) 611.
Alphonse, Matt J. "Father Virgil and the Social Institute." *Orate Fratres* 13 (22 January 1939) 135–38.
Alton Evening Telegraph. "Says Doctors Fail to Face Racial Problem." 12 November 1963, p. 18.
American Catholic Sociological Society. "Roster of the American Catholic Sociological Society." *American Catholic Sociological Review* 4 (December 1943) 219–24.
American Catholic Who's Who. 7th ed. Grosse Pointe, MI: Walter Romig, 1947.
A. M. N. Letter to the editor. *Chicago Sun-Times*, 16 February 1961.
Bogardus, Mrs. Hugh E., and Mr. James E. Davis. "Experience in Interracial Living: Western Springs, Illinois." *Social Action* (November 1957) 16–17.
Brantley, Geneva. "Our Lady of Solace Chapter." *Interracial Review* 5 (November 1932) 229.
Brophy, Mary Ligouri. "The Social Thought of the German Roman Catholic Central Verien." PhD diss., Catholic University of America, 1941.
Chicago Daily Tribune. "U. S. Enjoins Deerfield in Housing Row: Integration Issue in $750,000 Suit." 23 December 1959, p. A10.
———. "Peter Maurin to Appear Here at Discussions." 7 June 1936, p. NW8.
Chicago Daily Defender. "Calendar of Community Events." 24 May 1969, p. 13.
———. "League Head to Talk at Science Meet." 6 April 1964, p. 17.
———. "Negro Doctors Pleased with Court Agreement." 4 February 1964, p. 4.
Chicago Defender. "Voters Defeat Last Attempt Against Falls." National Edition, 25 July 1953, p. 5.
———. "Catholic School Joins Jim Crow Crowd; Bars Race Child." National Edition, 7 October 1933.
Cobb, W. Montague. "Hospital Integration in the United States: A Progress Report." *Journal of the National Medical Association* 55 (July 1963) 333-338.
Cogley, John. *A Canterbury Tale: Experience and Reflections: 1916-1976.* New York: The Seabury, 1976.
Day, Dorothy. "More Houses of Hospitality Needed." *New York Catholic Worker*, March 1938, pp. 1, 4.
Despres, Alderman Leon M. "Alderman Reports Integrating Medical Services." *Hyde Park Herald*, 13 October 1965, p. 4. Online: http://ddd-hph.dlconsulting.com/cgi-bin/newshph?a=d&d=HPH19651013.2.14&cl=&srpos=0&st=1&e=00-00-0000-99-99-9999—20—1——Sen.+Obama-all.
Farrell, Helen. "Chicago." *New York Catholic Worker*, May 1938.
———. "Chicago." *New York Catholic Worker*, April 1938.
———. "Chicago." *New York Catholic Worker*, January 1938, p. 6.
———. "Chicago Catholic Worker." *New York Catholic Worker*, November 1937, p. 3.
Gleason, John Philip. "The Central-Verein, 1900–1917: A Chapter in the History of the German-American Catholics." PhD diss., University of Notre Dame, 1960.
Green, Betsy J. *Western Springs Illinois.* Images of America Series. Chicago: Arcadia, 2002.
Hayes, John. Interview by Francis Sicius,14 June 1976. Cassette, Dorothy Day-Catholic Worker Collection, Marquette University, WI, Series W-9.1, Box C-3.
Jet. "Masses of Negroes Learn Thrift Through Credit Unions." 21 January 1965, p. 24.

Bibliography

———. "Chicago Couple Win Court Fight Over Home." 25 June 1953, 8.
Jones, Sidney, and Edward B. Toles. In *Chicago Defender*. "Dr. Falls Will Build in All-White Suburb," 20 June 1953, p. 4.
The Journal of Negro History. "Proceedings of the Annual Meeting and the Celebration of the Twentieth Anniversary of the Association for the Study of Negro Life and History in Chicago, September 9–11, 1935." Vol. 20 (October 1935) 373–78.
Mayor's Committee on Race Relations. *Race Relations in Chicago: December 1944*. Chicago: Mayor's Committee on Race Relations, 1944.
McCleary, Dixie Anne McCleary. "Vital Court Decision in Chicago: Judge Berkowitz Rule for Social Justice." *Catholic Interracialist*, July-August 1953, pp. 1, 6.
National Medical Association. "Chicago Court Agreement Reached." *Journal of the National Medical Association* 56 (March 1964) 205–6.
———. "Chicago Physicians Sue for Admission to Hospital Staff." *Journal of the National Medical Association* 53 (March 1961) 198–99.
———. "Chicago Enacts Hospital Anti-Discrimination Ordinance." *Journal of the National Medical Association* 48 (May 1956) 202.
———. "Chicago Ordinance Against Hospital Discrimination Introduced." *Journal of the National Medical Association* 48 (January 1956) 69.
Interracial Review. "New Editorial Board." Vol. 7 (October 1934) 118.
Lewis Memorial Maternity Hospital. "Lewis Memorial Maternity Hospital." *New World* 40 (29 April 1932) 6.
New York Catholic Worker. "Chi CW Holds Retreat, Makes Plea for Poor." October 1937, p. 2.
———. "New Branch of C.W. Opens in Chicago: Colored and White Work Together in South Side Center." June 1937, p. 2.
———. "Interracial." September 1935, p. 4.
Piehl, Mel. *Breaking Bread: The Catholic Worker and the Origin of Catholic Radicalism in America*. Philadelphia: Temple University, 1982.
Proctor, Lillian Steele. "A Case Study of Thirty Superior Colored Children in Washington, D.C." MA thesis, University of Chicago, 1929.
Reed, Christopher R. "'In the Shadow of Fort Dearborn' Honoring De Saible at the Chicago's World Fair of 1933–1934." *Journal of Black Studies* 21 (1991) 398–413.
Saunders, Doris E. "Confetti." *Chicago Daily Defender*, 10 February 1969, p. 12.
Schueler, J. O. "W. Springs Doctor Has a 'Better Idea' About Civil Rights." *Chicago Tribune*, 27 December 1968, clipping at Western Springs Historical Society, Western Springs, IL, Folder: Dr. Arthur G. Falls.
Sicius, Francis J. "The Chicago Catholic Worker." In *Revolution of the Heart: Essays on the Catholic Worker*, ed. Patrick G. Coy, 337–59. Philadelphia: New Society, 1992.
———. *The Word Made Flesh: The Catholic Worker and the Emergence of Lay Activism in the Church*. Lanham, MD: University Press of America, Inc., 1990.
Unsworth, Tim. "A Lonely Prophet Falls in Chicago." *National Catholic Reporter*, 3 March 2000, p. 18.
———. "Arthur Falls: Believing that 'Catholic' Means 'Universal.'" Chap. In *Catholics on the Edge*. New York: Crossroad, 1995.
Western Springs Times. "Drop Appeal of Park Condemnation Ruling." 17 July 1953, p. 1.
———. "Villagers Will Vote Next Friday on 3 Park Referendum Proposal." 3 July 1953, pp. 1–2.

Western Springs Villager. "Dr. Falls Chairman of Nat'l Meeting at University of Chicago." 17 March 1966, clipping of article available at Western Springs Historical Society, Western Springs, IL, Folder: Dr. Arthur G. Falls.

Who's Who in Colored America. 5th ed. New York: Who's Who in Colored America, 1940.

INTERVIEWS BY AUTHOR

Bright, Bill. Interview by author, 11 November 2011. Digital recording over phone, Milwaukee, WI to Western Springs, IL.

Davis, Cyprian. Interview by author, 13 June 2011. Digital recording over phone, Milwaukee, WI to St. Meinrad, IN.

Dowdle, Rev. David P. Interview by author, 12 December 2011. Notes, Western Springs, IL.

Gougiel, Joseph. Interview by author. 12 December 2011. Notes, Western Springs, IL.

Kravcik, Joan. Interview by author. 29 December 2011. Digital recording over phone, Milwaukee, WI.

Kravcik, John. Interview by author. 29 December 2011. Digital recording over phone, Milwaukee, WI.

Massingale, Bryan N. Interview by author, 8 September 2011. Notes, Milwaukee, WI.

O'Brien, Sr. Josephine. Interview by author. 14 December 2011. Notes, Western Springs, IL.

Scott, Dr. Rosalyn P. Interview by author. 5 January 2012. Digital recording over phone, Milwaukee, WI to New Jersey.

Sykes, Michelle. Interview by author. 26 January 2012. Digital recording over phone, Milwaukee, WI to New Jersey.

Wheeler, Zita. Interview by author, 23 January 2012. Digital recording over phone, Milwaukee, WI to Western Springs, IL.

Young, Dr. Quentin. Interview by author, 18 November 2011. Digital recording over phone, Milwaukee, WI to Chicago.

SOURCES FOR HISTORICAL BACKGROUND ON LIFE OF FALLS

Abu-Lughud, Janet L. *Race, Space, and Riots in Chicago, New York, and Los Angeles.* Oxford: Oxford University, 2007.

Adams, James Truslow. *The Epic of America.* Boston: Little, Brown, and Company, 1931.

Agar, Vin. "'Granny,' Born in Slavery—Lived Simply—and Died in Freedom: Aged Catholic Negress Mourned by La Grange Parishioners." *Chicago New World*, 14 February 1941, p. 6.

Archdiocese of Chicago. "Fr. Matthias Hoffman, Chicago Heights Pastor, Dies: Was Professor at Two Chicago Seminaries." Online: http://www.archchicago.org/news_releases/obituaries_05/obit_040105.shtm.

Avella, Steven M. *This Confident Church: Catholic Leadership and Life in Chicago, 1940-1965.* Notre Dame, IN: University of Notre Dame, 1992.

Bibliography

Baron, Dan. "Edward Toles, 1st Black Bankruptcy Judge." *Chicago Tribune*, 5 December 1998, p. 23.

Barton, Betty Lynn Barton. "The Fellowship of Reconciliation: Pacifism, Labor, and Social Welfare, 1915–1960." PhD diss., Florida State University, 1974.

Berrera, Albino. "The Evolution of Social Ethics: Using Economic History to Understand Economic Ethics." *Journal of Religious Ethics* 27 (summer 1999) 285–304.

Bethea M.D., Dennis A. Letter to the editor. *Chicago Daily Tribune*, 23 October 1939, p. 12.

Bielakowski, Rae. "You are in the World: Catholic Campus Life at Loyola University Chicago, Mundelein College, and De Paul University, 1924–1950." PhD diss., Loyola University Chicago, 2009.

Boston Pilot. "The Colored Catholic Memorial: The Eloquent Expression of Their Fourth Congress." 23 September 1893, p. 6.

Brady, Bernard, Kenneth Goodpaster, and Robert Kennedy. "*Rerum Novarum* and the Modern Corporation." *International Journal of Value-Based Management* 4 (1991) 57-75.

Bright, Bill. "Sharing Parishes." St. John of the Cross website. Online: http://www.sjcws.org/Organization.aspx?lngOrgID=34.

Cantwell, Daniel. Interview by Rev. Steven Avella. 14 December 1983. Transcript, Archives of the Archdiocese of Chicago, Box 43615.05, Folder Msgr. Daniel Cantwell.

Carey, Patrick. "Lay Leadership in the United States." *U. S. Catholic Historian* 9 (summer 1990) 223–47.

———. *People, Priests, and Prelates: Ecclesiastical Democracy and the Tensions of Trusteeism*. Notre Dame, IN: University of Notre Dame, 1987.

Chicago Daily Tribune. "Dr. Midian O. Bousfield." 17 February 1948, p. 21.

———. "5 New School Trustees Given O.K. by Council: Mayor Kelly's Appointees Pledged to Economy." 11 May 1933, p. 13.

———. "First Colored Democrat Named to State Law Post." 12 February 1933, p. 11.

———. "Interrace Group Opens Weekly Forum Series: Designed to Settle Problems." 6 November 1932, p. F4.

———. "Police Quell Trouble Over Car Extension." 17 September 1930, p. 15.

Chicago Defender. "125 Science Students Get Diplomas Sunday."18 September 1965, p. 35.

———. "Co-Op Hits $1 Million in Assets."1 February 1958, p. 9.

———. "Dr. Bousfield on School Board: Dr. Bousfield in Placed on School Board; Culminates 25-Year Fight Launched by Editor Robert S. Abbott." 28 October 1939, pp. 1–2.

———. "See Catholics Planning Jim Crow Church: Chicago Parishioners Fight Proposal." National Edition. 20 July 1935, p. 12.

———. "Catholic School Joins Jim Crow Crowd; Bars Race Child." National Edition. 7 October 1933, p. 12.

———. "List of Slain in Four Days Rioting." 2 August 1919, p. 1.

Chicago New World. "Father Flanagan's Boys Town Choir." 12 October 1951.

———. "Interracial Group Urged by Bishop." 19 December 1941, p. 1.

———. "Bill Overcomes Race Preference." 18 July 1941, p. 11.

———. "Meeting to Urge Better Relations Between the Races." 18 April 1941, p. 7.

———. "St. Elizabeth's H. S. Accredited." 14 September 1934.

Chicago Tribune. "Builder Ask Rehearing of Deerfield Suit." 28 May 1963, p. B17.

Integrated Education. "Chronicle of Race and Schools." Vol. 10 (July-September 1972) 20–32.

Cogley, John. *Catholic America.* Garden City, New York: Image, 1974.

———. "Archbishop Ousts Selma Priest Who Aided Voter Registration Drive." *New York Times,* 26 June 1965, p. 13.

———. "Negroes in Catholic Schools: 'Catholic Education in Catholic Schools for All Catholic Youth.'" *Chicago Catholic Worker,* August 1941, p. 3.

———. "Racial Prejudice is a Stupid Sin: Chicago Letter." *New York Catholic Worker,* September 1937 p. 3.

Davis, Cyprian. *Henriette Delille: Servant of the Slaves: Witness to the Poor.* New Orleans: Archives of the Archdiocese of New Orleans, 2004.

———. "Black Catholic Theology: A Historical Perspective." *Theological Studies* 61 (December 2000) 656–71.

———. "Reclaiming the Spirit: On Teaching Church History: Why Can't They Be More Like Us?" In *Black and Catholic: The Challenge and Gift of Black Folk,* edited by Jamie T. Phelps, 43–53. Milwaukee: Marquette University, 1997.

———. *The History of Black Catholics in the United States.* New York: Crossroad, 1990.

———. "Two Sides of a Coin: The Black Presence in the History of the Catholic Church in America." In *Many Rains Ago: A Historical and Theological Reflection on the Role of the Episcopate in the Evangelization of African American Catholics,* 49–62. Washington, DC: Secretariat for Black Catholics/National Conference of Catholic Bishops, 1990.

———. "Black Catholics in Nineteenth Century America." *U.S. Catholic Historian* 5 (1986) 1–17.

Day, Dorothy. *All the Way to Heaven: The Selected Letters of Dorothy Day.* Edited by Robert Ellsberg. Milwaukee: Marquette University, 2010.

———. "Liturgy and Sociology." *New York Catholic Worker,* December 1935, p. 4.

Deats, Richard. Introduction to *Peace is the Way: Writings on Nonviolence from the Fellowship of Reconciliation,* edited by Walter Wink, xv–xxii. Maryknoll, NY: Orbis, 2000.

De Hueck, Catherine. *Friendship House.* New York: Sheed & Ward, 1946.

De Lubac, Henri. *Catholicism: Christ and the Common Destiny of Man.* Translated by Lancelot C. Sheppard and Sister Elizabeth Englund, OCD. San Francisco: Ignatius, 1988.

De Young, Ruth. "Race Relations Parley to Open at World's Fair: Progress Made to be Topic of 2 Day Conference." *Chicago Daily Tribune,* 18 June 1933, WC 11.

Epiphany Catholic Church. "Monsignor John Hayes, The Priest." Online: www.epiphanychicago.org/index.cfm?load=page&page=160.

Frazier, E. Franklin. *The Negro Family in Chicago.* Chicago: University of Chicago Press, 1932.

Freeman, Ronald L. *The Mule Train: A Journey of Hope Remembered.* Nashville: Rutledge Hill, 1998.

Frisbie, Margery. *An Alley in Chicago: The Ministry of a City Priest.* Kansas City: Sheed and Ward, 1991.

Gardner, Burleigh B., Benjamin D. Wright, and Sister Rita Dee. "The Effect of Busing Black Ghetto Children into White Suburban Schools." Prepared for the Chicago Catholic School Board, Archdiocese of Chicago, July 1970. Online: http://eric.ed.gov/PDFS/ED048389.pdf.

Bibliography

Gula, Richard M. *Reason Informed by Faith: Foundations of Catholic Morality*. New York: Paulist, 1989.

Hayes, Diana L. "The Black Catholic Congress Movement: A Progressive Aspect of African-American Catholicism." In *What's Left? Liberal American Catholics*, edited by Mary Jo Weaver, 238–51. Bloomington: Indiana University Press, 1999.

Hecht, Robert A. *An Ordinary Man: A Life of Fr. John LaFarge, S.J.* Lanham, MD: Scarecrow, 1996.

Heise, Kenan. "Judge, Rights Crusader Sydney Jones Jr." *Chicago Tribune*, 11 November 1993, p. 15.

Hirsch, Arnold R. *Making the Second Ghetto: Race and Housing in Chicago 1940–1960*. Cambridge: Cambridge University, 1983.

Holy Family Parish. "Newsroom." Online: http://www.holyfamilychicago.org/newsroom/EditorialBackground.htm.

Honey, Michael K. *Going Down Jericho Road: The Memphis Strike, Martin Luther King's Last Campaign*. New York: Norton, 2007.

Jones, Dewey R. "Why Fight Segregation?" *Chicago Defender*, 24 March 1934, p. A10.

Johnston, M. "Colored Churches." *Chronicle: Official Organ of the Federated Colored Catholics of the United States* (February 1932) 26.

———. "Chicago, ILL." *Chronicle: Official Organ of the Federated Colored Catholics of the United States* 5 (January 1932) 15.

Johnson, Charles S. *The Negro in American Civilization: A Study of Negro Life and Race Relations in the Light of Social Research*. New York: Holt, 1930.

Johnson, Karen Joy. "The Universal Church in the Segregated City: Doing Catholic Interracialism in Chicago, 1915–1963." PhD diss., University of Illinois at Chicago, 2013.

Kelleher, Margaret M. "Liturgical and Social Transformation: Exploring the Relationship." *U. S. Catholic Historian* 16 (Fall 1998) 58–70.

King, Martin Luther, Jr. *The Trumpet of Conscience*. New York: Harper & Row, 1968.

———. *Where Do We Go From Here? Chaos or Community?* New York: Harper & Row, 1968.

Kirby, Joseph. "Rev. Martin W. Farrell: Aided Woodlawn Group." *Chicago Tribune*, 17 February 1991. Online: http://articles.chicagotribune.com/1991-02-17/news/9101150766_1_pastor-community-improvement-group-park-ridge.

Koenig, Harry C. *A History of the Parishes of the Archdiocese of Chicago*. 2 vols. Chicago: The Archdiocese of Chicago, 1980.

Lackey, Hilliard Lawrence. *Marks, Martin and the Mule Train*. Jackson, MS: Town Square, 1998.

Lewis, David Levering Lewis. *W. E. B. Du Bois: The Fight for Equality and the American Century, 1919–1963*. New York: Henry Holt, 2000.

McGreevy, John T. *Parish Boundaries: The Catholic Encounter with Race in the Twentieth-Century Urban North*. Chicago: University of Chicago, 1996.

McKanan, Dan. *The Catholic Worker after Dorothy: Practicing the Works of Mercy in a New Generation*. Collegeville, MN: Liturgical, 2008.

McKnight, Gerald D. *The Last Crusade: Martin Luther King, Jr., the FBI, and the Poor People's Campaign*. Denver, CO: Westview, 1998.

Merrill, Philemon. "The Theology of Racism." *Interracial Review* 19 (April 1946) 56–57.

Michel, Virgil. *Christian Social Reconstruction: Some Fundamentals of the* Quadragesimo Anno. Milwaukee: Bruce, 1937.

Miller, William D. *Dorothy Day: A Biography*. San Francisco: Harper and Row, 1982.

The Milton S. Eisenhower Foundation and The Corporation for What Works. *The Millennium Breach: Rich, Poorer and Racial Apart*. 2nd Edition. Washington, DC: Milton S. Eisenhower Foundation and the Corporation for What Works, 1998. Online: http://www.eisenhowerfoundation.org/docs/millennium.pdf.

Moeslein, Mark. "'That He Might Present Himself a Glorious Church, Not Having Spot or Wrinkle or Any Such Thing; But That it Would Be Holy and Without Blemish.'" *Chronicle: Official Organ of the Federated Colored Catholics of the United States* (February 1932) 54–55.

National Advisory Committee on Civil Disorders. *Report of the National Advisory Committee on Civil Disorders*. Washington, DC: U.S. Government Printing Office, 1968.

Nickels, Marilyn Wenzke. *Black Catholic Protest and the Federated Colored Catholics 1917-1933: Three Perspectives on Racial Justice*. The Heritage of American Catholicism Series. New York: Garland, 1988.

Noll, Bishop J. F. "Objectives for Catholic Action." *Our Sunday Visitor*, 7 October 1934, p. 8.

O'Shea, John S. "Becoming a Surgeon in the Early 20th Century: Parallels to the Present." *Journal of Surgical Education* 65 (May/June 2008) 236–41.

Piehl, Mel. *Breaking Bread: The Catholic Worker and the Origin of the Catholic Radicalism in America*. Philadelphia: Temple University, 1982.

Plotkin, Wendy. "'Hemmed In': The Struggle Against Racial Restrictive Covenants and Deed Restrictions in Post-WWII Chicago." *Journal of Illinois State Historical Society* 94 (spring 2001) 39–69.

Reitzes, Dietrich C. *Negroes and Medicine*. Cambridge: Harvard University, 1958.

Report of the National Advisory Committee on Civil Disorders. Washington, DC: U.S. Government Printing Office, 1968.

Rosen, Harry M., and David H. Rosen. *But Not Next Door*. New York: Ivan Obolensky, 1962.

Rudd, Daniel. Quoted in *Daniel Rudd: Founder of Black Catholic National Congresses*. VHS. Catholic Life in America Series. Directed by George Torok. Sparkill, NY: Hallel Videos; 1999.

———. In "Wednesday's Journal." *Three Catholic Afro-American Congresses*, No editor listed, p. 25–26. Cincinnati: The American Catholic Tribune, 1893.

Saint John of the Cross Catholic Church. "Sharing Parish St. Thaddeus Choir Visits SJC." Online: www.stjohnofthecross.org/event/sharing-parish-st-thaddeus-choir-visits-sjc/.

Satter, Beryl. *Family Properties: Race, Real Estate, and the Exploitation of Black Urban America*. New York: Metropolitan / Holt, 2009.

Seals, Connie. "Human Relations Beat." *Chicago Defender*, 6 February 1965, p. 5.

Seligmann, Herbert J. *The Negro Faces America*. New York: Harper, 1920.

Sharum, Elizabeth Louise. "A Strange Fire Burning: A History of the Friendship House Movement. PhD diss., Texas Tech University, 1977.

Slattery, John R. "The Hope of the Colored Race: Very Rev. J. R. Slattery's Sermon Points Out the Way to Prosperity." *Catholic Mirror*, 27 October 1894, pp. 1–2.

Southern, David W. *John La Farge and the Limits of Catholic Interracialism, 1911–1963*. Baton Rouge: Louisiana State University, 1996.

Bibliography

Spalding, David. "The Negro Catholic Congresses, 1889-1894." *Catholic Historical Review* 55 (October 1969): 337-57.
Steinfels, Peter. "John J. Egan, Priest and Rights Advocate, Is Dead at 84." *New York Times*, 22 May 2001, section C, p. 18.
Stocking, Luke. "When the Irish were Irish: Peter Maurin and the Green Revolution." MA Thesis, University of St. Michael's College, 2006.
Stritch, Cardinal Sameuel. "Interracial Justice in Hospitals." *Interracial Review* 28 (November 1955) 185-86.
Three Catholic Afro-American Congresses. Cincinnati: The American Catholic Tribune, 1893.
Troester, Rosalie Riegle, ed. *Voices from the Catholic Worker*. Philadelphia: Temple University, 1993.
Tuttle, William M., Jr. *Race Riot: Chicago in the Red Summer of 1919.1970*. Reprint. Urbana: University of Illinois, 1996.
Twomey, Mark J. *Seventy-Five Years of Grace: The Liturgical Press 1926-2001*. Collegeville, MN: The Liturgical, 2001.
Winslow, John Copley and Verrier Elwin. *Gandhi: The Dawn of Indian Freedom*. New York: Fleming H. Revell, 1931.
Wood, Robert N. Letter to the Editor. *New York Sun*, 29 June 1894, p. 6.
Young, Donald, ed. *The American Negro*. Philadelphia: American Academy of Political and Social Science, 1928.

ECCLESIAL DOCUMENTS ON RACE

Black Bishops of the United States. *"What We Have Seen and Heard": A Pastoral Letter on Evangelization from the Black Bishops of the United States*. Cincinnati: St. Anthony Messenger, 1984.
Flynn, Harry J. *In God's Image: Pastoral Letter on Racism* (12 September 2003). Online: www.archspm.org/reference/pastoral-letters-detail.php?intResourceID=158.
Leo XIII. Encyclical, *Rerum novarum*, 15 May 1891. Online: www.vatican.va/holy_father/ leo_xiii/encyclicals/documents/hf_l-xiii_enc_15051891_rerum-novarum_en.html.
National Conference of Catholic Bishops. *Brothers and Sisters to Us*. Washington, DC: United States Catholic Conference, 1979; revised to include *For the Love of One Another*, Washington, DC, United States Catholic Conference, 1991.
———. *The National Race Crisis*. In *The Pope Speaks* 13 (spring 1968) 175-79.
National Catholic Welfare Conference. *Discrimination and the Christian Conscience*. In *The Catholic Viewpoint on Race Relations*. Revised Edition. Edited by John LaFarge, 186-92. New York: Hanover House, 1960.
George, Francis. *Dwell in My Love: A Pastoral Letter on Racism*. Chicago: Archdiocese of Chicago, 4 April 2001.
Hughes, Alfred. *"Made in the Image of God": A Pastoral Letter on Racial Harmony* (December 2006). Online: www.arch-no.org/12.15_pastoral_final.pdf.
Melczek, Dale J. "Created in God's Image: A Pastoral Letter on the Sin of Racism and a Call to Conversion." Gary, Indiana, 6 August 2003. Online: http://www.dcgary.org/ pdf/Created-In-Gods-Image.pdf.
Pontifical Council for Justice and Peace. *Contribution to the World Conference against Racial Discrimination, Xenophobia and Related Intolerance*. Durban, August 31–September

7, 2001. Online: http://www.vatican.va/roman_curia/pontifical_councils/justpeace/documents/rc_pc_justpeace_doc_20010829_comunicato-razzismo_en.html.

———. *The Church and Racism: Toward a More Fraternal Society.* 3 November 1988. Online: www.ewtn.com/library/curia/pcjpraci.htm.

CONTEMPORARY THEOLOGICAL WORKS CONCERNING RACIAL JUSTICE
(Not Used for Historical Background)

Boff, Leonardo and Clodovis Boff. *Introducing Liberation Theology.* Translated by Paul Burns. Maryknoll, NY: Orbis, 1987.

Cone, James H. "Black Liberation Theology and Black Catholics: A Critical Conversation." *Theological Studies* 61 (December 2000) 731-47.

———. *Black Theology and Black Power.* Maryknoll, NY: Orbis, [1969] 1997.

———. *A Black Theology of Liberation: Fortieth Anniversary Edition.* Maryknoll, NY: Orbis, 2010.

———. *The Cross and the Lynching Tree.* Maryknoll, NY: Orbis, 2012.

———. *For My People: Black Theology and the Black Church.* Maryknoll, NY: Orbis, 1984.

———. *God of the Oppressed.* Revised Edition. Maryknoll, NY: Orbis, [1975] 1997.

———. *My Soul Looks Back.* Nashville: Abingdon, 1982.

———. *Speaking the Truth: Ecumenism, Liberation, and Black Theology.* 1986. Reprint. Maryknoll, NY: Orbis Books, 1999.

———. *The Spirituals and the Blues: An Interpretation.* New York: Seabury, 1972.

———. "Theology's Great Sin: Silence in the Face of White Supremacy." *Union Seminary Quarterly Review* 55 (2001) 1-14.

Copeland, M. Shawn. *Enfleshing Freedom: Body, Race, and Being.* Minneapolis: Fortress, 2009.

———. *The Subversive Power of Love: The Vision of Henriette Delille.* New York: Paulist, 2009.

———. "Foundations for Catholic Theology in an African American Context." In *Black and Catholic: The Gift and Challenge of Black Folk: Contributions of African American Experience and Thought to Catholic Theology,* ed. Jamie T. Phelps, 107-48. Milwaukee, WI: Marquette University, 1997.

———. "Racism and the Vocation of the Christian Theologian." *Spiritus* 2 (Spring 2002) 15-29.

———. "Guest Editorial." *Theological Studies* 61 (2000) 603-08.

———. "Tradition and the Traditions of African American Catholicism." *Theological Studies* 61 (December 2000) 632-55.

Cumming, Ryan P. "Contrasts and Fragments: An Exploration of James Cone's Theological Methodology." *Anglican Theological Review* 91 (summer 2009) 395-416.

Cummings, George C. L. "The Slave Narratives as a Source of Black Theological Discourse: The Spirit and Eschatology." In *Cut Loose Your Stammering Tongue: Black Theology in the Slave Narratives,* edited by Dwight N. Hopkins and George C. L. Cummings, 46-66. Maryknoll, NY, Orbis, 1991.

Floyd-Thomas, Stacey M. *Mining the Motherlode: Methods in Womanist Ethics.* Cleveland, OH: The Pilgrim, 2006.

Bibliography

Hopkins, Dwight N. "Introduction." In *Black Faith and Public Talk*, ed. Dwight N. Hopkins, 1–10. Maryknoll, NY: Orbis, 1999.

Kelsey, George D. *Racism and the Christian Understanding of Man*. New York: Scribner, 1965.

La Farge, John. *The Catholic Viewpoint on Race Relations*. Revised Edition. Garden City, NY: Hanover House, 1960.

———. *The Race Question and the Negro: A Study of the Catholic Doctrine on Interracial Justice*. New York: Longmans Green, 1943.

———. *Interracial Justice: A Study of the Catholic Doctrine of Race Relations*. New York: America, 1937.

Massingale, Bryan N. "The Dark Night(s) of Malcolm X: Catholic Spirituality and African American Sanctity." Presented at the Jesuit School of Theology, Berkeley, CA, in April 2012.

———. "Response: The Challenge of Idolatry and Ecclesial Identity." In *Ecclesiology and Exclusion: Boundaries of Being and Belonging in Postmodern Times*. Edited by Dennis M. Doyle, Timothy J. Furry, and Pascal D. Bazzell, 130–35. Maryknoll, NY: Orbis, 2012.

———. "Cyprian Davis and the Black Catholic Intellectual Vocation." *U.S. Catholic Historian* 28 (winter 2010) 65-82.

———. *Racial Justice and the Catholic Church*. Maryknoll, NY: Orbis, 2010.

———. "*Vox Victimarum Vox Dei*: Malcolm X as Neglected 'Classic' for Catholic Theological Reflection." *CTSA Proceedings* 65 (2010) 63–88.

———. "James Cones and Recent Catholic Episcopal Teaching on Racism." *Theological Studies* 51 (December 2000) 700–730.

———. "The African American Experience and United States Roman Catholic Ethics: 'Strangers and Aliens No Longer?.'" In *Black and Catholic: The Gift and Challenge of Black Folk: Contributions of African American Experience and Thought to Catholic Theology*, ed. Jamie T. Phelps, 79–101. Milwaukee, WI: Marquette University, 1997.

———. "The Social Dimensions of Sin and Reconciliation in the Theologies of James H. Cone and Gustavo Gutiérrez: A Critical Comparative Examination." Ph.D. diss., Academia Alphonsianum, 1991.

Nilson, Jon. "Towards the 'Beloved Community': The Church's Role in the Struggle Against Racism." *U.S. Catholic Historian* 28 (winter 2010) 83-91.

———. "Confessions of a White Catholic Racist Theologian." In *Interrupting White Privilege: Catholic Theologians Break the Silence*. Edited by Laurie M. Cassidy and Alex Mikulich, 15-39. Maryknoll, NY: Orbis, 2007.

———. *Hearing Past the Pain: Why White Theologians Need Black Theology*. New York: Paulist, 2007.

Raiser, Konrad. *Ecumenism in Transition: A Paradigm Shift in the Ecumenical Movement?* Geneva: WCC, 1991.

CONTEMPORARY NOTIONS OF RACISM IN THE SOCIAL SCIENCES

Alexander, Jeffrey C. *The Civil Sphere*. New York: Oxford University, 2006.

Bibliography

Appiah, Anthony K. "Identity, Authenticity, Survival: Multicultural Societies and Social Reproduction." In *Multiculturalism: Examining the Politics of Recognition*, edited by Amy Guttman, 149–63. Princeton NJ: Princeton University, 1994.
Bonilla-Silva, Eduardo. *Racism Without Racists: Color-Blind Racism and the Persistence of Racial Inequality in the United States*. Third edition. Lanham: Rowman & Littlefield, 2010.
Brown, Michael, Martin Carnoy, Elliot Currie, Troy Duster, David Oppenheimer, Marjorie Shultz, and David Wellman. *White-Washing Race: The Myth of a Color-Blind Society*. Berkeley: University of California, 2003.
Desmond, Matthew, and Mustafa Emirbayer. *Racial Domination, Racial Progress: The Sociology of Race in America*. New York: McGraw-Hill, 2009.
Emirbayer, Mustafa, and Matthew Desmond. *The Theory of Racial Domination*. Chicago: University of Chicago Press, *forthcoming*.
Feagin, Joe R., Hernan Vera, and Pinar Batur. *White Racism: The Basics*. Second edition. New York: Routledge, 2001.
Piven, Frances Fox. *Challenging Authority: How Ordinary People Change America*. Lanham, MD: Rowman & Littlefield, 2006.
Taylor, Charles. "The Politics of Recognition." In *Multiculturalism: Examining the Politics of Recognition*, edited by Amy Gutmann, 25–73. Princeton, NJ: Princeton University, 1994.

SOURCES FOR EXAMINATION OF SIN AND HERESY

Augustine. "Letter XCIII," in *A Select Library of Nicene and Post-Nicene Fathers of the Christian Church*. Edited by Philip Schaff and Henry Wace. Series 1. Vol. 1, *The Confessions and Letters of St. Augustin, with a Sketch of his Life and Work*. Grand Rapids: Eerdmans, 1956.
Canon Law: A Text and Commentary. Edited by Bouscaren, T. Lincoln and Adam C. Ellis. Milwaukee: Bruce, 1949.
Code of Canon Law: Latin-English Edition. Washington, DC: Canon Law Society of America, 1983.
Council of Nicaea. "The Canons of the 318 Holy Fathers Assembled in the City of Nice, in Bithynia." In *A Select Library of Nicene and Post-Nicene Fathers of the Christian Church*. Edited by Philip Schaff and Henry Wace. Series 2. Vol. 14, *The Seven Ecumenical Councils*, 8–45. Grand Rapids: Eerdmans, 1890.
———. "The Nicene Creed." In *A Select Library of Nicene and Post-Nicene Fathers of the Christian Church*, eds. Philip Schaff and Henry Wace. Series 2. Vol. 14, *The Seven Ecumenical Councils*, 3. Grand Rapids: Eerdmans, 1890.
———. "The Synodal Letter." In *A Select Library of Nicene and Post-Nicene Fathers of the Christian Church*, eds. Philip Schaff and Henry Wace. Series 2. Vol. 14, *The Seven Ecumenical Councils*, 53–54. Grand Rapids: Eerdmans, 1890.
Edwards, Mark. *Catholicity and Heresy in the Early Church*. Farnham, Surrey, England: Ashgate, 2009.
Irenaeus of Lyons. *Against the Heresies* (Book 2). Translated by Dominic J. Unger. New York: Newman, 2012.

Bibliography

Jennings, James R., ed. *Daring to Seek Justice: People Working Together: The Story of the Campaign for Human Development, its Roots, its Program and its Challenges.* Washington, DC: United States Catholic Conference, 1986.

Jerome. *St. Jerome: Commentary on Galatians.* Translated by Andrew Cain. Washington, DC: The Catholic University of America, 2010.

Maguire Daniel C. *The Moral Choice.* Minneapolis: Winston, 1979.

Mattox, John Mark. *Saint Augustine and the Theory of Just War.* London: Continuum, 2006.

McGrath, Alister. *Heresy: A History of Defending the Truth.* New York: HarperOne, 2009.

Merrill, Philemon. "The Theology of Racism." *Interracial Review* 19 (April 1946) 56-57.

Newman, John Henry Cardinal. *The Arians of the Fourth Century.* Notre Dame, IN: University of Notre Dame, 2001.

Nicholas V (Pope). Papal Bull, *Dum diversas,* 18 June 1452.

Noonan, John T., Jr. *A Church that Can and Cannot Change: The Development of Catholic Moral Teaching.* Notre Dame: IN: University of Notre Dame, 2005.

Rahner, Karl. *Foundations of Christian Faith: An Introduction to the Idea of Christianity.* Translated by William V. Dych. New York: Crossroad, 1984.

Schaff, Philip and Henry Wace, eds. *A Select Library of Nicene and Post-Nicene Fathers of the Christian Church.* Series 2. Vol. 14, *The Seven Ecumenical Councils.* Grand Rapids: Eerdmans, 1890.

Second Vatican Council. Decree on Ecumenism, *Unitatis redintegratio* (21 November 1964). Online: http://www.vatican.va/archive/hist_councils/ii_vatican_council/documents/vat-ii_decree_19641121_unitatis-redintegratio_en.html.

———. Declaration of Religious Freedom, *Dignitatis humanae* (7 December 1965). Online: http://www.vatican.va/archive/hist_councils/ii_vatican_council/documents/vat-ii_decl_19651207_dignitatis-humanae_en.html.

Stark, Rodney. *For the Glory of God: How Monotheism Led to Reformations, Science, Witch-Hunts, and the End of Slavery.* Princeton NJ: Princeton University, 2003.

Swift, Louis J. *The Early Fathers on War and Military Service.* Wilmington, DE: Michael Glazier, 1983.

Thomas Aquinas. *Summa theologiae.* Vol. 32, Consequences of Faith. Translated and edited by Thomas Gilby. Cambridge: Blackfriars, 1975.

Torrell, Jean-Pierrel. *Saint Thomas Aquinas.* Vol. 1, *The Person and His Work.* Revised. Edited and translated by Robert Royal. Washington, DC: The Catholic University of America, 2005.

OTHER WORKS CITED

Action Now. "About Us." Online: http://actionnowdotorg.wordpress.com/about-us/.

———. "Housing/Foreclosure." Online: http://actionnowdotorg.wordpress.com/housing-foreclosure/.

———. "In the News." Online: https://actionnowdotorg.wordpress.com/in-the-news-2/.

———. "Neighborhood Victories." Online: https://actionnowdotorg.wordpress.com/community-improvement/.

———. "Welcome to Action Now!" 31 March 2011. Online: http://actionnowdotorg.wordpress.com/2011/03/31/5/.

Bibliography

———. "Victory! New Vacant Property Ordinance Passes City Council," 25 July 2011. Online: http://actionnowdotorg.wordpress.com/2011/07/25/vacant-property-ordinance-update/.

Brown, Camille Lewis Brown. "Mother Mary Theodore Williams." In *African Saints, African Stories: 40 Holy Men and Women*. Cincinnati: St. Anthony Messenger, 2008.

CBS Chicago. "Women Dump Garbage From Foreclosed Home At Bank of America Offices." 11 October 2011. Online: http://chicago.cbslocal.com/2011/10/11/women-dump-garbage-from-foreclosed-home-at-bank-of-america-offices/.

———. "Ordinance Holds Banks Responsible For Maintaining Vacant Buildings." 28 July 2011. Online: http://chicago.cbslocal.com/2011/10/11/women-dump-garbage-from-foreclosed-home-at-bank-of-america-offices/.

Circuit Court of Cook County Mortgage Foreclosure Mediation Program. "About." Online: http://cookcountyforeclosurehelp.org/about/.

Clinton, Catherine. *Harriet Tubman: Road to Freedom*. New York: Little, Brown, 2004.

Cronin, John F. "Religion and Race." *America* 150 (30 June 1984) 472.

Donovan, John T. *Crusader in the Cold War: A Biography of Fr. John F. Cronin, S.S. (1908–1994)*. New York: Peter Lang, 2005.

Donovan, Lisa. "New County Fines of Up to $1,000 a Day for Problem Vacant Buildings." *Chicago Sun-Times*, 14 December 2011. Online: http://www.suntimes.com/business/9442567-420/new-county-fines-of-up-to-1000-a-day-for-problem-vacant-buildings.html.

Engel, Lawrence J. "The Influence of Saul Alinsky on the Campaign for Human Development." *Theological Studies* 59 (December 1998) 636–61.

Francoeur, Richard Benoit. "In Pursuit of a Living Wage." *Social Thought* 19 (1999) 1–14.

Fredal, Marian. "A Catholic Diocese's Initiative to End Racism: A Case Study." EdD diss., Cardinal Stritch University, 2007.

Glatz, Carol. "Pope Brings African-American Foundress One Step Closer to Sainthood." *Catholic News Service*, 29 March 2010. Online: http://www.catholicnews.com/data/stories/cns/1001298.htm.

Hanson, Joyce A. *Mary McLeod Bethune & Black Women's Political Activism*. Columbia: University of Missouri, 2003.

Hayes, Diana L. "Mother Elizabeth Lange." *Rite* 34 (Jan–Feb 2003) 14.

Houlihan-Skilton, Mary. "8 Years in Clark Beating." *Chicago Sun-Times*, 16 October 1998.

Jennings, James R., ed. *Daring to Seek Justice: People Working Together: The Story of the Campaign for Human Development, its Roots, its Program and its Challenges*. Washington, DC: United States Catholic Conference, 1986.

Lonergan, Bernard. *Early Works on Theological Method 1*. Toronto: University of Toronto, 2010.

———. *Macroeconomic Dynamics: An Essay in Circulation Analysis*. Toronto: University of Toronto, 1999.

———. *A Second Collection*. Edited by William F. J. Ryan and Bernard J. Terrell. Toronto: University of Toronto, 1996.

———. *Method in Theology*. New York: Herder & Herder, 1972.

———. *Insight: A Study of Human Understanding*. Toronto: University of Toronto, [1957] 1988.

Lowry, Beverly. *Harriet Tubman: Imagining a Life*. New York: Doubleday, 2007.

Loynes, Duane T., Sr. "Response to Drs. Nilson, Massingale, and Copeland." 2012 Lonergan on the Edge Conference, 22 September 2012, Marquette University,

Bibliography

Milwaukee, WI. Online: http://www.lonerganresource.com/pdf/contributors/LOE-2012-12d_Duane_Loynes.pdf.

Mattison, William C., III. *Introducing Moral Theology: True Happiness and the Virtues*. Grand Rapids: Brazos, 2008.

McAuliffe, Patricia. *Fundamental Ethics: A Liberationist Approach*. Washington DC: Georgetown University, 1993.

McCardell, Paul. "Mother Mary Elizabeth Lange: Founder and First Superior of the Oblate Sisters of Providence." *Baltimore Sun*, 14 February 2007. Online: http://www.baltimoresun.com/features/bal-blackhistory-lange,0,2431999.story.

McCarthy, John E. "Bishop John E. McCarthy." Diocese of Austin Website. Online: http://www.austindiocese.org/dept/bishops_office/mccarthy_bio.php (accessed 19 April 2011). Page no longer available.

McCluskey, Audrey Thomas and Elaine M. Smith, eds. *Mary McLeod Bethune: Building a Better World; Essays and Selected Documents*. Bloomington: Indiana University Press, 1999.

Morrow, Dianne Batts. *Persons of Color and Religious at the Same Time: The Oblate Sisters of Providence, 1828–1860*. Chapel Hill: University of North Carolina, 2002.

Passelecq, Georges and Bernard Suchecky. *The Hidden Encyclical of Pius XII*. Translated by Steven Rendall. New York: Harcourt Brace, 1997.

Porter, Jean. "Virtue." In *The HarperCollins Encyclopedia of Catholicism*, edited by Richard P. McBrien, 1316-17. New York: HarperCollins, 1995.

———. *The Recovery of Virtue: The Relevance of Aquinas for Christian Ethics*. Louisville: Westminster John Knox, 1990.

Preston, Jennifer and Colin Moynihan. "Death of Florida Teen Spurs Outcry and Action." *New York Times*, 21 March 2012. Online: http://thelede.blogs.nytimes.com/2012/03/21/death-of-florida-teen-spurs-national-outrage-and-action/.

Second Vatican Council. Pastoral Constitution on the Church in the Modern World, *Gaudium et sps* (7 December 1965). Online: http://www.vatican.va/archive/hist_councils/ii_vatican_council/documents/vat-ii_cons_19651207_gaudium-et-spes_en.html.

Sernett, Milton C. *Harriet Tubman: Myth, Memory, and History*. Durham: Duke University Press, 2007.

Strom, Roy. "Chicago Police Arrest 21 Protestors for Trespassing." Reuters, 12 October 2011. Online: http://www.reuters.com/article/2011/10/12/us-wallstreet-protests-chicago-idUSTRE79B0XI20111012.

Tessman, Lisa. *Burdened Virtues: Virtue Ethics for Liberatory Struggles*. New York: Oxford University, 2005.

Vogt, Christopher P. "Fostering a Catholic Commitment to the Common Good: An Approach Rooted in Virtue Ethics." *Theological Studies* 68 (2007) 394–417.

General Index

Action Now, 160–62
Airport Homes Riot, 72
Alexander, Jeffrey C., 128n19, 130
Alinsky, Saul, 63n151, 78
Allen, Richard, 19
American Catholic Sociological Society, 64–65
American League Against War and Fascism, xiii, 111
anti-Semitism, 27, 33–34, 73, 94, 103, 115, 116n117, 135–36
Arianism, 136, 139–41
Aristotle, 153
Augustine, Saint, 140

Baldwin, James, 27
Barrett, John, 81
Beloved Community, 25, 28, 144
Bennett, William J., 88
Berkowitz, Jacob, 75
Berry, William D., 39
Bethany Union Church, 43
Bethune, Mary McLeod, 10, 44
Beverly Hills, 43–44, 116
Billings Memorial Hospital, 117
black agency, xiv–xv, xvii, 1, 3–4, 6–9, 11–12, 17, 20, 22, 26, 29–30, 45n64, 123, 148
Black Catholic Congress, 49n80
Black Power Movement, 118–20, 125
Bousfied, Midian O., 43
Bowers, John, 62, 94n9
Boys' Town Choir, 73
Bright, Bill, 165

Brothers and Sisters to Us, 7–9, 16, 30
Brown, John F., 63n149
Brown v. Board of Education, 2, 4–5, 127
Byrne, Paul, 62

Canon law, 133, 138
Cantwell, Daniel, 71
Carey, Patrick W., vii, xi, 93
Cathars, 141
Catholic Worker, vii, xii–xiii, 32, 34, 45, 53–68, 70n180, 91, 93–95, 111, 121, 124, 153
Central Verein, 60
Cermak, Anton, 42
Chicago Board of Education, 84–85
Chicago Catholic Interracial Council, xiii, 54, 65, 71, 81
Chicago Commission for Human Relations, 65
Chicago Defender, xii, 84, 105, 109n86, 119
Chicago Inter-Student Catholic Action (CISCA), 66n160
Chicago New World, 73, 108
Chicago Tribune, 119
Chicago Urban League, xiii, 32, 40–45, 56, 61, 77, 87n259, 91–92, 111, 115n113, 119, 158
Childs, Vilma, xi, 47, 90
Church and Racism: Toward a More Fraternal Society, 14
Civil Rights Act, 84, 120
Civil Rights Movement, 8–9, 14, 24, 30, 38n26, 69, 86, 118–20

193

General Index

Cobb, William Montague, 80
Cody, John, 87
Cogley, John, 60–62, 65–66
Committee to End Discrimination in Chicago Medical Institutions (CED), 80, 82–86, 118
communism, 100, 107–8, 110–11
Cone, James H., vii, 1, 17–20, 24, 27–31, 47n70, 77n219, 115n115, 123, 125, 130, 132, 137–38, 142–43, 146–47, 158–60
Congress of Racial Equality (CORE), xiii, 68–69
Conrad, George, W. B., 54
Constantine, Emperor, 139–40
Contribution to World Conference Against Racism, 14–15
Cook County Hospital, 79
Cooperative Laboratory Program, 85
Copeland, M. Shawn, 1, 17, 21–23, 27, 30, 115n115, 123, 137–38, 144, 146–47
Corpus Christi Catholic Church, 46
Coughlin, Charles, 34n10
Council for Biomedical Careers, 85, 119
Crane Junior College, 33–34
Cronin, John, 4
Cunningham, Robert M., Jr., 82

Dailey, Edward B., 108
Davis, Cyprian, xiii, 8–9, 27, 47n70
Day, Dorothy, 54–55, 57–58, 61–67, 93
Deerfield, Illinois, 74n202, 76–77, 145
Delille, Henriette, 10, 14, 22–23, 30, 123, 146–47
DePaul University, 57
De Saible Club, 40–42, 119n135, 124
Desmond, Matthew, 126–30, 145
Dickerson, Earl, 42
discipleship, 92, 98–102, 121, 123, 144–45, 148, 157
Discrimination and the Christian Conscience, 4–5, 30
Docetism, 135
Doherty, Catherine de Hueck, 58n125, 69
Donatists, 140
Du Bois, W. E. B., 27, 41, 108–9

Du Sable, Jean Baptiste, 41–42
Dwell in My Love, 11

Eckert, Joseph, 40, 51–52
Edwards, Mark, 134
Egan, John, 63
Emirbayer, Mustafa, 126–30, 145
Englewood High School, 33n6, 34
Englewood Riot, 72

Falls, Arthur G., ix, xi–xiii, xv–xvii, 1, 31–126, 130–31, 133–37, 142–49, 151–52, 156–60, 162, 165
Falls, Arthur, Jr., 39, 47n68, 74
Falls, Leo, 44
Falls, Lillian Proctor, 37n21, 38–39, 41, 44, 45n66, 65, 68, 73, 75–77, 90–91, 112n104, 116, 120, 125, 163
Falls, Santalia A., 33, 40
Falls, William A., 33–35, 40, 91
Farrell, Martin William, 63
fascism, xiii, 111, 115–16
Federated Colored Catholics (FCC), xii–xiii, 2–3, 32, 41, 46–54, 56, 59, 91–92, 99, 105–6, 110, 113, 119n135, 124, 158
Fellowship of Reconciliation, xiii, 68
Fitzgerald, John, 73
Floyd-Thomas, Stacey, xvi
Flynn, Harry J., 11, 13
Foster, Albon, 40
Francis, Joseph A., 8
Friendship House, 58n125, 68–69, 75, 77, 94
Furfey, Paul Hanly, 58

Gandhi, 104, 159
Garvy, Arnold, J., 51–52, 104–5
George, Francis, 11–12
Gray, John, 110n95
Grier, William H., 118n133
Gutiérrez, Gustavo, 24

Hayes, John, 57, 58n123, 61–62
heresy, xiii, xv, 27, 97n24, 98, 115, 122–23, 131–44, 148, 157, 168
Hitler, Adolf, 94

General Index

Hoffman, Howard Matthias, 63
Holy Angels Catholic Church, 46
Holy Family Catholic Church, 51n92
Honey, Michael K., 5
hope, 30–31, 70, 99, 106, 109, 118, 122, 124, 129, 146–48, 150, 156, 158–63
Hopkins, Dwight N., 27
Howard, T. R. M., 80
Hueck, Catherine de, see Catherine de Hueck Doherty
Hughes, Alfred, 11, 13–14, 22

idolatry, 3, 115n115, 123, 136, 137n49
Innocent VIII, Pope, 136n48
interracialism, 2–3, 28–29, 40, 42–45, 48–54, 56, 65, 68–78, 81, 92–94, 100–102, 106–11, 116, 144–46, 151, 162
Interracial Review, xii, 42n47, 48, 107, 110, 112
Irenaeus of Lyons, Saint, 139

Jackson Park Beach, 45
Jacobs, Harriet, xvi
Jerome, Saint, 140–41
Jim Crow, xiv, 28, 67n165, 127
Johnson, Karen A., vii, 51n88, 69n174, 94n9
Johnson, Mrs. Walter, 80
Jones, Absalom, 19
Jones, Eugene Kinckle, 44
Jones, Sydney A., Jr., 74–75
justice, the virtue of, 150, 152, 156–59, 161–63

Kappa Alpha Psi, 73
Kells, George D., 71
Kelly, Edward J., 43, 71
Kiley, Roger J., 71
King, Martin Luther, Jr., 5–6, 16, 26, 28, 38n26, 63n151, 86

LaFarge, John, 1–3, 8, 30–31, 50–54, 56, 94–95, 112–13, 121, 123n1, 145, 157
Lange, Elizabeth, 10
Lewis Maternity Hospital, 82, 114n111

Licinius, Emperor, 139
Lightfoot, Claude, 110n95
Little Company of Mary Hospital, 63
Lonergan, Bernard, 24, 150–51, 154–56, 163
Loyola University Chicago, 57, 62, 66n160, 104

Maguire, Daniel C., vii, 131–32
Maguire, Robert C., 49
Malcolm X, 25–26, 123
Marciniak, Ed, 62, 65–66, 71n187
Marcion, 133, 135, 139
Maritain, Jacques, 58
Markoe, William, 2–3, 49n79, 50–52
Martin, Trayvon, xiv
Massingale, Bryan N., vii, xiv–xv, 1, 5, 7–11, 23–27, 29, 31–32, 115n115, 123, 128, 131n27, 132, 137n49, 143–44, 146–47, 160
Mattison, William, III, 158
Maurin, Peter, 54, 57
McCarthy, John, 6–7
McGrath, Alister, 133, 135
McNicholas, John T., 54
Medical Committee for Human Rights, 86
Melczek, Dale, xiv, 11–12
Merrill, Philemon, 97n24
Meyer, Albert G., 77, 82n237
Michael Reese's Sarah Morris Hospital, 79
Michel, Virgil, 58–59, 93, 121, 145
militancy, 54, 71n187, 102–6, 109, 114n112, 123, 130, 142, 150, 154, 156, 158–59, 161–63
Moeslein, Mark, 112–13
Mooney, Edward, 4
moral suasion, xiv, 2–3, 5, 16, 37, 67, 113–14, 116, 118, 125, 131, 142, 145, 158–59, 161–62
Morgan Park, 43–44, 116
Mundelein, George W., 46, 49, 52, 63n149, 70
Mundelein College, 57
Mystical Body of Christ, xiii, xv, 21, 49n80, 56, 58, 92–97, 109, 121, 123–24, 131, 136–38, 143–45, 148, 157

General Index

National Association for the Advancement of Colored People (NAACP), 56, 119
National Catholic Federation for the Promotion of Better Race Relations. See Federated Colored Catholics
National Race Crisis, 5–7, 16, 125n2
National Science Foundation, 85
Negro Catholic Congresses. See Black Catholic Congresses
Nicaea, Council of, 139–40
Nilson, Jon, vii, 1, 26–29, 132, 137–38
Noll, John F., 52–53
Northwestern University, 35, 36n16, 38, 73, 102, 106, 120

Obama, Barack, xiv, 127
Operation Hospitality, 87–88
Our Lady of Solace Catholic Church, 39n33, 40, 46, 47n68, 48, 52, 59

Perry, Joseph N., 11
Phelps, Jamie, 11, 27
Pius XII, Pope, 4
Piven, Frances Fox, 129
Plessy, Homer, 14, 25
Pontifical Council for Justice and Peace, 1, 14–16
Porter, Jean, 151, 157
Provident Hospital, 37, 43n52, 79

Queen of Heaven Catholic Cemetery, 91
Quigley Preparatory Seminary, 63n150

Rahner, Karl, 131–32
Red Summer, 34–35, 40, 46, 67n164, 72
Reinert, Joseph, 66n160
Reitzes, Dietrich, C., 78, 80, 82
Reser, Al, 62, 65
Riot of 1919. See Red Summer
Roach, Peggy, 63n151
Roosevelt, Franklin D., 42
Rosary College, 56
Ryan, John A., 70

Saint Alphonsus Catholic Church, 60n136
Saint Anselm Catholic Church, 46
Saint Cletus Catholic Church, 77
Saint Elizabeth Catholic Church, 40, 46, 51, 62, 70
Saint Elizabeth Chronicle. See *Interracial Review*
Saint Elizabeth High School, 33, 107
Saint Ignatius College, 57
Saint John of the Cross Catholic Church, xiii, 86–91, 165
Saint Joseph Colored Mission, 51n92
Saint Malachy Catholic Church, 46, 63n149
Saint Margaret of Scotland Catholic Church, 47
Saint Mary on the Lake Junior College, 63n150
Saint Monica Catholic Church, 33n2, 33n4, 34, 46
Saint Patrick Catholic Church, 57
Saint Raphael Catholic Church, 47n68
Saint Thaddeus Catholic Church, 88
Saint Teresa of Avila Catholic Church, 63n150
Saunders, Doris E., 119
Second Vatican Council. See Vatican II
Sheil, Bernard James, 49, 105
Sicius, Francis, 57n119, 62n146
Sign, xii, 113
sin, xv, 8, 12–13, 23, 27, 72, 92, 96–98, 121–24, 131–32, 137, 139
Smith, Vincent, 70
social sciences, 12, 29, 39, 43–44, 91–92, 112–16, 121, 124–31, 147, 157–58, 161, 168
Southern, David W., 2–3
Stein, Alfred B., 80
Stritch, Samuel A., 32, 69–73, 80–81
struggle, xiii, 19–20, 23, 29, 35, 42, 45, 49, 92, 101, 114n112, 116–18, 122–25, 130–31, 137–38, 142–48, 153, 156, 158–59
Sullivan, Tom, 60n136, 62
Swift, H. L., 117

General Index

Sykes, Michelle, 37n21, 47n68, 90n279, 120n141

Tarry, Ellen, 69n174
Taylor, Charles, 128n19
Tessman, Lisa, 150–51, 153–54, 156, 163
Theobald, Stephen L., 48
Thomas Aquinas, Saint, 97, 141, 157–60
Toles, Edward B., 74–76
Truth, Sojourner, xvi
Tubman, Harriet, 10
Tureaud, A. P., 14
Turner, Thomas Wyatt, 2, 48, 50–52, 91

University of Chicago, 39, 63n149, 117
Unsworth, Tim, 42n47, 47n69, 112n104

Valentinus, 133, 139
Vatican II, 7, 13, 49n80, 90n276, 133–34, 141, 151n3
Visitation Catholic Church, 72–73
Vogt, Christopher, 150–53, 155–56, 163

Waller High School, 85
Washington, George, 128n19
Wesley Memorial Hospital, 85
West, Cornel, 12, 27
Western Spring, Illinois, xiii, 32, 73–77, 86, 89–91, 116, 145, 165
What We Have Seen and Heard, 9–11, 16–17
Wheeler, Zita, 88
white privilege, 14, 25, 27, 80, 92, 114, 128, 132, 143
Williams, Mother Theodore, 10
Williams, Robert, 35
Winfrey, Oprah, 127
Wolfe, Edgar, 87–88
World Committee to Aid the Victims of German Fascism, 116n117

Yancy, John, 71
Young, Quentin, 36n15, 37n21, 79, 80n226, 83n241, 84.

197